Comparative-Integrative
Psychoanalysis

RELATIONAL PERSPECTIVES BOOK SERIES
LEWIS ARON AND ADRIENNE HARRIS
Series Editors

Rita Wiley McCleary
Conversing with Uncertainty:
Practicing Psychotherapy in a Hospital Setting

Charles Spezzano
Affect in Psychoanalysis: A Clinical Synthesis

Neil Altman
The Analyst in the Inner City: Race, Class, and
Culture Through a Psychoanalytic Lens

Lewis Aron
A Meeting of Minds: Mutuality in Psychoanalysis

Joyce A. Slochower
Holding and Psychoanalysis: A Relational Perspective

Barbara Gerson, editor
The Therapist as a Person: Life Crises, Life Choices,
Life Experiences, and Their Effects on Treatment

Charles Spezzano and Gerald J. Gargiulo, editors
Soul on the Couch: Spirituality, Religion, and Morality
in Contemporary Psychoanalysis

Donnel B. Stern
Unformulated Experience:
From Dissociation to Imagination in Psychoanalysis

Stephen A. Mitchell
Influence and Autonomy in Psychoanalysis

Neil J. Skolnick and David E. Scharff, editors
Fairbairn, Then and Now

Stuart A. Pizer
Building Bridges: Negotiation of Paradox in Psychoanalysis

Lewis Aron and Frances Sommer Anderson, editors
Relational Perspectives on the Body

Karen Maroda
Seduction, Surrender, and Transformation:
Emotional Engagement in the Analytic Process

Stephen A. Mitchell and Lewis Aron, editors
Relational Psychoanalysis: The Emergence of a Tradition

Rochelle G. K. Kainer
The Collapse of the Self and Its Therapeutic Restoration

Kenneth A. Frank
Psychoanalytic Participation: Action, Interaction,
and Integration

Sue Grand
The Reproduction of Evil: A Clinical and Cultural
Perspective

Steven H. Cooper
Objects of Hope: Exploring Possibility and Limit
in Psychoanalysis

James S. Grotstein
Who Is the Dreamer Who Dreams the Dream?
A Study of Psychic Presences

Stephen A. Mitchell
Relationality: From Attachment to Intersubjectivity

Peter G. M. Carnochan
Looking for Ground: Countertransference
and the Problem of Value in Psychoanalysis

Muriel Dimen
Sexuality, Intimacy, Power

Susan W. Coates, Jane L. Rosenthal, and Daniel S. Schechter,
editors
September 11: Trauma and Human Bonds

Randall Lehmann Sorenson
Minding Spirituality

Adrienne Harris
Gender as Soft Assembly

Emanuel Berman
Impossible Training:
A Relational View of Psychoanalytic Education

Carlo Strenger
The Designed Self: Psychoanalysis
and Contemporary Identities

Lewis Aron and Adrienne Harris, editors
Relational Psychoanalysis, Volume II

Sebastiano Santostefano
Child Therapy in the Great Outdoors: A Relational View

James T. McLaughlin
The Healer's Bent:
Solitude and Dialogue in the Clinical Encounter

Danielle Knafo and Kenneth Feiner
Unconscious Fantasies and the Relational World

Sheldon Bach
Getting from Here to There:
Psychoanalytic Explorations in Transitional Space

Katie Gentile
Eating Disorders as Self-Destructive Survival

Melanie Suchet, Adrienne Harris, and Lewis Aron, editors
Relational Psychoanalysis, Volume III

Comparative-Integrative
Psychoanalysis

*A Relational Perspective for the
Discipline's Second Century*

BRENT WILLOCK

The Analytic Press
Taylor & Francis Group

New York   London

The Analytic Press
Taylor & Francis Group
270 Madison Avenue
New York, NY 10016

The Analytic Press
Taylor & Francis Group
27 Church Road
Hove, East Sussex BN3 2FA

© 2007 by Taylor & Francis Group, LLC

Printed in the United States of America on acid-free paper
10 9 8 7 6 5 4 3 2 1

International Standard Book Number-13: 978-0-88163-460-0 (Hardcover)

Library of Congress Cataloging-in-Publication Data

Willock, Brent.
    Comparative integrative psychoanalysis : a relational perspective for the discipline's second century / Brent Willock.
        p. cm. -- (Relational perspectives book series)
    Includes bibliographical references and index.
    ISBN 978-0-88163-460-0 (alk. paper)
    1. Psychoanalysis. 2. Psychoanalysis--History. I. Title. II. Series.

BF173.W5476 2007
150.19'5--dc22   2007001305

Visit the Taylor & Francis Web site at
http://www.taylorandfrancis.com

and The Analytic Press Web site at
http://www.analyticpress.com

Freud was once asked what he thought a normal person should be able to do well. The questioner probably expected a complicated answer. But Freud, in the curt way of his old days, is reported to have said: "Lieben und arbeiten" (to love and to work). It pays to ponder on this simple formula; it gets deeper as you think about it.

(Erik H. Erikson, 1950)

for

陳
素
珍

&

T I C P

Contents

Acknowledgments   ix

Introduction   xi

Part I Innovation and Tradition in the Evolution of Psychoanalytic Thought

1 Revelations from a Triptych of Dreams   3

2 Toward Integrative Understanding   35

3 Mangy Mongrels or Marvelous Mutts? The Question of Mixed Models   65

Part II The Comparative-Integrative Point of View

4 Implications for Psychoanalytic Theory (and Organizations)   91

5 Significance for Psychoanalytic Practice   131

6 Significance for Psychoanalytic Education   147

7 The Class Struggle   175

8 The Comparative-Integrative Spirit   205

9 Last Words   211

References   213

Index   231

Acknowledgments

I am grateful to the following members of the Board of Directors of the Toronto Institute for Contemporary Psychoanalysis (TICP) with whom I have worked intimately and creatively over the past 17 years: Drs. Clarissa Barton, Don Carveth, Art Caspary, Sam Izenberg, Judi Kobrick, Nira Kolers, Roy Muir, John Munn, Gary Rodin, Gary Taerk, Sarah Turnbull, Scott Bishop, Gail White, and, *prima inter pares*, Dr. Hazel Ipp who has done more than her share to foster the Institute with heart and soul, time and energy, skill and competence, enthusiasm and devotion. Striving collectively to contribute to and advance our field, locally and beyond, all board members helped nurture the perspective portrayed in this book. Without their friendship, collegiality, and commitment, this volume would not have been written. Thanks are also due to many members of our faculty, advisory board, and the Toronto Society for Contemporary Psychoanalysis for support and participation in this endeavor over the years. I am grateful, too, to my partner Elizabeth for facilitating my involvement in this time-consuming profession and to the rest of my family for their assistance over the years. In the realm of wishes come true, one could not hope for a more supportive, challenging, respectful, encouraging editor than Dr. Lewis Aron. He works tirelessly and with astounding efficiency to facilitate the birth of new ideas. Possessing qualities not omnipresent in our fractious field, he is able to discern and welcome contributions even when they may not necessarily be completely congruent with his own current views. Thanks are also due to Dr. Paul Stepansky, Editor-in-Chief of the Analytic Press, for many years of devotion to publishing new psychoanalytic ideas. As you can see, it takes a village to raise a book.

Introduction

The mind must be made ready to receive the quantum idea, and this can be done only by systematically expanding the scientific spirit.

—Gaston Bachelard, *The New Scientific Spirit*

Pondering penning prefatory remarks suitable for setting the tone to launch this treatise, a familiar figure emerged in the mental mist that enveloped my mind. This gregarious, supportive individual was our longtime, inspiring colleague, Stephen Mitchell. His unbidden, most welcome presence illuminated the inner landscape as he had previously enlivened the outer. Brilliant conceptualizer, superb author, masterful instructor, he had helped kindle necessary hope and determination in our local psychoanalytic group. From our initial encounter more than 20 years ago, a spark of comradeship had arced between Mitchell and us. He had a similarly beneficial impact on many other kindred spirits throughout North America and the world.

My last, "real-time" conversation with Mitchell transpired 3 months before his unexpected, untimely, unnerving death in December 2001. Despite his towering stature on the leading edge of disciplinary development, he was always down to earth, approachable, engaging, and encouraging. Devoted to facilitating others' endeavors to acquire knowledge, skill, and contribute to the field, he inquired on that occasion as to what I was currently writing. Expressing genuine interest in my thoughts on comparative-integrative psychoanalysis, he urged me to send the manuscript to him on completion for consideration for the innovative book series he had founded. Although my ideas are not identical to his, absence of perfect symmetry did not stand in the way of his finding them intriguing. I was grateful for his interest and encouragement and appreciated his graciously joining me on the psychic plane as I prepared to compose this introduction. Certain ideals can be counted on to hold up through time.

In honor of Stephen Mitchell's contributions to the field and to our group in particular, and, no doubt, to facilitate our mourning and related transformational processes, the TICP established an annual Stephen Mitchell Memorial Lecture. The first one was delivered by his close colleague and friend, Dr. Lewis Aron, head of the renowned Postdoctoral Program in Psychoanalysis and Psychotherapy at New York University. On that inaugural weekend, embodying the same lively curiosity and supportive interest as his dear friend, Aron likewise inquired about my writing and encouraged me to forward my manuscript to him in his new role as Coeditor-in-Chief (with Dr. Adrienne Harris) of the Relational Perspectives Book Series. It was, therefore, with significant history and the fondest of feelings that I finally mailed this product of many years' labor to Aron.

Our field's division into diverse schools of thought had long struck me as intriguing, problematic, and in need of attention. This state of the discipline struck me afresh one day while perusing one of Kohut's contributions to our literature. This particular piece of his, for reasons detailed in chapter 1, helped consolidate my resolve to give more formal shape to my ideas on this fractious state of affairs with its many conceptual conundrums. I am grateful to the founder of self psychology for having provided this immediate intellectual stimulation.

The purpose of this book is not to criticize any particular perspective. Critique is, however, intended for any and all theoretical frameworks to the extent that they isolate themselves from open, authentic discourse with alternative points of view. Despite declaring this credo clearly and up-front, because the primary illustration I have selected to commence this inquiry emanates from a particular orientation, this treatise may be viewed by some as prejudiced against that perspective. I would be chagrined, but not totally surprised by that reaction. It is part of the problem of having separate (but often unequal) schools of thought (and not-thought). Not just convenient, useful, even necessary divisions, these groupings easily devolve into hypervigilant, antagonistic camps. Freighted with exquisite sensitivities and hyperaggressive potential, these gradients in our field can become as calcified and conflicted as can the components of Freud's tripartite structural model.

Hair-trigger reactions manifested by passionate adherents of diverse schools reflect difficult individual and organizational histories. Politics, economics, narcissistic investments, personal and group psychologies are all intimately involved, reinforcing antagonistic positions in this troubled stew. These confluent variables create a highly inflammable mixture, a potent brew that can bring one's temperature to a boil, mobilizing essential qualities of the beast that might be corralled under the rubric of Freud's (1901/1960) fond references to "the psychopathology of everyday life." In the possibly quixotic hope of allaying angst and soothing that irritable brute, I extend my hand toward his nostrils by way of introduction in hopes that the creature will be able to discern nonpersecutory intent. I am, of course, acutely aware that his olfactory organ is located in close proximity to his primary means of aggressive defense, his mouth. Teeth notwithstanding, via this gesture, I seek to communicate my wish to not offend any particular association except in so far as I would challenge the limitations of them all.

To question the problematic nature of a field fragmented into multiple, competing domains is not to be without sympathy for this devilish situation; nor does it preclude perceiving some value in it. Nonetheless, we have been advised by a credible source that love is not enough (Bettelheim, 1950). To this adage, we might add that empathy is insufficient, and sympathy will not suffice. Something more than all these is needed. Consequently, in this volume, I have critical things to say about our current state of disciplinary disunion. These pages provide a polemical playground for exploring a tougher love I think we need.

For purposes of organizational clarity, I have divided the text into two sections. In the first, I present a significant problem in the nature of the evolution of psychoanalytic thought. I consider difficulties our field has repeatedly encountered when faced with challenging, innovative ideas. I discuss some explanations for this situation. I initially present this material in a manner familiar to all analysts, that is, through exploring clinical data, making inferences, and evaluating them with respect to alternative hypotheses. The latter part of this section goes a little beyond our customary modes of thought by drawing on insights from neighboring disciplines to shed additional light on our problem. I believe this excursion outside the usual borders of our field to be an interesting, perhaps essential endeavor, even though one can rarely, if ever, be as knowledgeable of other domains of scholarship as one is of one's own. Awareness of this regrettable reality expands the pathos of intradisciplinary, psychoanalytic diversity into the far greater fragmentation of knowledge into highly specialized, scholarly worlds.

Part I thus begins to create the case for our need, after a century of disciplinary development, to move beyond delineated schools. I propose a term, a method, and a goal (comparative-integrative psychoanalysis). I elaborate on this desideratum in detail in Part II, where I explore its implications with respect to theory, organizations, practice, and pedagogy. Some readers may find Part I most intriguing because of its familiar, clinically based investigation into the nature of thought and its intrinsic problems. Part II may strike others as most directly applicable to our everyday concerns with doing ever better work, be it in the consulting room, classroom, or in and between the various organizations in which we labor, love, and sometimes drive each other to distraction.

I

INNOVATION AND TRADITION IN THE EVOLUTION OF PSYCHOANALYTIC THOUGHT

The scientific spirit is essentially a way of rectifying knowledge, a way of broadening the horizon of what is known. Sitting in judgement, it condemns its historical past. Its structure is its awareness of its historical errors. For science, truth is nothing other than a historical corrective to a persistent error, and experience is a corrective for common and primary illusions. The intellectual life of science depends dialectically on this differential of knowledge at the frontier of the unknown. The very essence of reflection is to understand that one did not understand before.

—**Gaston Bachelard,** *The New Scientific Spirit*

1

Revelations from a Triptych of Dreams

Sooner or later scientific thought will become the central subject of philosophical controversy.

—Gaston Bachelard, *The New Scientific Spirit*

INTRODUCTION

Periods of both smooth and disjunctive evolution have characterized the past century's developments in psychoanalysis. Theoretical conflicts have sometimes generated lively, fruitful debate. Other times, handled in a less amicable, dialogical spirit, controversies have culminated in feelings of estrangement embodied in dissociated schools of thought. These contrasting approaches and outcomes with respect to the confrontation between innovative and traditional ideas bespeak the promise and pitfalls that continue to characterize the path of our young science.

The current intellectual climate within our field and beyond (e.g., postmodernism) affords propitious circumstances for contemplating the nature of this ofttimes tumultuous evolution of analytic thought. Such reflection should enable us to better situate ourselves so that we might more creatively manage the future development of our discipline.

ENTER THE SELF

A major participant in the recent evolutionary epoch of psychoanalysis has been Heinz Kohut. His seminal contributions fomented a great deal of excitement as well as controversy. Analysts wondered and debated whether his perspective could be integrated into the existing mainstream(s) of analytic thinking or whether it constituted a separate theoretical/clinical approach requiring distinctive organizational structures to protect and promote its development. Kohut's ideas and their mixed reception furnish us with an outstanding, contemporary opportunity to study issues central to the nature of the conjunctive and disjunctive possibilities encountered during the development of analytic thought.

THE NEW AND THE OLD

In his final contribution to the burgeoning, increasingly pluralistic, psychoanalytic literature, Kohut (1984) articulated some astute observations apropos scientific evolution. Every explanation, he wrote, "must not only be considered a gain, but also a barrier to further thought, a potential obstacle to seeing the new and appreciating the unexpected" (p. 125). Underscoring this assertion, he continued to say that progress in science "is impeded more by our commitment to old knowledge than by our incapacity to acquire new knowledge" (p. 125).

Perceptive, important, and valid, Kohut's perspective on the relationship between new and old is, at the same time, significantly incomplete. In this chapter, therefore, I endeavor to demonstrate a crucial, seemingly opposite, but actually complementary proposition: Excessive commitment to new explanatory models and to innovation can also constitute surprisingly powerful obstacles to understanding that which continues to be valid and valuable in the preexisting body of knowledge. Scientific progress may be impeded as much by one-sided emphasis on innovation as by rigid adherence to convention.

Ironically, the core clinical case presented by Kohut in the very chapter in which he enunciated his insightful ideas on scientific progress can be fruitfully studied and utilized equally well to illustrate this opposite thesis. Kohut's case is especially fortuitous for this purpose because he carefully considered the relative merits of analyzing his clinical material both from the traditional and from his innovative, self psychological viewpoint. Processing his patient's productions from these dual perspectives, he concluded, inter alia, that this case provided no significant support for certain fundamental tenets of classical analysis (e.g., the Oedipus complex). My contention is that his conclusion (particularly with respect to the oedipal) was invalid (notwithstanding other merits in his approach). If my dissenting view is supported by reanalysis of his data, then the inability of such an outstanding investigator to perceive the abundant, phallic-oedipal material suffusing his analysand's productions would furnish an illuminating illustration of how a new clinical perspective and commitment to innovation can militate against the possibility of adequately evaluating data in terms of a prior theoretical framework despite one's best intentions.

Had Kohut merely been endeavoring to demonstrate the nature and utility of the self psychological approach without regard for how the classical perspective might elucidate the material, most readers would simply have found his perspective interesting, useful, or otherwise. If that had been his sole intention, it would not have been so startling to discover that he had overlooked so many classical interpretive possibilities. The fact that he committed himself to exploring his material from both perspectives (while also focusing on their possibly different understandings of resistance and defense) makes his inability to perceive copious oedipal manifestations striking, important, and above all, intriguing.

If fundamental perceptual and cognitive operations can be subject to such serious blocking in someone as knowledgeable of traditional analysis as Kohut, the danger of similar deficits manifesting themselves in analysts less expert, less conversant with classical thinking, is likely far greater. This probability has important implications for training. In this chapter, however, I am content if I can make a case for my primary hypothesis that the new can seriously impede access to valuable aspects of the old. I leave it to later in the book to explore in greater detail the nature of the processes involved in these impediments to clinical apperception and the evolution of analytic thought together with their pedagogic implications.

CAVEAT LECTOR

Conversation between self psychologists and analysts of other persuasions has often been and frequently still is problematic. Feelings frequently have run high. Mutual misunderstanding and suspicion, a sense of abuse, and excommunicative tendencies have often overpowered more constructive, collegial, communicative desires. Apart from the cruder forms of dismissal, merely questioning, let alone criticizing, one side rather than simply embracing and idealizing it has often been taken as tantamount to persecutory devaluation. Not surprisingly, such perceived or imagined degradation has ofttimes been responded to with correspondingly defensive counterattack. Once these processes are in motion, participants become increasingly hard of hearing.

As so often happens when one has something to say that differs from received wisdom, self psychologists have had to struggle valiantly against considerable odds to make space for their point of view. Due to the endless skirmishes and bitter battles they have faced and managed to survive, some self psychologists may feel slighted by a treatise, such as this one, that uses some work by their preeminent personage for illustrative purposes. I wish, therefore, to underscore that Kohut's writing has been chosen primarily because it is relatively contemporary and therefore especially well suited for exploring the idea that the new can block access to still important aspects of the old. This contention could be equally well illustrated with examples from other schools of thought. Such illustrations would, however, probably be less well known and consequently less evocative, engaging, and interesting for readers. Alternative vignettes would likely be regarded as more historically or locally significant rather than constituting cutting-edge concerns of real import to contemporary psychoanalysis.

If this book were to alienate any colleagues strongly identifying with Kohut's perspective, I would be chagrinned indeed. This disappointment would be particularly intense with respect to those whose professional identities have been forged in the heat of battles that required individualism, character, and courage on the part of dissidents. My sympathies tend to be more with those who dare to think, speak, and advocate for interesting alternative points of view rather than with those comfortably ensconced in old positions who seek to protect themselves against disequilibria by branding upstarts as deviants in a malicious sense of the word.

My hope is that rather than seeing red, or even pink, recent revolutionaries will instead find the ideas in this book of considerable interest. Ideally, they will grasp that my views are not directed toward any single perspective but rather constitute a necessary, worthwhile challenge to our field as a whole. It would please me to know they understood my argument could be founded equally well on other important moments in the evolution of analysis. For example, Freud's shift from his traumatogenic, seduction theory to a more drive-based, intrapsychic, conflict model might have served these purposes almost as well. That exemplar from the end of the 19th century would, however, leave it to the reader to apply the lessons learned from that historic situation to current controversies. Rather than argue mostly from that relatively remote, now fairly safe past, if we can tolerate a more contemporary discussion, it will increase our chances of being able to apply the lessons we may learn to the most important period, that is, to the present and future, as we attempt to advance our knowledge base.

Should books be received more frequently on electronic monitors in the future, the preceding caveat could be programmed to pop up every 30 pages. In the absence of such cooling flashes, should anyone temporarily lose sight of this "heads up" and start to feel annoyingly alienated, perhaps the much maligned wonders of suggestion and conditioning will come to the rescue, bringing this message to mind, reducing the tendency to see scarlet, permitting the full spectrum of colorful thought to return.

In sum, this volume is not about the presence or absence of the Oedipal complex (or self–object transferences, or any other singular phenomenon). It is about the presence of complexity. Cognizant of our inclination to shift to a paranoid-schizoid, defensive, battle-ready posture, it is useful to endeavor to keep open the contemplative space of the alternative (so-called depressive) position. If we can make room for the depressive position to complement the paranoid–schizoid position, we may be able to play with ideas and make conversation, not war.

EXIT OEDIPUS (OR NOT)

Three dreams that emerged over a 3-month period during the fourth year of an analysis constituted the heart of Kohut's (1984) illustrative case in chapter 7 of *How Does Analysis Cure?* Asserting that he used to be highly skilled at formulating in terms of incompletely resolved Oedipal complexes, and still could do so, he declared that such traditional conceptualizations were simply not borne out:

> Despite my openness to discern the Oedipal complex in this patient's analysis and thus come face to face with the resistances that constitute clinical manifestations of the defenses against castration anxiety, I was unable to discover this classically pivotal configuration, at least not in its role as a nucleus of psychopathology. I was not only unable to find evidence of a pathogenic Oedipal complex in the material pertaining to the three dreams I am examining, but also in the material that preceded them and followed them right up to the end of the patient's long analysis. (Kohut, 1984, p. 126)

In contrast to Kohut, Freud (1905/1953b) was unambiguous with respect to his belief in the importance and ubiquity of the oedipal complex; a footnote he added in 1920 to his "Three Essays on the Theory of Sexuality" (1905/1953b) asserted this construct's continuing centrality to the psychoanalytic edifice: "The importance of the Oedipus complex has become more and more clearly evident; its recognition has become the shibboleth that distinguishes the adherents of psycho-analysis from its opponents" (p. 226). With these words, he inscribed a line in the sand with certainty and, one might say, panache.

Freud's radically innovative idea served as a keystone at the heart of his theoretical system. Kohut's conclusion that there was no pathological Oedipal complex discernable in his case and perhaps in others as well, for he did not appear to regard his analysand as particularly unusual, constituted a provocative challenge to the classical perspective. If valid, his findings could be construed as falsifying (Popper, 1959/1968), or at least going a considerable way toward substantially challenging, fundamental Freudian theory. Due to this potentially significant effect, his assertions merit careful consideration.

Prerequisite for either accepting or rejecting Kohut's iconoclastic conclusion would be a thorough examination of the three specimen dreams at the heart of his clinical presentation. Undertaking that review, I shall simultaneously explore the alternative hypothesis that Oedipus may have actually been staring Kohut in the face, repeatedly, but he could not discern this phenomenon because his innovative model inactivated core perceptual-cognitive processes despite his conscious openness to this fundamental, orthodox construct; his long-standing, thorough familiarity with it; and his conscious search for its possible manifestations. Again, if this hypothesis is supported, it would not be a criticism of Kohut but rather a useful drawing of attention to an intriguing phenomenon to which we are all prone.

The preceding Kohutian citation concerning the absence of the Oedipal complex, in addition to its relevance to my central hypothesis concerning possible inadvertent interferences between new and old, raises, en passant, questions as to whether his understanding of the oedipal may have been too heavily organized around the idea of castration anxiety. He may have given that significant component of the construct inordinate emphasis relative to other, equally important aspects of the complete complex (other affects, fantasies, object relationships, passions, multiple shifting identifications, etc.), to the detriment of his capacity to utilize this rich, multifaceted construct to elucidate clinical material. If one is mostly looking for "resistances that constitute clinical manifestations of the defenses against castration anxiety" (Kohut, 1984, p. 126) to decide whether or not oedipal dynamics are psychopathologically present and significant, one's conceptual apparatus may have become too narrowly focused, too restricted to have much likelihood of obtaining samples of the much broader array of data (triadic object relationships, feelings of exclusion with relevant affective reactions, etc.) that could help answer the question.

Also en passant, some analysts felt Kohut may have had a tendency to bypass rather than interpret resistance (Levy, cited in Jessee, 1995). If so, this proclivity may also have contributed to his not coming face-to-face with oedipal resistance in this case. Despite the importance of such technical questions, for reasons of space, focus, and clarity, in this chapter I confine its examination primarily to matters of observation and formulation. Tantalizing technical questions must be temporarily sidelined other than to state my conviction that what one sees (and does not see) influences (significantly) how one can intervene.

THE INTERPRETATION OF DREAMS

Latent Manifesto

In presenting his three dream specimens, Kohut omitted most associations. If emphasizing what he elsewhere referred to as "self-state dreams" (1977, p. 109) reduces attention to associative material, this might be another way in which a new construct could curtail access to established modes of conceptualization and data collection that could otherwise illuminate clinical material. Nonetheless, as Freud (1916/1972) skillfully demonstrated (e.g., with the famous dream of wartime "love services"), one can learn a great deal from manifest content: "If we are acquainted with the ordinary dream symbols, and in addition with the dreamer's personality, the circumstances in which he lives and the impressions which preceded the occurrence of the dream," then, he opined, "We are often in a position to interpret the dream straightaway" (Freud, 1916/1972, p. 115).

Although some analysts might chastise Freud for being insufficiently Freudian with respect to the absolute necessity of collecting and utilizing abundant associations, a considerable clinical and research literature has supported the founder's conviction that both the content and structure of manifest dreams can be richly mined (e.g., Brenneis, 1975; Erikson, 1954; Fine, Moore, & Waldhorn, 1969; Freud, 1900/1953a; Hatcher & Krohn, 1980; Krohn & Mayman, 1974; Langs, 1966; Palombo, 1984; Pulver, 1987; Rosenbaum, 1965; Saul, Snyder, & Sheppard, 1956; Spanjaard, 1969; Stewart, 1967).

Our ofttimes bivalent regard for the merely manifest was pithily portrayed by Erikson (1954) in his insightful distinction between actual versus advertised, idealized modes of practice. In his classic contribution, "The Dream Specimen of Psychoanalysis," he noted: "Officially, we hurry at every confrontation with a dream to crack its manifest appearance as if it were a useless shell and hasten to discard this shell, in favor of what seems to be the more worthwhile core" (p. 17). In contrast, he observed, "Unofficially, we often interpret dreams entirely or in parts on the basis of their manifest appearance" (p. 17). With wry wit, bred of much experience, he underscored the significant gap between official and actual practice.

Believing real conduct to be more valid than prescribed doctrine, Erikson asserted that, on careful inquiry, the radical differentiation between a manifest and a latent dream "defuses in a complicated continuum of more manifest and more latent items which are sometimes to be found by a radical disposal of the manifest configuration, sometimes by a careful scrutiny of it" (p. 34). Reminding his readers that the Rorschach Thematic Apperception Test and other projective techniques had convincingly demonstrated that any behavior reflects the whole, he emphasized the principle that a continuum of dynamic meaning connects surface and core.

In Lansky's (1992) contribution to his own compendium on *Essential Papers on Dreams,* he concurred with Erikson: "In actual practice, there is a tendency to use an interplay of manifest and latent content" (p. 14), he asserted.

In a study of analysts of various persuasions in the United States and Britain, V. Hamilton (1996) found that with the exception of a handful of Freudians and British Independents, the majority in all orientations no longer focus on gathering associations to individual dream elements. This "new normal" would, no doubt, shock and dismay many analysts belonging to what is now apparently the associational minority. V. Hamilton's data suggested that in clinical and educational settings today, analysts of diverse persuasions apparently feel they can work with predominantly manifest content to good effect. This reality does not, of course, negate the possibility that one might function to even better effect by collecting more associational material. In that regard, it was interesting to hear that more than one analyst in V. Hamilton's study admitted they did not really feel competent to work intensively with dreams. I address such intriguing findings more in later sections of this book concerned with psychoanalytic training.

Erikson (1954) believed compulsive adherence to official mantras deriding the manifest seriously "hindered a full meeting of ego psychology and the problems of dream life" (p. 17) to the detriment of both theory and practice. In a similar vein, Lansky (1992) asserted that such dogmatic rigidity had adverse consequences not only for theory and clinical practice but that the "legacy of contempt for and suspicion of" (p. 15) the manifest had also systematically undercut psychoanalytic research.

Studying clinical reports, one sometimes wishes for more associative material. Nonetheless, in the case I am scrutinizing, considering the variables cited by Freud (1916/1972) as frequently sufficient for meaningful interpretation, it can be said that Kohut provided ample information concerning his analysand's "personality, circumstances in which he lives and the impressions which preceded the occurrence of" (p. 115) at least some of the dreams. Furthermore, Kohut proffered not just one nocturnal hallucination, but a sequence of three (plus relevant historical and transferential material). I will endeavor to meticulously mine these confluent, mutually enhancing data sources to explore Kohut's hypothesis and my own.

Via Regia

Through the medium of three dreams, Kohut served his readers a concentrated glimpse into the complex psychic reality of his analysand. Their significance and utility reminds one of Erikson's (1958) astute comment in another of his penetrating contributions, "The Nature of Clinical Evidence":

> The experienced dream interpreter often finds himself "reading" a dream report as a practitioner of medicine scans an x-ray. Especially in cases of wordy or reticent patients or of lengthy case reports, a dream often lays bare the stark inner facts. (p. 257)

My experience working with Kohut's dreams (including the progression of meaning evolving across them) strongly accords with Erikson's insight.

Each nocturnal phantasy presented by Kohut can be contemplated separately. Each contains enough food for thought to constitute a meal on its own. Alternatively, the dreams may be enjoyed as integral parts of a more encompassing, sumptuous, three-course repast. Both perspectives have merit. I approach the buffet both ways. With this in mind, let us venture to the banquet and delve deeply into Kohut's account to see what we can learn.

PRIMO FANTASIA—A DISCORDANT NOCTURNE

In the first dream, Kohut's analysand, a middle-aged lawyer, described

> [a] summer resort, a hotel or motel or bungalow. The patient, however, was sleep-
> ing not inside the building but on the front lawn. He was ill at ease, uncomfortable,
> thrashing about restlessly with the result that he became uncovered. People began
> to walk by. He was dismayed by the thought that they would see him partially
> uncovered. (p. 116)

First Approaches

The dreamer's initial words served to establish the setting for his phantasy. In a resort's relaxed ambience, one may experience some liberation from everyday responsibilities and constraints. Correspondingly, there may be greater opportunities for sensuous, motoric release.

The subsequent sequence of domiciliary images (hotel, motel, bungalow) suggests progression from large public places (suitable, nonetheless, for private encounters) to more intimate abodes. Restlessly, and unusually stationed vis-à-vis the more obvious living quarters, the dreamer may have felt excluded from cozier sleeping arrangements. Uncomfortably distanced, yet so close, his placement is analogous to a child's spatial/emotional relationship to the conjugal bedroom. From this perspective, his tense thrashing about may have embodied and enacted agitated, perhaps masturbatory fantasies, a means of coping with the stress experienced by the oedipal "outsider" (sexual arousal, separation, anger, loss, feelings of inferiority, vicarious participation, etc.).

Supporting the possible sexual significance of this dream, the patient worried that his body was becoming "uncovered," exposed to the view of others. From a transferential perspective, those onlookers could include the analyst, a prominent proponent of intensive, "uncovering" therapy.

Discomfort about being observed is often proportional to conflictual, exhibitionistic desires. The night before the dream, the analysand had wanted to keep the lights on during intercourse. His wife thwarted this incandescent desire. Traditional thinking, Kohut noted, might postulate that the patient's frustrated exhibitionistic urge intensified and had therefore to be defensively censored, contributing to shame in the dream. Even here, however, Kohut downplayed phallic elements: "None of the patient's associations ever led to phallic or anal exhibitionism in early life" (p. 121).

Although Kohut discussed blocked exhibitionism in the day residue, voyeurism was equally stymied. In the dream, too, the analysand's wish to observe may have been frustrated by his being isolated, "in the dark" with regard to what may have been transpiring inside the bungalow. His voyeurism may, however, have been gratified later when, in the guise of passersby, he got to view the partially naked individual (in phantasy, perhaps more than one person) thrashing about, splendidly in the grass.

Both these partial instincts, voyeurism and exhibitionism, are centrally important to infantile sexuality. "Scoptophilia is the main component in children's sexual curiosity," Fenichel (1945) noted. The counterpart, exhibitionism, usually appears together with it, he (pp. 71–72) observed. These component instincts went hand in hand in the analysand's first dream. His initial phantasy appears, therefore, to involve core issues from the foundational realm of infantile eroticism.

Consistently, Kohut overlooked or minimized the possibility not only of early partial instincts but also of oedipal elements. The patient's fundamental desire was not simply to observe a naked woman. "His voyeuristic wish was in the main that of watching the woman looking at him" (p. 120). Based on that sophisticated statement, one could say that the analysand (observing ego) wanted to watch two people (experiencing/performing self plus observing female) interacting sexually. This triangular fantasy might relate to or derive from earlier wishes to observe intercourse between another endlessly fascinating couple, his parents. This latter, committed, compelling investigation is an integral part of what Freud (1905/1953b) referred to as the crucial, engrossing, "sexual researches of childhood" (p. 194). From this perspective, the analysand's desire to observe an aroused woman looking at him in all his naked glory—a central organizing component in his character structure and in the day residue—provides additional support for my hypothesis that the dream may represent a conflictual drama pertaining to interest in and feelings of exclusion from the primal scene.

Kohut was attuned to the significance of the sexual fantasies and frustrations between the patient and his wife on the night preceding the dream. He seemed less inclined to contemplate how such fantasies (and the dream) might relate to unconscious material, particularly childhood fantasies. Yet dream formation, in Freud's (1916/1972) evocative analogy, requires cooperation between entrepreneur (day residue) and capitalist (repressed infantile wish). Attending to the day residue while minimizing the phallic, especially the oedipal, particularly with regard to early developmental roots, Kohut may have been expressing a preference to exercise his talents more at the entrepreneurial level.

In keeping with this possibility, Mitchell (1997) noted that, for Kohut, the most significant meaning is to be found in the way the analyst manages the surface. In contrast, reminiscent of Erikson, Mitchell emphasized that surface and depth, conscious and unconscious, meanings that are apparent and meanings that are elaborated, are mutually enriching. I too believe that insufficient attention to the relationship between manifest and latent, between data and theory, can be both theoretically and clinically impoverishing. This is not to say that important work cannot be done on either side of the street. It is, rather, to suggest that one can achieve even more if one takes the middle road, working both sides of the street.

Solo, Duet, Trio, Quartet

Traditional analysis has been criticized for being a one-person perspective. Self psychology (and some other orientations) have been said to promote a superior, two-person point of view. Examination of the first dream suggests Kohut had some difficulty seeing his patient in triangular terms. Classical analysis furnishes a constant, valuable reminder of the importance of "three-person" psychology— or more, if we recall Freud's (1954) ideas concerning ordinary psychosexual bisexuality: "I am accustomed myself to the idea of regarding every sexual act as a process in which four persons are involved" (p. 289). With respect to those inevitable ghosts in the bedroom, there may be far more presences than even the founder fathomed. "Freud's 'four,'" Shengold (1989) opined, "is pitifully inadequate" (p. 35).

Controversy between monadic and dyadic perspectives is not new. Over a half century ago, Rickman (1950/1957a, 1951/1957b) had differentiated one-, two-, three- (oedipal), four-person (sibling rivalry as an oedipal side issue), and multibody (group) psychologies. Noting that traditional, academic, one-person psychologists were unable to predict much about two-person situations, he believed their knowledge was "almost useless in a clinical situation, particularly the analytic situation" (p. 221). Especially germane to the material I am considering, he commented that "A two-person psychologist who *shut his mind to those transference manifestations which brought in the third party* [italics added] would not be able to make many useful predictions concerning three-person psychological situations" (p. 222).

In contrast to the usual debate between allegedly one- and two-person psychologies, Morrison (1994) wryly advocated a one-and-a-half-person psychology. In his cleverly integrative notion, the subjective self is one person, whereas the "other" is partly an objectively perceived being, partly a created image. The half objective, half subjective other is composed not only of who she or he is as a person, that is, what she or he brings to the table, but also who she or he is imagined to be in terms of what needs and fears she or he is expected to fulfill. The other is inevitably imbued with transferences from the past, with qualities that are wished for, dreaded, or required. Morrison's perspective might be considered as usefully reminding one of the transitional domain (Winnicott, 1952/1971b) between phantasy and reality.

Shifting emphasis from a natural scientific, objectivist model to a more hermeneutic, relational, constructivist framework, contemporary analysts speak less about prediction, power, and control than Rickman did. Still, it is the power of understanding that enables them somewhat to predict and control, that is, to intervene intelligently and influence patients. In this sense, Rickman's warning about the cost of closing one's mind to the oedipal dimension continues to be valid and timely. My emphasis, however, is not so much on shutting one's mind but rather on one's mind closing inadvertently. One might be surprised and intrigued if this unknown foreclosure were pointed out by a friendly critic.

Cultures that only have words for the numerical concepts one, two, and many may intimate that beyond dyadic intimacy (with its at-one-ment) lie the inevitably more stressful, triadic, and larger group experiences (with their propensities to split and exclude). In common parlance, two's company, three's a crowd. Triads and larger associations jostle one with new affects, conflicts, and challenges.

Concordant with Freud's hypothesis concerning the routine augmentation of the couple in the boudoir, groups appeared in each of Kohut's dreams. His analysand was always observed by some aggregate in painful, excited, and ambiguous ways. The omnipresence of the larger social unit might reflect the centrality of his patient's struggle with postdyadic object relations including conflictual wishes to be part of the group (primal) scene, participating, watching, being seen, stimulated, and seeking release.

Kohut only mentioned the primal scene concept once, and then only in a negative sense, ruling out the possibility that his analysand's voyeuristic-exhibitionistic features could have been derived from "frightening primal-scene observations" (p. 125). As with his previously noted, seemingly excessive emphasis on castration anxiety in his understanding of the Oedipus complex, here, too, Kohut seemed to focus exclusively on anxiety-laden aspects of the primal scene at the expense of appreciating its more complex significance (e.g., arousing, sexual, and aggressive features; its role in children's crucial sexual research including fantasies concerning who has which genitals, who does what to whom and why; dysphoria related to exclusion, etc.). If one is searching exclusively for indications of frightening primal scenes, one may overlook other significant signs of this entity including manifestations more attractive than repulsive, more saddening (re exclusion) than anxiety producing, and so on. Reduction in the richness of the primal scene construct curtails one's ability to utilize it to understand and assist patients.

Among analysts in the various relational traditions, Kohut would be by no means alone with respect to overlooking or minimizing the complex role of infantile sexuality. In a superb article on the internalized primal scene, Aron (1995), a leading relationalist, noted that such "concepts seemed to be underemphasized, if not altogether lost, in contemporary relational theory" (p. 250). The relational discourse came to be dominated by what Loewald (1979) called "The Waning of the Oedipus Complex." Moving away from a drive-discharge model and focusing on pre-oedipal phenomena, analysts working in relational traditions have shifted away from the sexual and oedipal imagery that had characterized psychoanalytic discourse for half a century, Aron observed. Aron lamented and labored to redress this loss. Infantile sexuality, primal scene, Oedipus complex, and other such constructs are important, clinically rich metaphors to be utilized by analysts independent of any commitment to drive-discharge metapsychology, Aron argued. Furthermore, relational approaches add depth and complexity to our understanding of these central psychoanalytic ideas, Aron believed. In terms of the direction of influence between classical and relational perspectives, it can be a two-way street.

End of First Movement

Convinced that mental disturbances (irritability, restlessness, fatigue, failure to concentrate) were caused by feces, the analysand's mother administered enemas to her children until they approached adolescence. Thereafter, they would have to attend to such matters on their own. Her theory and practice would, no doubt, influence her offspring's psychosexual fantasies during their formative years and beyond.

In nocturnal hallucination, Kohut's analysand exhibited the very sorts of disturbance (ill at ease, uncomfortable, thrashing about restlessly, tired but unable to concentrate on sleeping) that his mother liked to treat with enemas. His agitated display, right on the lawn, may have been unconsciously calculated to seduce her away from other affairs. Stimulating her desire to approach and even enter him, his subsequent submission to her potent, intrusive intervention might signify a cunning oedipal victory. This phallic mother (analyst in maternal transference) may have been depicted by the crowd (in the familiar manner of representing one by many) intruding into the analysand's personal domain as he thrashed about, partially uncovered. This seemingly unwanted invasion may have been secretly desired even though, consciously, the dreamer may simply have wanted the crowd to "butt out."

INTERMEZZO—NOTES ON REASONING SCIENTIFICALLY

Along with the formulation of theory, challenging its own theories is the essence of any science.

Roy Schafer, *A New Language for Psychoanalysis*

There were no indications that Kohut raised any of the preceding hypotheses about the first dream, not even to rule them out. He did not appear to consider that this nocturnal reverie might reflect intense interest in the parental relationship, understood in terms of early developmental, component instincts like displaying and watching (id) coupled with a painful sense of exclusion (superego prohibition); giving rise to a variety of compensatory fantasies aimed at reversing the dreamer's predicament (ego defense); setting himself at the center of a new scene emphasizing agonizing, exhibitionistic-voyeuristic gratification (compromise formation), tension discharge, restoration of narcissistic balance, and so forth.

These omissions are a wellspring for wonderment given that Kohut scrutinized his material from both classical and self psychological points of view. Had he simply processed his data with self psychological lenses, one might not be so taken aback by his not perceiving and discussing the cornucopia of classical interpretive possibilities. In the more comparative context he adopted, it is hard not to be astounded (and intrigued) by his assertion that despite openness to discerning the oedipal, there was no significant evidence for it, neither in the dreams nor anywhere else throughout years of analysis.

In the course of their investigations, scientists make bold conjectures. Subsequently, they subject them to rigorous tests, enabling them to conclude whether they stand up better than rival hypotheses (Popper, 1959). Basic to the scientific evaluation of evidence is a comparative process in which each side needs to be explored with comparable care and precision (Campbell & Stanley, 1963). Similar methodological precepts were emphasized by Edelson (1984) in promoting eliminative inductivism to test analytic hypotheses by case study and other methods.

In the context of discovery (Popper, 1959), Kohut made bold conjectures. In the context of confirmation, he subjected them to processes of comparison with rival explanations derived from traditional theory. Unfortunately, in the instance we are considering, his devotion to the new appeared to have interfered with his capacity to access the old domain of appropriate alternative explanations. Consequently, he was unable to adequately create the necessary rival arguments, neither during the analysis, for the patient's benefit, nor subsequently for his readers. In the absence of a judicious process of comparison, his boldly asserted findings (nonsightings) about the Oedipal complex do not appear to meet the rigorous standards that accord with the basic and best canons of scientific reasoning. His assertion about the lack of significance of the oedipal does not seem scientifically sound.

Lest these comments be misconstrued as a critique of Kohut or his oeuvre, allow me to reiterate that the preceding difference of opinion is but a focal criticism. It is not directed at Kohut per se but rather at more general reasoning processes and liabilities to which all are vulnerable. Kohut merely provides an illustration that, because he is Kohut, is more interesting and compelling than would be a similar example selected from the work of "Jane Doe." This being said, one might otherwise replace the word, Kohut, with the name, Everyman.

THE PSYCHOANALYTIC RESEARCH TRADITION

Our concern with how commitment to innovation can block access to important aspects of the traditional and with how this interference can lead to unsound scientific reasoning that may seriously undermine the clinical inference process might be viewed in relation to a thesis advanced by Stepansky (1983). In his article on dissent and the psychoanalytic research tradition, he drew on Laudan's (1977) differentiation between global theories or research traditions (e.g., psychoanalysis) and the more delineated theories that fall within and exemplify such traditions. A research tradition specifies modes of procedure that constitute legitimate methods of inquiry and provide guidelines for the development of theory in accordance with the requirements of the tradition.

Stepansky asserted that Kohut understood psychoanalysis to be a research tradition radically discontinuous with the content of its specific theories. For Kohut, analysis as an investigative tradition encompassed no more than the specific methodology appropriate to its subject matter, namely, depth psychology, the inner life, the domain of complex mental states. That methodology he defined as introspection and empathy. He therefore regarded self psychology as a new theory solidly within the psychoanalytic research tradition.

Stepansky raised the crucial question: How does one know whether empathy is being employed scientifically in the analytic setting? Presumably one knows, he answered, when the analyst obtains data that in accordance with the analyst's understanding of psychoanalytic theory, can be ordered into explanations and interpretations that are therapeutically efficacious. Stepansky therefore believed an adequate definition of the psychoanalytic research tradition must incorporate not only a methodology but also an ontology circumscribing the ordering principles, that is, the theories that fall within the research tradition. In his opinion, Kohut neglected to provide an epistemological basis for imputing scientific status to explanations and interpretations proceeding not just from a data-gathering process, however precise and objective, but also from an ordering operation. By presupposing rather than critically elucidating the scientific status of the analyst's ordering of data, Kohut's perspective on the psychoanalytic research tradition provided no basis for ascribing validity to clinical theories that underlie the dynamic and genetic interpretations that proceed from empathic data gathering, he argued.

Stepansky concluded that self psychology can legitimately retain the psychoanalytic appellation to the extent that it can equate analysis with a research tradition radically discontinuous from the content of specific psychoanalytic theories. He, however, viewed Kohut's operational perspective as epistemologically incomplete because it addressed only the methodology that informs psychoanalytic observation and ignored the ontology that circumscribes the nature of distinctively psychoanalytic theories.

In his analysis of the dream material, what Stepansky described as Kohut's lack of concern with scientifically sound principles for ascribing validity (and invalidity) to clinical theories made it easy for him to slip scientifically and, perhaps, clinically. Insufficient attention to the manner in which empathic data gathering relates to explanatory theories made it easy for Kohut's commitment to the new to interfere with his capacity to access the old, thereby compromising his scientific reasoning and possibly his clinical efficacy.

On the basis of this single dream, one can raise serious questions in relation to Kohut's assertion about the lack of significance of the Oedipal complex in this case (and, by implication, in others). In fairness, however, it is necessary to examine all three dreams to see whether the totality of available evidence constitutes a significant challenge to Kohut's bold conjecture.

SECONDO FANTASIA—HALLELUJAH!

The climax of the first dream was heralded by the arrival of onlookers. The dénouement was not portrayed. Like the passersby, we were not privy to the narrative's unfolding. The door to the dream theater closed. Paralleling the position of the protagonist excluded from the bungalow, our situation only permitted us to wonder what might have transpired beyond that opaque portal. Fortunately, subsequent dreams enable us to reenter the analysand's fantasy world, affording opportunities for ascertaining whether the rival conjectures I proposed (bold as Kohut's) are additionally supported, or refuted, by further data in the context of confirmation/disconfirmation.

Proudly, the patient reported behaving more maturely during a recent disagreement with his spouse. Rather than becoming enraged, he cancelled an engagement to allow her to attend a concert with a friend. He proceeded to describe a dream about his law society:

> Although he himself had not heard … that he was to be honored, the man sitting next to him told him about it and also explained … that, as a compromise, he was sharing the prize with someone else. The patient then went to the podium and was given the award; it was a camera. To the surprise of everyone, he lifted the camera and took a picture of the audience. The audience was stunned. (p. 116)

As in Dream 1, triangularity (analysand, spouse, companion) is suggested in the day residue. Once again, Kohut did not comment on this oedipal trend. The patient's wife and friend observed others making beautiful music while he stayed home. Significantly, however, he was no longer simply a victim of exclusion (from bungalow, illuminated sex, concert). Now he was the explicit maestro of extrusion (his, theirs). He orchestrated the scene so he would be separate from the couple when the lights went low. This time, he did not have to thrash about to discharge mounting tension, playing second fiddle to his wife's preferential attunement to her friend. Conducting himself differently, he exhibited his splendid new matu-rity to his analyst. Rather than feeling diminished by extrusion, he swelled with pride. Aggrandized by voluntary exclusion, he transmuted oedipal trauma into maturational triumph.

As in the first dream, the analysand distinguished domestic from public milieus. (Dream 3 blends public and private.) His concern with this distinction might have roots in earlier developmental efforts to comprehend boundaries between what was open and shared in his original home, particularly in his rela-tionship with his parents, as opposed to that which was closed and from which he was excluded. Discriminations between public and private places (and acts) are often associated with corresponding notions of public versus private parts of bodies. Such highly charged zones of differentiation, exclusion, and privileged access frequently stimulate fantasies of transgression. Exhibitionism and voyeur-ism provide nifty vehicles for exciting, transborder excursions.

Mitchell (1988) made similar points when he noted that

> The very privacy, secrecy, and exclusion in one's experience of one's parents' sex-uality makes it perfectly designed to take on meanings concerning a division of interpersonal realms, the accessible versus the inaccessible, the visible versus the shadowy, surface versus depth. Sexuality takes on all the intensity of passionate struggles to make contact, to engage, to overcome isolation and exclusion. (p. 103)

Assuming both public situations (concert and award ceremony) may have been related (unconsciously equivalent), the patient may have arranged it so that in attending the law soirée, he could observe what others (wife and partner or, more fundamentally, mother and father) were doing at night. Instead of just his wife and her mate witnessing gratifying nocturnal events, he did so, too, with a gentleman at his side.

No sooner had the analysand accepted the reasonableness of boundaries than he found a way of traversing them, thereby compensating himself handsomely for any temporary loss that might have been incurred in his maturational advance. The very night the conductor mounted his podium, the patient, in scintillat-ing symmetry, ascended his own podium to accept a prize. His developmental achievement—accepting the reasonableness of subordinating his desires to the needs of the couple—received ample recognition, perhaps with his wife, certainly in the dream, and subsequently, through proudly parading his progress before his analyst.

Having set the scene in prefatory associations about his spouse and friend going out, the analysand expressed, via the dream, that he would not long remain even a willing oedipal outsider. In Dream 1, he moved from periphery (vis-à-vis the bungalow) to the center of attention. In Dream 2, likewise, he injected himself onto the principal stage, assuming a key part in the evening's main event, transforming himself from oedipal loser to winner. No longer excluded from the inner sanctum (e.g., relegated to the lawn of the last resort), he was now securely inside, coupled with a friendly gentleman "in the know" (conceivably Kohut in paternal transference). This gentleman explained what might be understood as a message that the analysand would not instantly become a full-fledged oedipal victor. Rather, "as a compromise he was sharing the prize with someone else." He would not have to bear the guilt of full oedipal triumph nor the pain of total exclusion. Such compromise formations are a hallmark of oedipal resolutions (Brenner, 1955).

Arabesque

At the most highly charged moment at the law society soirée, the analysand deployed his prize to photograph the audience. One could understand their being surprised or amused; to be "stunned," however, seems extreme. Kohut did not comment on this discrepancy. To a classical analyst, such strong affect might suggest the situation represented some unconscious scenario in which the emotional reaction might make more sense, for, as Edelson (1988) noted, psychoanalysis "especially raises questions about causal gaps ... about the inexplicability of the contents of particular mental states" (p. xxv).

In contrast, Kohut (1984) simply asserted that his patient

> surprised and shocked them ... to convert the uncomfortable situation of being looked at into a situation in which it was he who did the looking and thus made those who looked at him feel uncomfortable. He (visually) counterattacked when he began to feel (visually) attacked; he embarrassed (shamed) others when he experienced the discomfort of being embarrassed (shamed). (p. 121)

Although Kohut's analysis fits his understanding of narcissistic difficulties, it is not otherwise clear what led him to believe his patient felt mainly persecuted rather than gratified by this public honoring.

Classical analysts would consider this material differently. The analysand loved illuminated intercourse. Tending to feel deprived and diminished by his wife's preference to keep him in the dark, in his wish-fulfilling hallucination, his frustration and belittlement were replaced by gratification and aggrandizement. He became a star. Basking in the limelight, he looked without restraint and was seen, reciprocally, in very positive terms. Finally granted his just desserts, he ate up the whole experience *con gusto.*

For his sacrifice the previous evening, the analysand was richly rewarded not only with peer recognition but also with a special viewing device. This prize provided the perfect means for enacting a desirable derivative of his core sexual phantasy. Through the eye of the camera, he was able to observe aroused spectators admiring him enthusiastically in his moment of glory. This experience was marvelously isomorphic with his most cherished desire of "watching the woman looking at him" (p. 120). Symbolic realization of this highly cathected wish might account for that moment having been so electrifying, so meaningful. His photograph would preserve this peak experience forever.

A fine evening of observing and being observed led to steadily mounting excitement. As he gripped his perfect prize possession, concentrating, escalating tension culminated in a divinely climactic experience. Erecting his gift from the gods (of the law society), poised to shoot, it would scarcely have sufficed for his audience to have been simply surprised, merely amused. The only concordant response capable of doing justice to the fantasy embodied in his stunning, phallic display would be for the audience to be correspondingly stunned. At their finest moments, law societies can be counted on to be attuned to such matters of balance and justice.

Veni, vidi, vici:. The analysand came, saw, and conquered. Whereas life frequently frustrates, in the theatre of the dream, wishes can come true.

In the Eye of the Beholder

Classical analysts comprehend dreams by elucidating how manifest content reflects underlying wishes, particularly infantile ones. "Something is added to the day's residues, something that was also part of the unconscious, a powerful but repressed wishful impulse; and it is this alone that makes the construction of the dream possible" (Freud, 1900/1953a, p. 226). In contrast, Kohut may have overemphasized attunement to conscious experience as opposed to unconscious processes requiring more theoretically informed inference (Levy, cited in Jessee, 1995; Richards, 1992; Stepansky, 1983). One can learn a great deal by focusing on the surface. If, however, one remains too much in the domain of the "entrepreneur," one will likely miss some capital ideas. Without sufficient access to such core psychoanalytic principles, one is unlikely to fully understand the structure and meaning of dreams.

As with Dream 1, it was remarkable that Kohut did not entertain any of these possible oedipal interpretations (letting the women leave to have a gallivanting good time; enjoying watching turned-on spectators admiring him; sharing the prize, etc.). He did consider that sharing might relate to sibling rivalry. It might have served him well, however, if he had recalled Rickman's (1951/1957b) remark apropos "sibling rivalry as a side issue in the examination of the Oedipus complex" (p. 220) or Freud's (1916/1972) earlier reflection:

> When other children approach the scene the Oedipus complex is enlarged into a family complex. This, with fresh support from the egoistic sense of injury, gives grounds for receiving the new brothers and sisters with repugnance and for unhesitatingly getting rid of them by a wish. It is even true as a rule children are far readier to give verbal expression to *these* feelings of hate than to those arising from the parental complex. (p. 333)

Sometimes we, too, may be more at ease with issues of sibling rivalry than with oedipal complexities.

Kohut noted the defense of turning passive to active both in photographing the audience and also in proceeding from being painfully observed in Dream 1 to inflicting observation in Dream 2. He did not, however, note the key progression from seeming to passively suffer exclusion in Dream 1 to actively deriving pleasure by excluding himself in Dream 2, then actively reinserting himself onto center stage (as he had also done in the earlier dream, although then in a more masochistic manner).

Despite awareness of the importance of exhibitionism and voyeurism in his patient's sexual life, Kohut did not articulate the parsimonious possibility that his analysand might actually have enjoyed the audience's admiration (in accordance with Freud's fundamental theorem of dreams as wish fulfillments). Although cognizant of the importance of looking and being looked at in his analysand's preferred foreplay, Kohut did not consider that being observed and admired in the dream might also have functioned as desirable forepleasure, spurring the analysand on to even greater feats of phallic exhibitionism. Seized with the idea that his patient may have experienced the audience's enthusiasm as traumatic, Kohut seemed unable to contemplate that he might, on the contrary, or in addition, have enjoyed the experience to such an extent that he may have been stimulated to strive for an even more stunning finale, reaching for a means of discharge that would enable him to leave the limelight not with a whimper but with a bang.

The analysand's dramatic exit was reminiscent of a patient of mine who, for a period of time, experienced emptiness at the end of sessions. He protested poignantly that he had to leave "with nothing but my dick in hand." Rather than experiencing such deflating dysphoria, Kohut's analysand chose to leave triumphantly, with dick/head/camera held high, proudly erect. To maintain a grip on his feelings, exerting control over the affectively charged situation, he may have experienced an irresistible urge to proffer a clever parting shot, a spirited spurt, more like a second coming than a dismal, anticlimactic, fading into the dark anonymity of the night.

Patients with such vulnerabilities strive against succumbing to the rather depressive philosophy enshrined in the famous dictum, *Post coitus omnes animales tristes sunt* (after intercourse all animals are sad). Following an hour of analytic intercourse or law society celebrations, these analysands seek more uplifting options. Their counterdepressive strategies suggest mildly manic, defensive operations.

Although Kohut noted that the "camera is, of course, a symbol of the eye—of being looked at, of looking" (p. 121), he did not mention that this device can also symbolize a fascinating, phallic apparatus. Its protruding lens may be conveniently stimulated to stick out even further simply by fingering the right button in the appropriate manner. This intriguing, corporeal extension is ever ready to rise to the occasion, pointing toward others who arouse interest. It can, therefore, stand not only for the eye but also, as the vernacular would have it, the one-eyed trouser snake (the pet name bestowed by some phallic aficionados on their favorite character in the oedipal drama).

Although trouser snakes should usually be discretely concealed, this analysand enjoyed toying and flirting with the public/private boundary. Not wanting to be restricted to revealing his amazing prize possession strictly in camera, he wished to exercise his inalienable right to flash it occasionally in public in the pursuit of happiness. His wife subscribed to a more puritanical philosophy whereby private parts should not be so proudly aired in prime time. Genital appreciation ought be restricted, not placed in the limelight. Let there be darkness, she decreed. Slippery snakes should generally lie contentedly concealed beneath flat stones or other opaque objects rather than becoming uppity, getting their rocks off, basking brazenly in the warm, sensuous glow of the sun.

The Latin word *pudere,* to be ashamed, gave rise to our term *pudenda,* which signifies external genitalia. Kohut's analysand manifested shame in Dream 1, maintaining the fig leaf of his covers at least partly in place. In Dream 2, however, he was unabashedly cocky (*impudent*). In contrast to his wife's inhibitory, nocturnal philosophy, this prince of darkness was determined to assert and express himself. He seemed more enamored than she with the famous 1960s, Dionysian credo, "Let it all hang out."

GLISSANDO—THE COURT JESTER

Bisexual Brouhaha

After reflecting on the camera, Kohut reported some transferential interactions. His analysand ended one session with unprecedented emotion, sharing that he could now converse freely with colleagues and relate warmly with his wife and children. He noticed he occasionally spoke with his analyst's voice, words, and humane attitude. These gains he attributed to his therapist's influence. Kohut responded that he was glad to hear of all this.

Launching the next session with a vigorous attack, the analysand alleged that dogmatic, sometimes deranged, analysts forced opinions on patients. Kohut suggested this tirade related to the analysand's gratitude in the previous session.

An analyst approaching this material from a classical perspective might hypothesize that the patient's new feeling of masculine, identificatory closeness may have stimulated homosexual fantasies, anxieties, and defenses. Although fervently desired, greater relaxation, openness, and emotionality might simultaneously have made the analysand feel more feminine—a vulnerable position to be in with a potentially "crazy" analyst.

The specter of a beloved, but possibly eccentric, unstable therapist forcing opinions on a troubled, dependent patient may have been reminiscent of the analysand's mother forcing her queer beliefs concerning enemas into him. He had come to realize that his mother was "a little crazy" (p. 142). He frequently viewed analysis in identical terms. Fear of rectal assault by a not always easily understood, phallic, intrusive parent may have stimulated a counterdependent, aggressively guarded, anal expulsive defense now manifested in his tirade about crazy psychoanalysts.

These two sides of the coin (wish–fear, masculine–feminine, active–passive) recall the symbolism of the camera. Like other objects that can penetrate the surrounding, yielding medium while also having a capacity to contain (e.g., cars, boats, shoes), it can be a bisexual symbol. Both phallic and feminine, it is like the penetrating/receptive eye itself. In keeping with its feminine facet, the word *camera* comes from the feminine, Latin noun *camera*, meaning a vaulted room (enclosed, feminine space).

Whether proudly exhibiting new capacities for warm, open, emotional, verbal intercourse with men, women, and children in front of his analyst or flashing his box-like device with its prominent, protruding, central aperture at the aroused, admiring audience, the analysand may have been tempted to drop his defenses, relax his emotional sphincter even further, leaving his little shutter ajar for more than a split second, allowing more than a little light to penetrate his dark hole, the symbolic portal, perhaps, to the unexplored, "dark continent" (Freud, 1926/1959b, p. 212) of his femininity. Such risky temptations may have stimulated anxiety/desire that his analyst, no doubt crazy like some others he had heard about, might in turn be tempted to force more than just a rigid opinion into him much as his mother had inserted more than simply her views about the anal etiology of mental disturbances into his posterior invagination.

Bridge over Troubled Waters

"Without any logical bridge" (Kohut, 1984, p. 122), Kohut's patient proceeded to recount a vivid memory of a grueling mock court from his student days. Terrified, he had turned the tables on the usually brutally critical audience by pursuing a seemingly erroneous route and then revealing suddenly, to everyone's surprise, that he had misled them. As a result of his cunning coup de théâter, the usual critique following the trial bypassed the analysand to his great relief. From this tale, Kohut concluded that the analysand's habit of shaming and stunning others when he feared being shamed and stunned was deeply engrained.

By now it will perhaps not be surprising to find that Kohut did not allude to the fact that his patient had, yet again, managed to underscore the triadic nature of his object relational conflict. On this occasion, triangularity was represented by the highly charged relationship between prosecution, defense, and audience. The latter entity—somewhat excluded, keenly observing, action-oriented—watched in a heightened state of arousal, ever ready to pounce on the other participants (with scathing criticism). Clearly the spectators got off on this passionate mode of involvement.

In a self-protective tour de force, the analysand may have led not only the mock court down the garden path but his analyst as well. This evocative trial memory emerged after Kohut interpreted the defensive (paranoid) need to mount a vigorous attack following unprecedented expression of warmth. The analysand's previous therapist had been given to waxing enthusiastically about anality including anal orgasm. That gentleman's orientation may have been reminiscent of the patient's mother's fondly held theory of the anal etiology of mental disturbances, with her corresponding passion for inserting tubes into posterior portals. Given the well-known associations between paranoia, homosexuality, and anality, the analysand may have had unsettling premonitions as to where Kohut's seemingly gentle interpretive line about his paranoia may have been heading.

Introducing the mock trial memory "without any logical bridge," the crucial *psychological* bridge may have been the need to hoodwink Kohut, to lead him astray with a stunning red herring, exactly as he had once thrown the prosecution off his tail. Adroitly conjuring up a time when, on behalf of the "defense," a clever stratagem had served him well in warding off intensely persecutory, phallic anxieties, these tried and true defenses appeared to have worked equally well with his second analyst.

Testing, Testing

In terms of control-mastery theory (Weiss, Sampson, & the Mount Zion Psychotherapy Research Group, 1986), Kohut's patient may have sprung a subtle test on his analyst when he launched his verbal assault after having expressed unprecedented warmth and gratitude. Correctly intuiting that this rant was reactive to that progress, Kohut interpreted this likelihood. By not having taken offense and not adopting a persecutory counterattack, Kohut passed that exam. Kohut's therapeutic skill was, no doubt, simultaneously reassuring and threatening to the patient because it would help him to relax, drawing him closer to his admired analyst.

Because of the continuing element of anxiety intrinsic to Kohut's having survived the tirade test, the analysand may have felt a need to resort to a new line of defense. The analysand may have felt compelled to create a subsequent, subtler exam. This second test, embedded in the mock trial memory, may have been intended as a real, continuing trial of his analyst, an experiment aimed at misleading Kohut away from more threatening issues. In Trial 2, we, the readers, become the keenly observing spectators in the case of analyst versus artful dodger.

Advocating for the defense of his status quo, the analysand would have wanted to win this *control-mastery trial* (a term that unintentionally but neatly evokes the sexualized, dominance-submission, transferential struggle). This desire to come out on top would obtain even if it mocked not only the analyst but also the analytic process, culminating in mere Pyrrhic victory.

At another level, control-mastery theory would posit that the analysand would also have longed to be found out. He would have yearned for a masterful analyst who could uncover his fantasies, skillfully penetrating his defenses, so he would not keep getting away with such rearguard actions, turning the same old tricks that kept him all too securely imprisoned in his ultimately unsatisfying, missionary position. Kohut may not have passed this subtle, second test. (Of course, he may have passed it on subsequent occasions.)

(Don't) See Me, Hear Me, Touch Me, Feel Me

Kohut selected this patient for publication to ground his effort at reformulating the concepts of resistance and defense. He presented his case for the superiority of self psychological formulation to the court of public appeal. In the halls of justice, his readers assume the role of the critical spectators in the case of Kohut versus classical analysis. He did not articulate why this patient seemed especially suitable for this project. Perhaps he sensed that this analysand's self-protective maneuvers were particularly pervasive, interesting, subtle, or challenging. The mock trial memory suggests this may have been the case as does the elusiveness to Kohut of the patient's psychosexuality, particularly his Oedipal complex. Kohut may have intuited that even though he never came "face to face with the resistances that constitute clinical manifestations of the defense against castration anxiety" (p. 128), such factors may, nonetheless, have been operative. Taking him literally, he never said those issues were absent, only that he could not discern them. Consciously, he believed these defenses and the underlying complex were simply not there. Unconsciously, he may have sensed otherwise. (It would be hard to imagine, for example, that Kohut did not, at some level, entertain the hypothesis of dreaded/desired sexual violation when he interpreted his patient's postgratitude assault on the analytic process, although one cannot know for certain.)

A prominent London Kleinian, O'Shaughnessy (1989), criticized Kohut's tendency to consider that when an Oedipus complex is not apparent, it does not exist and his consequently advocating a restoration technique. In contrast, she stated the Kleinian view that when an Oedipus complex is "invisible," it is not because it is unimportant but "because it is so important and felt by the patient ... to be so unnegotiable that he employs psychic means to make and keep it invisible" (p. 129). In reviewing O'Shaughnessy's essay, Chasseguet-Smirgel (1991) concurred that this was "a point no non-Kohutian analyst would want to question" (p. 729).

These considerations give rise to the following query: How can what is invisible to one analyst be so visible to another? The popular tale of the emperor's magnificent new duds may be relevant. Musing with respect to those who do not believe in childhood sexuality, Freud (1916/1972) noted that "It calls for real ingenuity not to see all this or to see it differently" (p. 316). Ingenuity perhaps or, I argue, an inadvertent epiphenomenon of commitment to a new theoretical model excessively separated from other frameworks. I take up these vital questions pertaining to seeing and not seeing in detail in chapter 2.

Common Ground

The analysand's father was blessed with impressive "masculine assets" (Kohut, 1984, p. 130). The father had garnered many athletic and vocational trophies. Distant and forbidding, he was not an easy model for identification. In contrast, the patient had clearly come to feel closely identified with Kohut. This positive libidinal development stimulated intense fantasies, anxieties, and defensive processes apparently related to the admirable, exciting, yet potentially abusive facets of imposing masculine assets.

By Dream 2, the analysand may have been more comfortable identifying with men in general and with his father and analyst in particular. Receiving an award for career prowess, as his father had done, he shared the prize. As in the transference, this identificatory closeness with father (older gentleman sitting next to him) may have aroused homosexual anxiety, stimulating a need to seize control, sticking it to the audience counterphobically (especially to the gentleman/father/Kohut). This sexually tinged fear of attack, provoking defensive counterattack, constitutes an alternative (complementary) hypothesis to Kohut's assertion that the audience's admiration was simply experienced as a shameful, stunning assault requiring retaliation in kind.

Kohut's chapter sought to reconceptualize the fundamental ideas of resistance and defense. Classical analysis, the *fons et origo* of these concepts, continues to have much to offer to their elucidation even in analyses conducted primarily along other lines. Approaches estranged excessively from our rich tradition may miss crucial insights pertaining, for example, to phallic-oedipal, impulse-defense configurations. Restoration of continuing valid aspects of the classical perspective might eliminate some shortcomings, thereby magnifying the power of Kohutian formulation. Admiring looks and comments from analyst or audience might, for example, from a combined Freudian/Kohutian point of view, be experienced as pleasurable, even intensely so, and also as having potential to lead to shameful, stunning attack, especially if they are unconsciously associated with conflictual fantasies of (homo)sexual interest and invasion. Integrating self psychological with Freudian interpretation may afford more comprehensive, satisfying, therapeutically useful formulations and interventions.

Over a half century ago, Fenichel (1945) was among those who strove to integrate theories of instinct and narcissism: "Exhibitionism remains more narcissistic than any other partial instinct" (p. 72), he wrote. "Its erogenous pleasure is always connected with an increase in self-esteem, anticipated or actually gained through the fact that others look at the subject" (p. 72).

A quarter of a century before Fenichel, Freud (1920/1955b) himself, when he discussed the ending of infantile sexuality, observed that "loss of love and failure leave behind them a permanent injury to self-regard in the form of a narcissistic scar, which ... contributes more than anything else to the 'sense of inferiority' which is so common in neurotics" (pp. 20–21).

In a similar vein, Gedo and Goldberg (1973) noted that Freud regarded the threat of castration as a danger of narcissistic injury:

> The gradual reduction of the child's grandiosity comes to include his phallus last of all, so that phallic exhibitionism, as well as its counterparts in females, continues to be subject to the excessive vulnerability that characterizes every aspect of the grandiose self. ... A prerequisite for the resolution of the Oedipus complex is sufficient maturation along the paths of transformation of narcissism to permit the child to tolerate the mortification caused by the collapse of his phallic grandiosity. (p. 84)

More recently, Aron (1995), following Ikonen and Rechardt (1984), noted that the primal scene involves both narcissistic injury and relational deprivation. "It therefore serves as an internal structure regulating both narcissism and object relations" (Aron, 1995, p. 207).

This longstanding interest of Freud, Fenichel, Gedo, Aron, and others in integrating theories of infantile sexuality and narcissism continues to be an important project. My contribution, like theirs, suggests and supports the idea that these realms can be complementary rather than combatively opposed.

TERZO FANTASIA—AFFAIRS OF THE HEART (CRESCENDO)

His friend   was with the patient during the analytic session   lying next to the patient on the couch. There were other people in the room too, quite a few of them. Somebody seemed to have a heart attack. The patient sprang into action to help that man—an older person—doing mouth-to-mouth resuscitation. (Kohut, 1984, p. 116)

Culminating a sequence of fantasies expressing increasingly overt sexuality, this third dream has prominent oedipal (including homoerotic, negative oedipal) elements. Dream 1 introduced the patient alone (albeit next to a dwelling, perhaps feeling excluded from parental sexual life, possibly attempting to lure phallic mother away from father to relieve loneliness, isolation, distress, and tension with her cure-all, penetrating enemas). Dream 2 presented sexual pairs more directly, generally as same sex couples. (The analysand cancelled an engagement so his wife and girlfriend could go out, then he sat beside a gent at an exciting function. Later, he coupled with someone else, sharing a trophy.) In Dream 3, coupling and triangularity became even more explicit. The analysand lay intimately with his friend, whereas the older generation (analyst) was cast into the role of observer—a classic oedipal reversal.

Flashing a camera now seems tame compared to springing this epiphany on his analyst. The patient's overload of jealousy, excitement, exclusion, and homosexual anxiety appear to have been projected into the old man (analyst/father). Burdened by these highly charged evacuations, the elderly gentleman could scarcely contain the stimulation. His heart succumbed. As he went down, the perfect opportunity arose for the analysand to leap into action (as he did, less dramatically, in both previous dreams), going down on his analyst. Abandoning his mate to link up with the slightly removed, third party, the patient transcended separation, exclusion, and distress. In this grand finale, all passivity (feminine receptivity) was conveniently projected into the analyst as was all the dis-ease that had perturbed the patient in the original dream.

Although Kohut said nothing about it, consistent with his tendency to largely overlook sexuality in these dreams, mouth-to-mouth activity might be viewed as disguised eroticism, a splendid opportunity for short-circuiting the gap between the couple and the excluded one. Likely for defensive reasons, this event was portrayed as a medical necessity, like mother's enemas that may also have provided a sensational means for obliterating the generation gap, drawing one party away from other dyadic coupling. In contrast to such medically compelling rationales, only "psychotic" (p. 122) analysts would perceive passion in resuscitation, thrusting such gross ideas down patients' throats. If anyone were going to force anything into any orifice on anybody, the analysand preferred to be on top, in control, in the active, penetrating, heavy-breathing role.

Silent regarding the possibility of such sexual connotations, Kohut (1984) suggested "The revival of the father-analyst ... invited interpretation in terms of a death wish and reaction formation against it" (p. 146). He quickly dismissed that Freudian interpretation, asserting that "in reality, however, the active resuscitation expressed the patient's wish to transform the analyst from an old, sick, dying man into a living, vital, and responsive ideal" (p. 146). Once again, Kohut's view of traditional analysis underscored frightening, hostile oedipal elements (castration anxiety, terrifying primal scenes, and now death wishes) at the expense of other components of the complex, including erotic, loving aspects in all their complexity and depressive anxieties related to exclusion from the sexual arena.

By Dream 3, the analysand had come a long way from lonely thrashing. From isolation outside a room (exclusion, inferiority), he had progressed to a prominent position inside (phallic narcissism) and then to a triangular, oedipal, object relationship right in the consulting room. In this journey from the periphery, he finally fulfilled his ardent desire to include himself in all the frantic, carnal action, the paroxysms of the heart. No longer left to fantasizing and other solitary modes of release, he was, at last, passionately involved with a beloved, transference parent. He could shift attention freely from one partner to the other, as diverse needs and inclinations arose. Kohut did not say anything about this impressive progression.

The Complete Oedipus

The negative oedipal suggested in this patient's material is but one pole of the complete complex. "In each case the two coexist in dialectical relation to each other, and the task of the analyst is to ascertain which the different positions are which the patient takes up as he assumes and resolves his Oedipus complex" (Laplanche & Pontalis, 1973, p. 284). In keeping with that idea, I described the progression of positions this analysand assumed, and resisted, in his dreams. Kohut appeared mostly to have missed these manifestations. The reason for this oversight may have been that constrictions in his oedipal model and, especially, his commitment to a new framework cut him off from these jewels of classical thought. With a particularly strong drive to innovate, the treasure house of traditional insights is subject to being misperceived to an excessive extent as *The Prisonhouse of Psychoanalysis*, to borrow Goldberg's (1990) provocative phrase. Understandably, one would want to escape from a jail rather than attempt to integrate its ambience into postpenitentiary life.

With respect to these gems, particularly the one that could be described as the jewel in the classical crown, Freud (1900/1953a) warned that

> The Oedipus complex can ... be developed to a greater or less strength, it can even be reversed; but it is a regular and very important factor in a child's mental life, and there is more danger of our underestimating than overestimating its influence and that of the developments which proceed from it. (p. 207)

This investigation suggests Freud's cautions continue to be relevant.

To Err Is Helpful

In his splendid article on slips, Rothenberg (1987) encouraged analysts to do with their errors what creative artists do, namely, welcome and even court them. Mistakes provide a unique way for material from the unconscious to enter into art or therapeutic dialogue. Slips are not simply to be passed over, corrected, or understood. They can be used, woven into the very fabric of art or analysis. This approach to the value of error holds true for scientific dialogue as well.

Rothenberg urged us to articulate our errors, that is, separate them, then connect them with the creative context. In that spirit, I separated Kohut's error from his study, allowing it to speak as another important voice. In the following chapters, I connect this voice ever more strongly to a broader context, a creative endeavor, the evolution of psychoanalytic thought.

Neither phase of this articulation process constitutes personal criticism of Kohut. To the extent that he slipped, he merely revealed his humanity. His oversight provides us with a rich opportunity for learning. As can be the case with art, his error is arguably the most unique, important element in his entire chapter.

"In formal logic, a contradiction is the signal of defeat: but in the evolution of real knowledge it marks the first step in progress towards a victory," Wittgenstein declared (as cited in Mitchell & Black, 1995, p. 206). I contradicted Kohut's assertion that there was no evidence of significant oedipal conflict in his patient's dreams. The purpose for articulating this contrary position was not to imply victory or defeat for any individual or point of view but rather to point the way to victory for our field.

Awareness of this conflict between Kohut's data and his conclusion opens a path toward a significant advance in understanding crucial processes in the evolution of analytic thought. This contradiction is therefore, for me, the pièce de résistance in his chapter. It is the penicillin in his petri dish. With an eye toward this larger picture, that serendipitous opposition between his clinical material and formulation is not a phenomenon to be overlooked or dismissed as insignificant. It is, rather, one to be worked with and understood.

CONCLUSION

Kohut was unable to discern any pathogenic oedipal manifestations in his analysand's dreams or anywhere else "in the material that preceded them and followed them right up to the end of the patient's long analysis" (p. 126). In contrast, I found each dream and the surrounding clinical material contained prominent, phallic-oedipal dynamics. Furthermore, dramatic progression over the three-dream sequence powerfully underscored the importance of the phallic-oedipal dimension.

This remarkable evolution across the dreams correlated with noteworthy, corresponding, clinical progress. Proudly reporting that he could now warmly engage in kind ways with family and colleagues, the analysand conveyed his advance in relational capacity from an awkward, tense, isolated condition (like outside the motel) to a more comfortable, although still somewhat distanced, position in which his needs to be attended to and admired were met (as at the law society) and, finally, to a closer, compassionate, more intimate, clearly postdyadic relationship (as in the triangular setting linking the bustling consulting room with the outside world).

Kohut's attachment to his framework and to ongoing innovation seemed to have interfered strikingly with his ability to tap into the revelatory and explanatory powers of traditional psychoanalysis. In consequence, his capacity to more fully comprehend his analysand appears to have been compromised. Powerful investment in promoting and extending the power and explanatory range of new formulations can insidiously close our minds to crucial, hard-won insights. Scientific progress may be obstructed as much by overemphasizing innovation as by rigidly adhering to tradition.

Kohut's difficulty evaluating the relative utility of classical and self-psychological perspectives, despite his conscious attempt to do so, suggests the cognitive processes underlying such constriction of thought operate outside our ken (cf. Gedo, 1984, p. 110). Mental operations always begin outside awareness, Freud (1912/1958c) maintained. Only some become conscious. In this chapter, I endeavored to bring a searchlight to bear on certain important, unconscious processes and their significant sequelae so that we can begin to gain greater control over them rather than being subject to their silent machinations. By increasing our understanding of such subtle operations, we can augment our chances of preventing, or at least catching, such crucial cognitive slippage.

The magnitude of discrepancy in perception and formulation between Kohut and myself is, in this instance, highly significant. This substantial variance brings one face-to-face with the core problem in clinical inference—reliability—the question of whether two or more independent investigators can make the same judgment as to what is (and is not) present in a sample of data (Bolgar, 1965). Dramatic divergence between qualified observers raises disturbing questions pertaining to the nature, soundness, and scientific integrity of the psychoanalytic enterprise. Opponents of analysis would readily draw disparaging conclusions about this state of affairs. We should be able to do much better than that in terms of making sense of, and learning from, this perturbing, intriguing situation.

In the next chapter, I therefore discuss how it could be possible for a superb, classically trained analyst not to perceive profuse, phallic-oedipal material, particularly when searching for it for purposes of comparative analysis. Beyond seeking insight into this enigma, in subsequent chapters, I utilize the knowledge gained from this investigation to explore and develop implications for psychoanalytic education, for clinical practice, and for forging a less disjunctive approach to the evolution of analytic thought and organizational structures.

2

Toward Integrative Understanding

What would be needed, then, would be an ontology of complementarity less sharply dialectical than the metaphysics of the contradictory

—Gaston Bachelard, *The New Scientific Spirit*

INTRODUCTION

Rapaport (Schafer, 1983) often referred to his work as "thinking about thinking; he could envision nothing more worthwhile" (p. xi). Rapaport's student, Schafer, continued this cognitive project "now, however, in connection with the clinical analyst at work" (p. xi). My treatise, too, constitutes an investigation of psychoanalytic thinking. Like Schafer's contribution, this book is also about the clinical analyst at work, albeit in a wider range of settings, including the consulting room, writing room, classroom, and professional associations

In the previous chapter, I contemplated Kohut's (1984) illustrative case in which he reported his inability to discern any evidence of a significant Oedipal complex. A review of his data revealed an abundance of phallic-oedipal material virtually leaping from his data like the patient himself as he thrashed about partially naked in Dream 1, sprung his camera on the startled audience in Dream 2, then vaulted right off the couch in Dream 3. Driven by increasingly peremptory needs that could no longer be kept even partially under wraps, in the final dream, the analysand brought a friend to lie with him on the analytic couch and then thrust himself onto his transference parent to engage in a form of passionate breathing, mouth-to-mouth, his analyst lying intimately beneath him. This triptych of nocturnal hallucinations portrayed a dramatic advance from uncomfortable, solitary, motoric discharge of tension to exuberant, public flashing, to increasingly overt, triangular, oedipal intimacy.

Despite Kohut's commitment to evaluating his data from both classical and self psychological perspectives, he seemed strikingly unable to understand the material in the traditional ways in which he had originally been trained. In this chapter, I endeavor to comprehend how an eminent investigator could fail to perceive such an efflorescence of phallic-oedipal material, especially when he was open to its presence, even looking for it. His oversight raises disquieting questions about the nature and quality of psychoanalytic science. It is far preferable for us to detect and address such conundrums rather than leaving ourselves open to potentially damning criticism from others. In this chapter, therefore, I seek to explicate this enigma.

Scientific Challenges

Epistemological difficulties encumber the approach to the question of the importance of the Oedipal complex in psychopathology and treatment (Simon, 1991). "The interplay of theoretical expectations, clinical observations, therapeutic conceptions, and even how and what one reports of clinical work produces a virtually impenetrable thicket" (p. 643), Simon wrote. Furthermore, "It becomes difficult, perhaps even impossible, to specify what constitutes the data relevant to whether or not the Oedipus complex is central." How then can we "move from the subjectivity of the psychoanalytic situation to the intersubjectivity of firm and agreed-upon knowledge?" Simon asked. "Is it possible that the very nature of psychoanalytic knowledge makes such a move impossible?" (p. 643) he wondered.

Although the methodological problems are substantial, intersubjective agreement (reliability) and validity are surely not beyond the realm of the achievable. Psychoanalysis may sometimes seem to be an impossible profession, but surely it is not an impossible science. Our methods must, of course, be sufficiently powerful so that in the context of confirmation (Popper, 1959), we accurately generate consensus (or disagreement) rather than achieving false positive (or negative) concurrence.

In evaluating Kohut's contention that there was no evidence of significant oedipal conflict, the dreams proved particularly useful in rendering the thicket of his clinical observations and formulations "penetrable." This finding supports the wisdom of the American Psychoanalytic Association Committee on Scientific Activities' recommendation for authors to report sufficient clinical material to enable others to "consider, debate, agree, and/or modify" (Klumpner & Frank, 1991, p. 545) the presenter's conclusions. This value one finds in Kohut's raw data simultaneously underscores the enduring utility of Freud's (1900/1953a) characterization of dreams as the royal road to the unconscious. At the same time, this investigation extends Freud's finding beyond the domain of clinical practice into the more contentious arena of scientific debate.

Anticipating the "commonly expressed fear that including too much information only provokes purposeless second guessing" (Klumpner & Frank, 1991, p. 545), the Committee on Scientific Activities argued convincingly that such anxiety is based on a misunderstanding of scientific discourse and processes for generating knowledge. With Kohut's dreams and related material, we found, in strong agreement with the Committee, that such consideration, testing, and reevaluation of clinical data is anything but "purposeless."

In contrast to the optimistic outlook concerning the possibility of evolving beyond the subjectivity of the psychoanalytic situation to intersubjective agreement, Holt (1992) held a more pessimistic view of the past, present, and future of our science: "Psychoanalysis makes little if any theoretical progress" (p. 380), he bluntly stated. This dismal state of affairs, he believed, was due to the fact that psychoanalysis "has no way of detecting and abandoning errors, no way of settling controversies objectively" (p. 380). As a result, psychoanalysis "lacks the great advantage that scientific method can bestow: escape from the danger of self-deception" (p. 380).

In contrast to Holt's harsh, albeit understandable and at least partially correct judgment, in the previous chapter, I considered some important factors contributing to and impeding theoretical (and clinical) progress. I went to considerable length to demonstrate, contra Holt, that we have some rather robust ways of detecting mistakes, working to settle controversies, and abandoning errors. In this chapter, I continue that train of thought on a complementary, although more experience-distant, level (i.e., no longer grappling with actual clinical data).

Any investigator or school of thought can slip into moments, even prolonged phases, of self-deception. A corrective process will, however, emerge, sooner or later. This self-righting (Lichtenberg, 1995) will take place in the arena of and through processes of scientific reasoning and debate. This eventuality reflects the importance of the broader scientific community as opposed to the role of the lone investigator or isolated school of practitioners/theoreticians. This chapter and the previous one exemplify the nature of our discipline's self-correcting process.

This field need not lack that summum bonum of scientific method cited by Holt, namely, protection from self-deception. Self-deception happens as does group self-deception. It is unlikely, however, that the entire scientific community will succumb to such illusionment. If it appears to, one can rest assured that illusion/delusion will not last forever. As Abraham Lincoln pithily put it, you can fool all the people some of the time, and some of the people all the time, but you cannot fool all the people all the time. In science, this adage, adapted to the vagaries of self-deception and group deception, implies the importance of ongoing, vigorous dialogue in a broad, diverse community of scholars committed to constructive criticism and self-criticism.

Psychoanalytic investigators, like any others, are subject to parapraxes (slips of the conceptual apparatus) and other functional problems. We are determined to value and learn from such phenomena as we do in the consulting room. One can gain as much or more from errors and failed experiments as from smoothly evolving ones. Seeking to comprehend what went awry in Kohut's (or anyone's) experimentation with new thought forms can help elucidate important features and vulnerabilities in our science and practice. Insight gleaned from such investigation will enable us to forge a stronger, more robust, valid, clinico-scientific enterprise. Erring is human; learning from such experience is divine.

EXPLANATORY FRAMEWORKS—PERSONAL AND ABSTRACT

Unable to access the full scope and richness of traditional theory to illuminate his data, Kohut attempted to fit his analysand's productions into relatively ill-suited aspects of the classical model rather than into others that would have accommodated them easily. How could his once powerful, refined capacity to draw on the broad array of classical conceptual tools have become so constricted?

His colleague, Gedo (1986), observed that "Kohut was less and less inclined to *give weight* to the oedipal material he encountered in Tragic Man as he gained confidence in the power and relevance of his own contribution to clinical psychoanalysis" (p. 106). By the time of Kohut's final contribution, from which I derived my example, Kohut seemed unable to consistently perceive, let alone give weight to, the phallic-oedipal dynamics permeating his clinical material.

Increasingly prizing the new theoretical outfit he was fashioning that enabled him to move with ease, Kohut decreasingly cherished the old, heavyweight mode. When a formerly valued, substantial suit is relegated to the back of the closet in favor of a more stylish, comfortably fitting one, one may no longer perceive any merit in the seemingly outdated model. In fact, one may never see that ensemble again as it settles into the black hole at the rear of the cupboard.

Discussing the intrinsically problematic, narcissistic investment in new paradigms, Rothstein (1980) alerted us to a similar phenomenon. Narcissistic cathexis inevitably interferes with realistic perception and testing of reality, he wrote. His thesis is pertinent to this discussion (previous chapter) of Kohut's inability to conduct an appropriately rigorous, objective test of his conjecture, meeting scientific standards, because of his inability to adequately create the necessary, rival argument based on the classical model he could no longer access or "get into" fully.

Although not necessarily renowned for sartorial splendor, analysts are inclined to wrap themselves in highly cathected, deeply cherished theories. The fabric of these constructs may become second nature, functioning in some ways like second skin (Bick, 1968). If these fabrications—what Schafer (1983) and Freud (1926/1959b, p. 194) called "fictions"—are questioned, we may respond in a touchy, thin-skinned manner. Our narcissistic rage with respect to these old and new school ties can sometimes be easily provoked. At other times, we seem

firmly ensconced in Teflon™-coated character armor, narcissistically imperme-
able to challenge.

Liberating himself from old restrictions that he felt impeded scientific progress and clinical practice, Kohut would not have wanted to lose anything essential. He may, however, have inadvertently thrown out some of the baby with the
bath water. Attempting to clean up messy conceptual areas, he addressed some
stagnant, troublesome zones. He managed to inject fresh, invigorating fluid into
the theoretical discourse. Hypercathecting self psychology, he may, however, have
decathected or countercathected classical analysis far more than he realized, cur-
tailing his access to still valuable concepts and modes of analyzing data. As the
eminent historian of science, Thomas Kuhn (1970), noted, "There are losses as
well as gains in scientific revolutions, and scientists tend to be particularly blind
to the former" (p. 167).

From one accounting perspective, the positive gain from Kohut's new outlook,
combined with the negative gain due to loss of worthy aspects of the old point
of view, may have yielded a net clinical/scientific advance of approximately zero.
From a different (comparative-integrative) accounting perspective, the bottom
line would be much more satisfying.

Had we been contemplating ideas of a less distinguished investigator, we
might have speculated that Kohut's classical training may have been less than
ideal, that his exposure to traditional modes of formulation may have been somewhat mechanical, lacking in sensitivity, empathy, and respect for the complexity of data and the intricacies of the clinical inference process. Notwithstanding
Kohut's complaints about some of the supervision he received (Cocks, 1994),
there are no grounds for such ad hominem considerations.

Continuing to entertain explanations at the personal level, one might hypothesize a subtle problem in the fit between Kohut's character and traditional theory.
Long ago, Abraham (1924a) suggested that

> Persons with an oral character are accessible to new ideas, in a favorable as well
> as an unfavorable sense, while the anal character involves a conservative behavior
> opposed to all innovations—an attitude which certainly prevents the hasty aban-
> donment of what had been proved good. (p. 403)

Based upon Abraham's insight, one might argue that Kohut, self psychologists,
and even our entire cultural epoch are more oral whereas Freud, Freudians, and
their cultural milieu are more anal. These characteristics may have influenced the
degree of attachment of both sides to old ideas and their corresponding receptivity to new ones.

Balint's (1955) discussion of the different developmental roots of the attachment styles of ocnophilic (clinging, dependent) versus philobatic (adventurous)

scientists/artists/thinkers would also be apropos when considering factors at the personal level that could influence psychoanalytic theorizing.

Schafer (1983) too believed that different personalities favor different forms of theorizing, perceiving, and empathizing over others. "Nobody can analyze every type of analysand. At least one cannot do so equally well in all instances" (p. 290). He warned against postponing recognition of the narcissistically difficult fact that "there are certain types of empathizing in certain types of situations that are simply not your cup of tea" (p. 291).

Schafer's reflections dovetail with Rapaport's (1951/1967b) penetrating insights that span the personal and the more general:

> So it is in the development of science. For every achievement we pay dearly by turn-ing away and indeed cutting ourselves away from other possibilities and facts. No individual and no school can encompass the riches of phenomena in any science. … None of us can behold all aspects of man at once. … He [Schilder] makes it easier for us to understand why, in exploring cultural influence … one is prone to forget basic motivation by showing us that a high price has to be paid, by every one of us, for what we would discover.
>
> This price is determined by what our interest centers on, and our interest in turn flows from our character and personal proclivities. It is a different person with partly different values who is possessed with the discovery of basic motiva-tion, from the one who finds defensive and socializing motives to be the ultimate ones. So with Schilder too: personal proclivities, values, and urges, determined ultimately the choice of the price he paid. (p. 381)

Although individual proclivities are germane to this discussion, my explora-tion arose from a somewhat more global, abstract proposition, seemingly tran-scending idiosyncratic taste, values, and narcissism. Kohut had asserted that every scientific explanation is a potential barrier to further thought. Progress is hindered by commitment to old ideas. His thesis seemed incomplete, like the formulation of his illustrative case. It therefore seemed necessary to propose the complementary theorem that powerful commitment to new models and to innovation can interfere equally severely with the ability to appreciate what is of enduring value in the traditional body of knowledge.

This threat to perceptual integrity and progress is particularly important to bear in mind when the new is regarded as a radical departure from the old. When change is viewed as revolutionary rather than evolutionary, Kuhn's (1970) cau-tions about losses, gains, and blindness in scientific revolutions are particularly apposite.

In the very case in which he attempted to evaluate his clinical material from two perspectives, Kohut proved surprisingly incapable of analyzing data from the traditional perspective. His case presentation served as backbone for a chapter in which he critically examined the classical concepts of resistance and defense. He wished to cast off outdated aspects of ego-psychological conceptualization to advance the self psychological point of view. In this innovative thrust, he lost hold of far more than he realized.

THOUGHTS FROM A YOUNG OLD DISSIDENT

The definiteness and directedness that characterize the conscious mind are extremely important evolutionary acquisitions, Jung (1916/1969a) noted. These products have rendered humanity the highest service. Without them, science, technology, and civilization would be impossible. Humanity has, however, acquired these qualities of mind at a very high sacrifice, he averred.

On the down side, directedness requires the inhibition or exclusion of all psychic elements that appear to be or really are incompatible with it. (Here, Jung [1916/1969a] seems to have drawn from Breuer & Freud's [1895/1955] earliest view of the ego and repression, enriching it with new ideas concerning adaptation that did not find a secure place within psychoanalysis until Hartmann's [1939/1958] contributions to ego psychology.) Material is deemed incompatible by an act of judgment that determines the direction of the path that is chosen and desired. This judgment is inevitably "partial and prejudiced" (p. 70) because it chooses one particular possibility at the cost of all others.

Particularly germane to this discussion, Jung (1912/1969b) noted that "The directed process necessarily becomes one-sided, even though the rational judgement may appear many-sided and unprejudiced" (p. 70). Here, he points to the importance of psychological processes that exert their influence from beneath, and in contrast to, conscious intention.

Although Jung's observations are very apposite to my endeavor to comprehend certain omissions that arose in the course of Kohut's pursuit of his project, in another regard, he was of the same mind as Kohut. Jung observed that the fatal act of judgment that primes one's prejudices is "always based on experience, that is, on what is already known. As a rule it is never based on what is new, what is still unknown, and what under certain conditions might considerably enrich the directed process" (p. 70). Here, Jung foreshadows Kohut's declaration that commitment to old ideas is the major impediment to scientific advance. Their agreement could relate to the fact that they were both innovators. Regarded critically as dissidents, each endeavored to forge a new path unencumbered by excessive adherence to older (Freudian) commitments.

Freud on Formulation

The complexities of clinical observation and interpretation have challenged our field ab initio. Freud's (1912/1958d) historic shift in emphasis from seduction theory to the realm of the Oedipus complex and psychic reality exemplified his grand struggle with the treacherous conundrums inherent in these activities. He learned much about pitfalls pertaining to observation and formulation during that crucial phase in the evolution of analytic thought. His experiences enabled him to address issues germane to this discussion. "As anyone deliberately concentrates his attention," he (1912/1958d) wrote, "he begins to select from the material before him; one point will be fixed in his mind with particular clearness and some other will be correspondingly disregarded, and in making this selection he will be following his expectations or inclinations" (p. 112). He went on to emphasize that "If he follows his expectations he is in danger of never finding anything but what he already knows; and if he follows his inclinations he will certainly falsify what he may perceive" (p. 112).

The risk Freud identified in which following expectations one may never discover anything different from what one already knows relates to Kohut's concern about old ideas impeding progress. The contrasting danger Freud described of inclinations leading to perceptual falsification pertains to the concern about new ideas blocking access to older ones.

Working with clinical data, Kohut (1984) laudably committed himself "to postpone closures" and "to consider as great a variety of explanations as possible" (p. 125). As a scientist, he valued an objective, multiperspective, comparative stance. Nonetheless, one may assume he was not without "expectations or inclinations." He may have increasingly anticipated finding self psychological postulates more useful than traditional ones for formulating clinical material, contributing to a growing tendency to find "what he already knows."

Kohut would certainly not consciously "falsify what he may perceive." I noted in chapter 1, however, ways in which his sense of the phallic-oedipal construct highlighted certain perturbing features (castration anxiety, frightening primal scenes, death wishes) while seeming to minimize or ignore other, equally important facets (multiple identifications, sexual curiosity, gratification, feelings of inferiority, exclusion, and so forth). This loss of the cohesive richness of this central, classical tenet may relate to the tendency to disregard certain points when others are "fixed in his mind with particular clearness." Shifting processes involving hypercathexis, decathexis, and countercathexis (selective inattention) may lead inadvertently to falsification by omission.

Had our field been able to fully grasp Freud's (1912/1958d) conclusions concerning observation and interpretation, we would not have become stuck in quite so many clinical, theoretical, and organizational quagmires. Because we lacked sufficient capacity to hold in mind and utilize his prudent observations, these axioms need to be reiterated and applied more rigorously. We should, however, not necessarily feel too badly about our failure to live by Freud's insights; he himself had difficulty abiding by them.

Kohutian Formulation

In his efforts to make sense of the complexities of clinical data, Kohut (1984) shared that it had become

> a deeply ingrained aspect of my own cognitive style—to construct first, however tentatively, a hypothesis concerning the structure of the patient's nuclear self, the outline of its central program, of the basic means by which the program is to be realized, and only subsequently to assess such details as psychic mechanisms against the background of this tentative overview of the personality. (p. 127)

A provisional model is part of the mind; one might even say part of the self, particularly when one is deeply invested in that model. As a product of the self's creative endeavors, the provisional model is subject to forces aimed at maintaining, restoring, and developing it—processes that have been well delineated by articulate self psychologists (e.g., Fosshage, 1983). Consequently, holding "fixed in his mind with particular clearness" (Freud, 1912/1958d, p. 112) a tentative self psychological portrait of an analysand might favor searching for material to shore up that model, making it more substantial, cohesive, less tentative, fragmented, flimsy. In this manner, provisional formulations can become self-fulfilling hypotheses.

Similar processes were likely on Edelson's (1985) mind when he wrote that "The difficulty in achieving intersubjective agreement in psychoanalysis follows from the preoccupation with seeking confirming instances, without regard to the problem of excluding plausible alternative explanations of the occurrence of such instances" (p. 584). Pessimistic about clinicians' capacity to be skeptical of their ideas, he suggested that how determined an author of a case study, or any research, is to be critical of his/her hypothesis can only be decided from tests carried out by others.

Such an external verification process characterized my approach in chapter 1 to Kohut's belief concerning phallic-oedipal material. He presented his conviction in a quiet, thoughtful manner, as if it had been repeatedly tested and corroborated not just with respect to his three specimen dreams but throughout the entire analysis. His hypothesis had become for him an established, solid, reliable, well-founded conclusion. A review of his evidence suggested, however, that his conclusion warranted a different description. His repeated confirmations—that is, his failure to find evidence supporting the rival, oedipal hypothesis—were, unwittingly, false confirmations.

This chapter is part of a quest to comprehend not only why it is so difficult for scientists and clinicians to be skeptical of their ideas but also why, even when they make a determined effort to be open minded, comparing their novel formulations with alternative (conventional) modes of conceptualization, they may, nonetheless, fail to do so in a manner meeting scientific standards. These issues are not only important and interesting in and of themselves but also because the soundness of clinical practice is predicated on the validity of the underlying science.

McGill University's preeminent psychologist, Hebb (1958), put this latter matter succinctly: "Before one can have applied science, one must have a science to apply" (p. 17). Needless to say, that science must be sound, that is, highly reliable and valid. Important though this connection between the integrity of science and ensuing clinical practice is, I must largely confine myself in this chapter to the former. Later, I permit myself to ponder clinical implications in greater detail.

Hermeneutic Considerations

"It is not the parts that explain the meaning and significance of the whole but the whole that explains the meaning and significance of the parts," Kohut (1984, p. 127) asserted. In terms of this axiomatic hegemony he gave to the gestalt, Kohut's provisional formulation of a patient's nuclear self might rather easily function as a "whole," screening data ("the parts"), lending heightened significance or insignificance to clinical material in terms of the postulates of that whole. What began as a provisional entity could thus rather easily slip into becoming a nonprovisional entirety.

A more balanced perspective on part–whole relationships was offered by Steele (1979). From the vantage point of hermeneutic methodology, knowledge of the parts is necessary to understand the whole. The parts, in turn, can only be understood as aspects of the whole that envelops them with meaning. Nine postulates comprise the "hermeneutic circle" (p. 391), a concept encompassing the constant, dialectical movement between parts and whole. In the interpretive enterprise, hermeneuticists strive for harmony of constituents with gestalt with respect to consistency, coherence, and configuration. These principles, Ricoeur (1977) believed, may constitute validation criteria sufficiently rigorous to serve as "the proof apparatus in psychoanalysis" (p. 869).

Determined to construct as soon as possible a tentative self psychological model of his patients, Kohut may have tended to give undue weight to such a whole, as opposed to the parts, creating an imbalance in the hermeneutic process. His provisional gestalt would lend meaning to parts, but the parts might then be insufficiently empowered to contribute autonomously and adequately to the understanding of the whole. Deficiently endowed with respect to the vital momentum needed to attract allied parts to bombard and challenge the membrane of meaning afforded by the provisional formulation, the dialogue between constituents and gestalt might be insufficiently rigorous, allowing the envelope of meaning to seal prematurely.

Such foreclosure appears to have occurred in Kohut's approach to his analysand, despite his admirable, conscious desire "to apply closures tentatively, to observe the analysand's reactions to our (tentative) interpretations" (p. 125), and so forth. Similar processes of premature sealing may account for the fact that no oedipal conflicts were detected in the six analyses presented in the Chicago casebook (Goldberg, 1978). In those instances, Gedo (1981) believed "The interpretive technique used clearly precludes the detection of *any* significant childhood constellation beyond the ones described by Kohut, once one of the 'selfobject' transferences has been recognized" (p. 45).

Finding value in hermeneutic principles does not, of course, constitute blind embrace of any unduly narrow, nonscientific conception of psychoanalysis. Hermeneutic postulates concerning part whole relationships are simply part of our broad, disciplinary endeavor that is, among other things, an interpretive science. Recent interest in our field in hermeneutics is just another example of integrating principles, methods, and data from the humanities and sciences, something that has long been a hallmark of psychoanalysis. As Gedo noted,

> It is a measure of Freud's genius that he was able to successfully forge a discipline that is a fusion of science and humanism by finding an intermediate level of inquiry, focusing on the intrapsychic world that can and should be approached simultaneously from the biological and the hermeneutic viewpoints. (p. 309)

PRINCIPLES FROM OTHER FIELDS: FROM PHYSICS TO FINE ARTS

In accord with Gallic sensibility, the philosopher William Barrett (1958) noted that "The price one pays for having a profession is a *déformation professionelle*" (p. 4). For example, doctors and engineers tend to see things from the viewpoint of their specialty. They "usually show a very marked blind spot to whatever falls outside this particular province" (p. 5).

Although one might like to reduce the limiting impact of our professional socialization, it is, of course, beyond the scope of this contribution to comprehensively survey other fields with respect to what they might have to say on the subject that concerns us. Nonetheless, it would surely be beneath a contribution about integrative understanding to not at least mention some findings from other disciplines that can help us better understand phenomena in our own. Some brief excursions into other domains of research and scholarship may expand our vision, thereby aiding us in deconstructing our *déformation professionelle*.

The Natural (Physical) Sciences

Freud's cautionary remarks concerning dangers to analytic perception and formulation are congruent with core principles of modern physics. For example,

Heisenberg's uncertainty principle alerts us, as did Freud, to the fact that observational methods influence what we see. Psychoanalysis does not generally rely on complex, mechanical/electronic apparati for examining the objects of its study. Our observing instrument is primarily the mind, including the sensory-perceptual apparatus that furnishes the psyche with mentational data. Theoretical orientations are crucial components of this complicated, cognitive-perceptual instrument.

Theories clothe the bare mind, the naked eye, in psychoanalysis and all sciences. Just as raiment may make the man, theoretical wardrobes also create illusions. Models of mind may make some things appear and others disappear. "Whether or not you can observe a thing depends upon the theory that you use. It is the theory which decides what can be observed" (Einstein, 1998, p. 23).

The eminent biologist Lewontin (1997) stated similarly that

> There can be no observations without an immense apparatus of pre-existing theory. Before sense experiences become "observations" we need a theoretical question, and what counts as a relevant observation depends on a theoretical frame into which it is to be placed. Repeatable observations that do not fit into an existing frame have a way of disappearing from view. (p. 30)

Freud (1893/1962, p. 13) cherished Charcot's maxim: "*La théorie c'est bon, mais ça n'empêche pas d'exister.*" (Theory is good, but it doesn't prevent things from existing.) One might amend the French neurologist's aphorism in a radical, yet complementary manner, much as I did with Kohut's idea of what impedes scientific progress. The revised Charcotian principle would state that theory is good, but it can prevent things from existing, in psychic reality and in clinical and theoretical discourse.

Analytic perceptions and formulations will be affected—data will be highlighted, downplayed, or obliterated—whether guided by an old or new framework. Kohut was keenly aware that classical theory can be limiting in these ways: He appeared less cognizant of how radical movement away from tradition can be equally constraining.

Kohut's advocacy of a strategy to allow the emergence of transference paradigms essential to the treatment of narcissistic patients led some to wonder whether this stance emphasized such transferences at the expense of others that might be obscured by the analyst's empathic immersion in the patient's experience (Gedo, 1991; Levy, as cited in Jessee, 1995). If so, this would be another illustration of how modes of data collection influence the nature of the data collected.

"Freud's discoveries have led us to see more clearly that 'reality' can only be perceived through the prism of the observer's self-organization" (Gedo,

1981, p. 368). Viewing material with self-psychological lenses and organizing principles, Kohut experienced satisfaction. Examining data through classical optics, a prescription that fit less well as his vision changed, the emerging picture seemed less clear, coherent, and compelling: in short, less to his taste.

Contemplating the classical framework (or any component thereof such as the concepts of resistance and defense), Kohut would inevitably do so from his new, preferred point of view. Consequently, the traditional framework might not appear in such sharp focus or in such good light. His laudable attempt to evaluate his patient's productions (and certain core, classical constructs) from two points of view unwittingly demonstrated the difficulty of setting aside a favored mode of observation and formulation to adopt a less congenial one.

When one has a preferred vantage point, it tends to alter one's view of the less favored, possibly devalued framework such that it may be difficult, if not impossible, to view data through the "outdated," déclassé, conceptual apparatus. Preference slips easily toward prejudice (prejudgment). In a sense, one's old framework no longer exists (*ça empêche d'exister*).

This principle concerning interference between new and old accords with Kuhn's (1970) adjudgment that scientists cannot shift freely between traditional and innovative perspectives, unlike the way one can oscillate easily between radically different views of Gestalt psychology drawings such as the well-known picture that can be seen either as a vase or as two faces in profile. Kuhn did not fully explain this lack of scientific freedom. This study helps elucidate this phenomenon. Flexibility declines with hardening of commitment to conceptual categories.

The eminent philosopher of science, Michael Polanyi (1958/1964), noted similarly that once a scientist has made a discovery, he will never again see the world as before. His eyes have become different. He has made himself into a person seeing and thinking differently. Furthermore, in sharing their discoveries, creative scientists change the world one sees irrevocably.

Another principle from modern physics, complementarity, informs us that phenomena can seem inconsistent, as if having different natures at different times. Light, for example, has been understood as being composed of either particles or waves. In different scientific eras, one view or the other has held sway. Phenomena are, however, often too complex to be encompassed by single (new or old) modes of observation/formulation. Bohr's principle alerts us to the advantages of both/and rather than either/or thinking. Kohut may have slipped a bit too much into the latter, more restrictive mode.

Psychological Sciences and the Humanities

Human eyes are built to seek complete figures, respected art historian James Elkins (1996) noted. Presented with a "triangle" missing midsections in its sides, we complete the figure to perceive a triangle. Whereas Charcot declared theory does not prevent things from existing, here we might say reality does not prevent things from existing (in our minds).

Neuropsychologists refer to such phenomena as subjective contour completion. "We instinctively repair fragments into wholes and search for continuous contours and closed curves," Elkins wrote.

> Shards present our eyes with a problem, and unwittingly we cast around for patterns, assembling pieces into shapes. Our eyes prefer practically any object to a borderless scatter of points . . . On a deeper level, subjective contour completion answers to a desire for wholeness over dissection and form over shapelessness. (p. 125)

These comments differ from, but are interestingly consistent with developmental ego psychological emphasis on the drive to create constant objects, Kleinian underscoring of the need to advance from part to whole objects and to repair damaged objects, and self psychological stress on cohesion and restoration of the fragmented self. In a similar vein, we discussed how Kohut, in his method of clinical formulation, emphasized the importance of the whole as compared to the parts. Elkins reminded us how fundamental this whole-seeking tendency is.

Seeing is incessant searching, Elkins averred. We are passionate hunters, constantly scanning the environment to find percepts that match underlying search images. Freud (1900/1953a), too, discussed the organismic need to establish "perceptual identity" (p. 566) between preexisting internal images and external data. If we do not find what we wish/expect to see, we may even "hallucinate" it, Elkins, like Freud, noted. For example, if a building were half hidden by branches, we would literally see fragments (like the fragmented "triangle" or a painting presented as triptych), Elkins pointed out. If one were to mentally subtract the tree, one would be left with a partly floating collection of building pieces, a mosaic. Instead, our eyes complete the puzzle and we see the edifice whole. (In rare instances, one might find oneself struggling for a few minutes to see an unfragmented whole. I did so recently while contemplating a painting where long hair fell over an arm. That latter appendage looked weirdly fractured until it became "obvious" that it was a perfectly normal arm.)

This capacity to subtract the interfering tree (or hair) to see the building (or arm) as an undisturbed, undisturbing whole is relevant to clinical formulation. If one is attempting to assemble a model of a patient that is cohesive rather than fragmented (concepts vitally important to Kohut), one may experience a powerful need to disregard certain branches and certain phenomena that might otherwise get in the way, dissecting, confusing, and confounding one's efforts.

A tree in front of an edifice, like any sight, is perceived by continuous, darting eye movements. We shift rapidly between left, right, up, down, figure, ground, and so forth. Processes of integration, fragmentation, and defragmentation occur continuously. Winnicott's (1969) disquieting belief that we constantly destroy (and create) objects makes sense on this fundamental, perceptual level.

One usually thinks of blindness as the opposite of seeing. It turns out, however, that "Blindness also happens alongside seeing ... *while* we are seeing," Elkins (1996, p. 205) asserted. "Blindness is like a weed that grows in the center of vision, and its roots are everywhere. There are things we do not see and things we cannot see and things we refuse to see" (p. 205).

The weed of blindness is like the tree in front of the building. It blinds us to the wholeness of the edifice, so we pluck it from our perceptual field. At that moment, we become blind to the sprawling weed. In clinical formulation, we might pluck oedipal weeds to see a preoedipal, self psychological flower or vice versa. We may do this so automatically and effectively that we do not realize what we have done. In such cases, it would be difficult or impossible to put the ousted flora back into the picture.

Complicity between blindness and sight resides at the heart of Elkins's argument. Blindness is right there in the act of seeing, working to ensure that some things are not seen, he believed. "Each act of vision mingles seeing with not seeing, so that vision can become less a way of gathering information than avoiding it" (p. 201).

We are, furthermore, blind to our blindness: "These twin blindnesses are necessary for ordinary seeing: we need to be continuously partially blind in order to see. In the end, blindnesses are the constant companions of seeing and even the condition of seeing itself" (p. 13).

Elkins's belief about blindness being built into the act of seeing has found surprising, dramatic confirmation by perceptual psychologists studying "inattentional blindness" (Mack & Rock, 1998). "This research is showing us something we didn't think was the case—that we can fail to perceive very major things going on right in front of our eyes," remarked Brian Scholl (in Carpenter, 2001, p. 54), a cognitive psychologist at Yale University. "These studies are truly surprising for both scientists and lay people because they're so at odds with how we assumed vision worked" (p. 54).

Striking examples of this illuminating research come from studies conducted in 1999 by Harvard psychologists Simons and Chabris. They instructed participants watching a basketball film to count how many times the ball passed between members of one team. Half the observers did not notice that anything unusual transpired during the game. In reality, a gorilla (a person in costume) had sauntered into the middle of the court, halted to face the camera, thumped his chest, and then walked away. The ape spent 9 seconds on screen.

"I think every serious person in psychology has always believed that we don't consciously perceive everything that happens to us," Chabris (as cited in Carpenter, 2001, p. 56) commented. "The shocking thing was that you could show that so little is being perceived" (in Carpenter, 2001, p. 56). Even psychoanalysts would be impressed by those examples of cathexis/hypercathexis/anticathexis and selective attention/inattention.

For better or worse, cognition is similar to perception: "Like seeing, thinking is intermittent, unreliable, and difficult. Both take place in darkness and both depend on light. Blindness is their constant accompaniment, the precondition of both thought and sight" (Elkins, 1996, p. 226). Freud (1916/1972) seemed in touch with this phenomenon when he stated that "In writing I have to blind myself artificially in order to focus all the light on one dark spot. ... My eyes, adapted as they are to the dark, probably can't stand strong light or an extensive range of vision" (p. 45).

A few other psychoanalysts concerned with similar problems have come to similar conclusions. For example, in their classic text, Greenberg and Mitchell (1983) observed that "the drive/structure model, like other models, by positing a clearly defined hermeneutic system, directs our attention to certain aspects of a situation and away from others" (p. 43). Similarly, Schafer (1997b) noted that "Each approach equips us with instruments of thought that bring both light and darkness to its subject matter" (p. 12). A school of thought rarely, if ever, advertises the darkness it can bring to the clinical situation.

From the work of Elkins and of Mack and Rock, Simons, Chabris, and others on inattentional blindness, we begin to understand how powerful this attention channeling can be. These processes can blind us to major phenomena staring at us, right in front of our eyes, even while we are seeing other things with admirable clarity. One is reminded of the catchy title Kubrick selected for his final film, *Eyes Wide Shut*.

An interesting detail emerged in these studies on inattentional blindness. Subjects were more likely to notice an unattended object if it bore some similarity to the attended ones. They were more likely, for example, to notice the gorilla if they were focused on players wearing black uniforms. From this finding, one might extrapolate that a self psychologist focused on, say, idealizing transference would be more likely to notice distant but related self psychological phenomena than matters more central to other frameworks even if these model-alien phenomena were large and glaring.

Why do we continue to see so little when we want to see so much? Elkins (1996) queried. We wondered the same while pondering Kohut's unintended illustration of partial blindness. "Perhaps ordinary vision is less like a brightly lit sky with one blinding spot in it than like the night sky filled with stars. Maybe we see only little spots against a field of darkness" (p. 206), Elkins mused. Clinicians commonly refer to another clinician's blind spots. That term may reverse the nature and underestimate the magnitude of the problem.

Struggling to comprehend psychoanalytic formulation and scotoma, one resonates readily with Elkins's aphorism that seeing is not simple: "It is not easy to do, it is not easy to control, and it is certainly not easy to understand" (p. 124). Far from it, "Vision is immensely troubled, far more than a neurophysiological experiment or a psychoanalytic meditation could ever uncover" (p. 201). Although I heartily concur with these sentiments, I do, however, believe our psychoanalytic meditation has uncovered quite a bit, contributing something important to this overall, multidisciplinary project, much as Elkins's work itself has done.

Educational Implications

Clinicians educated traditionally prior to founding new schools of psychoanalytic thought have often succeeded in illuminating complex phenomena. They challenge us to extend or modify our frameworks. In contrast to the creator of the innovative perspective, individuals trained predominantly in one of these newer orientations sometimes convey a more limited grasp of the history, scope, and profundity of analysis. If one lacks sufficient sense of the field's development and complexity, one may simply regard one's perspective as the ultimate blossoming of thought. Enchanted by one flower, one may have less grasp of the stem, leaves, root, soil, climate, and other, more distal, yet important factors. Ensorcelled by the new, one may lose sight of (even derogate) still vital aspects of the disciplinary tree and its ecological niche.

Derived from the Greek *historia*, the word *history* means "learning or knowing by inquiry" (from an even earlier root meaning simply "to know"). Similarly, *science* came from the Latin, *scientia,* meaning knowledge (from *scire,* to know). Thus science and history, as ways of knowing, are linked at their etymological roots. *Education* that does not lead (*educare,* to lead forth) from familiarity with the past, through the present, toward the future is ahistorical. It fosters an island of knowing founded on a sea of not knowing.

A similar vision was articulated by the poet and literary critic T. S. Eliot (1919/1951) when he wrote that "The historical sense involves a perception, not only of the pastness of the past, but of its presence" (p. 14). An individual is not likely to know what is to be done, he believed, "unless he lives in what is not merely the present, but the present moment of the past, unless he is conscious, not of what is dead, but of what is already living" (p. 22).

Kohut has often been criticized for paying insufficient attention to the contributions of others, failing to cite their works, and neglecting to indicate the roots of his ideas in their findings. He may have been inclined to break a bit too *radically* (Latin *radix,* root) with history and tradition. At times he may have mistaken aspects of "what is already living" (and still vital) for the dead or the dying that would be better off deceased.

In agreement with one aspect of Kohut's attitude toward the liability of established knowledge, Eliot (1919/1951) averred that "If the only form of tradition, of handing down, consisted in following the ways of the immediate generation before us in a blind or timid adherence to its successes, 'tradition' should positively be discouraged. ... Novelty is better than repetition" (p. 14). He was, however, quick to emphasize that

> Tradition is a matter of much wider significance. It cannot be inherited, and if you want it you must obtain it by great labor. It involves, in the first place, the historical sense, which we may call nearly indispensable to anyone who would continue to be a poet beyond his twenty-fifth year. (p. 14)

Speaking from the vantage point of his discipline, Eliot noted that the historical sense

> compels a man to write not merely with his own generation in his bones, but with a feeling that the whole of the literature of Europe from Homer and within it the whole of the literature of his own country has a simultaneous existence and composes a simultaneous order. This historical sense, which is a sense of the timeless and of the temporal together, is what makes a writer traditional. And it is at the same time what makes a writer most acutely conscious of his place in time, of his own contemporaneity. (p. 14)

Endorsing a "conception of poetry as the living whole of all the poetry that has ever been written" (p. 17), Eliot noted that the mature poet must

> be aware that the mind of Europe—the mind of his own country—a mind which he learns in time to be much more important than his own private mind—is a mind which changes, and that this change is a development which abandons nothing *en route*, which does not superannuate either Shakespeare, or Homer, or the rock drawing of the Magdalenian draughtsman" (p. 16).

In contrast to this appreciation for tradition, Eliot noted

> Our tendency to insist, when we praise a poet, upon those aspects of his work in which he least resembles anyone else. In these aspects or parts of his work we pretend to find what is individual, what is the peculiar essence of the man. We dwell with satisfaction upon the poet's difference from his predecessors, especially his

immediate predecessors; we endeavor to find something that can be isolated in order to be enjoyed. (p. 14)

We regard not only poets but also psychoanalytic authors in this way.

In contradistinction to this common view, Eliot believed that

If we approach the poet without this prejudice we shall often find that not only the best, but the most individual parts of his work may be those in which the dead poets, his ancestors, assert their immortality most vigorously. (p. 14)

Winnicott's (1971a) approach to the relationship between tradition and innovation was historical and developmental like Eliot's. "It is not possible to be original," Winnicott opined, "except on the basis of tradition" (p. 117). At the same time, tradition for him was most useful if it provided opportunity for innovation (Phillips, 1988). Flexible regard for the value in both the old and the new provided him a secure base (Bowlby, 1979) from which he could venture forth and be profoundly creative.

Like Eliot (1919/1951) and Winnicott (1971a), Bachelard (1960/1969) seems to have had a similar respect for the relationship between new and old. Bachelard (1960/1969) considered that connection mutually vitalizing: "The new age awakens the old. The old age comes to live again in the new" (p. 25). In this vision, the new does not simply superannuate or bury the old. Rather, it stimulates, changes, revivifies, and preserves it.

In a similar spirit, at a conference dedicated to exploring ways to best recognize and develop scientific creativity, Kuhn (1959) stressed his belief that we are most likely to achieve these important goals if we recognize the extent to which the creative scientist must also be a firm traditionalist (p. 351).

Grasping this fructifying link between tradition and innovation has profound implications for analytic training. As analysts, we are fond of the idea that education inevitably leads to improvement, to greater breadth and depth of understanding. We are inclined to believe pedagogy always adds something, that it is intrinsically positive. We therefore focus little, if at all, on what it might subtract. Looking on the sunny side, we ignore the shadow.

In contrast to this rosy perspective, Kuhn's (1970) research led him to bluntly conclude that professional training leads to "an immense restriction of the scientist's vision" (p. 64). Analysts might not like to believe this seemingly paradoxical, potentially depressing assertion could be true of our prized, tripartite, educational process. We might, however, see merit in Kuhn's provocative point in relation to "rival" fields that we may regard as simplistic or wrong headed (e.g., radical behaviorism or reductionistic biological psychiatry). Scientists from these domains would, reciprocally, have little difficulty seeing how psychoanalytic training might not only expand but also restrict our vision.

Like all founders and promoters of schools of thought, Kohut and his collaborators created their own continuing education project. Although they believed this process to be marvelously expansionary, we established grounds in the previous chapter for suggesting that their ongoing investigations and training may at times have simultaneously constituted "an immense restriction of the scientist's vision." Our exploration of Kohut's case illustration supports Kuhn's disquieting dictum.

Freud (1916/1972) himself was fond of a fable in which a landlord's daughter developed a neurosis that "cheated her of marriage and her hopes in life" (p. 353) because she had "come under the influence of education and accepted its demands" and ideals, reducing "her interest in the feminine part which she was destined to play" (p. 354). In contrast, the caretaker's daughter escaped education and lived a happy life, unburdened by neurotic affliction. Freud understood that one's outlook is not simply expanded but can simultaneously be constricted and contorted by pedagogy. "Evil results," Freud (1916/1972) warned, are "a risk with all education" (p. 355).

In a similar vein, the eminent sociologist Ernest Becker (1973) believed that "In order to function normally, man has to achieve, from the beginning, a serious constriction of the world and himself. We can say that the essence of reality is the refusal of reality" (p. 16). Although education certainly has constructive aims, it can also assist with this goal of constriction. Schools of psychoanalytic thought have tended to teach modes of refusal along with paths of acceptance. Promulgating political, subcultural, and conceptual correctness based on preferred parochial standards has exacted considerable cost in terms of cognitive constriction.

The respected philosopher William Barrett (1958) cautioned similarly that "We know one thing at the cost of not knowing something else, and it is not simply true that we can choose to know everything at once" (p. 39). He referred to this unfortunate state of affairs as "the pathos of knowledge" (p. 38). His reflections provide a sobering balance to our more usual enthusiasm for the joys of learning.

Scientific paradigms suppress observations that might be subversive to their commitments, Kuhn (1970) found. They specify what the universe contains and, by implication, what it does not. Work within a paradigm constitutes a "strenuous and devoted attempt to force nature into the conceptual boxes supplied by professional education" (p. 5). Phenomena "that will not fit the box are often not seen at all" (p. 24).

These peculiar processes were powerfully exemplified in the constriction of vision and thought observed in Kohut's work. Such conceptual narrowing is encountered not only in innovators—Rapaport's (1951/1967b) high price each of us must pay for what we would discover—and in individuals educated in new orientations insufficiently grounded in the fertile substrate of the past but also in those who are rigidly tradition bound.

Kuhn's (1970) pithy observations on science and education might sound cynical. Kuhn believed, however, that they were confirmed repeatedly over centuries. It would not be difficult to locate recent evidence supporting his iconoclastic conclusions. For example, when psychiatry took its relatively recent, biological turn, psychopharmacology came to be regarded in many quarters not just as an additional mode of understanding and intervening but as the only scientifically and politically correct approach. Biochemical/genetic perspectives replaced "outdated," psychodynamic points of view in many academic/professional circles. As new biological information was acquired, a vast amount of hard-won, depth psychological knowledge was lost in many a milieu. Similar evidence of new ideas obliterating old ones can be discerned through studying the growth of systemic family therapy, cognitive behaviorism, and other fields of inquiry. In the evolution of science, an advance can simultaneously constitute a setback.

Kuhn's challenging findings about the dangers intrinsic to science and education should, like Freud's research, disturb the sleep of the world. Whereas one would not wish insomnia on anyone, neither should one valorize somnambulism. Elaborating and demonstrating the validity of some of Kuhn's assertions with respect to our field may contribute something to this desirable deconstriction and awakening process.

CULTURAL CONTEXT

Darwinian Deep Structure and Superficiality

In principle, Kuhn believed, there were no reasons why assimilation of a new theory required rejection of an older one. In practice, however, he found such development virtually always involved conflict between competing schools and attempts to destroy prior paradigms. Based on these observations spanning several centuries of scientific evolution, he went so far as to assert that there is no other effective way to generate discoveries. His was a bold conjecture, indeed.

Goldberg (1984b) concurred. He cited an eminent philosopher of science in support of his belief that paradigm clash is inevitably a fight to the finish: "Popper (1963) feels that any theory worth its salt would necessarily overthrow the old one because it must, by definition, be revolutionary and, thus, a really new finding cannot long exist in the confines of an old theory" (p. 379). New models are "essentially incompatible," Goldberg (p. 386) asserted.

From this survival of the fittest perspective, the emergence of self psychology necessarily entailed a primal challenge to tradition. Its birth inevitably initiated fundamental conflict demanding destruction of the extant. From this point of view, it is not surprising that the new might lunge for the jugular of the old. In classical analysis, one conceptual jugular is the Oedipus complex, "the shibboleth that distinguishes the adherents of psychoanalysis from its opponents" (Freud, 1905/1953b, p. 226). It is not, therefore, unexpectable that a new school might regard this vessel as particularly well suited for at least covert attack.

This propensity within science for the innovative to spearhead deadly assaults on the traditional resonates with broader social trends. "The culture of our time is predominantly a cult of innovation" (Polanyi, 1958/1964, p. 220). In this trendy zeitgeist, the old must die, or at least be put out to pasture, so the new can flourish.

With customary aplomb, Oscar Wilde chided Western culture for rushing from barbarism to decadence without passing through the stage of civilization. Bearing in mind the Freudian view of civilized maturity as the ability to both love and work, it is not hard to detect considerable barbarity, fused with moral decay, in certain contemporary cultural practices. Leaving aside the obviously grotesque 20th- and 21st-century reasons for and modes of war, one might choose a slightly more subtle illustration from the vocational battlefield. For example, one could consider the recent fashion of for extruding "old" employees who, by age 55, are increasingly regarded as undesirable material clogging corporate pipes. Highly educated (in the narrowest, Kuhnian sense) corporate plumbers must regularly flush organizational systems, moving "yesterday's men" swiftly along to make space for fresh input.

In this anal/hydraulic model, those resisting routine processing may be regarded as "old farts" by higher ups holding their nostrils erect. Such salty slang sometimes unmasks the barbarism institutional doublespeak strives to conceal with platitudes: We are just downsizing and rightsizing; to do otherwise would be "dumbsizing" and "wrongsizing." Trained to follow orders and not question, to focus on production, to expedite movement of labor units through the corporate digestive tract, managers serving the cult of innovation believe systemic vitality depends on prodding stubborn ones into going with the flow. Obstinate curmudgeons must be squeezed to the back door to be dropped off unceremoniously without further ado.

Higher up the flow chart, executives are inclined occasionally, if not regularly, to "kick ass" (as first President Bush proclaimed with respect to Saddam Hussein when the latter ceased behaving like a good employee). Concerned with the short term, bottom line, corporate executors, sometimes known as hatchet men, favor potent, anal expulsive modes. Ends justify means. Feeling their derrière might soon be on the line, they cover it tightly, shifting the focus and feared trauma to someone else's. This mode of thinking gives new meaning to the concept of a posteriori reasoning.

Advertising (Henry, 1963) plays a hefty role in the culture of innovation. It famously exploits basic desires (phallic narcissism, grandiosity, etc.) and insecurities (e.g., phallic-competitive inferiority, annihilation anxiety) to achieve its ends. Both the beleaguered and the ambitious are constantly encouraged to reject the old and consume the new to avoid the fate (extinction) of those who cannot keep up with "progress." In our throwaway culture, everyone is prompted to believe they need the latest, "all new" model—the biggest, brightest, best. Purchasers are led to believe they will partake of these grand qualities by association, osmosis, and symbiosis. When old and new are virtually indistinguishable, purveyors of innovation cheerily exploit the "narcissism of minor differences" (Freud, 1918/1957c, p. 199). Anyone not on the latest bandwagon (of glittery products, services, ideas, techniques) may fear being left hopelessly behind. A "culture of narcissism" (Lasch, 1978) offers convenient consumer (cf. Fromm, 1947, 1955) solutions (addictive fixes) to those seeking to escape ontological insecurity (Laing, 1960). Sometimes the sales pitches of psychoanalytic schools of thought bear more than a slight resemblance to tactics polished and preferred by purveyors of laundry detergent.

Climbing steadily toward the top of the material heap, dynamic managers fuse consumer and organizational psychology to create potent messages. Touting new, lean, mean models, they encourage frightened survivors of downsizing and rightsizing to "buy into" the latest innovations in corporate groupthink (and don't think). Groupthink itself is offered as a labor-saving device designed to eliminate the necessity of real thinking. With yesterday's corpses—the corporate disappeared—still and perhaps forever unmourned, the blinding beat goes on in relentless "repetition compulsion" (Freud, 1920/1955b), a way of dealing and/or not dealing with corporate trauma. Reflection and the sense of history succumb under the pressure of impulsive, mind-numbing action.

The ability to love, the other major pillar of civilized maturity, may also take a beating in the disposable culture. For example, except for certain fundamentalists, few would argue for the benefits of sentencing citizens to life imprisonment in dysfunctional marriages. At the opposite extreme lies the perhaps too ready discarding of relationships that have begun to lose their luster. "We drifted apart ... I outgrew him/her ... I needed a new, different, more exciting, younger model." Such statements have gained the status of clichés by their frequent use. Congruent with the values and structure of the cult of innovation, these attitudes are valorized in the cult of celebrity that encourages people to be mesmerized by the short-lived, serial marriages of the stars. Love affairs with theoretical models may suffer similar fates in a time favoring freely mobile cathexes, instant gratification, death wishes, and other manifestations of primary process rather than reflection and cultivation of more enduring, complex commitments.

Introducing the New

It can be difficult to obtain a hearing for a new scientific model replete with foreign concepts and terminology, yet one cannot convince others to abandon a framework if one argues within their terms, Polanyi (1958/1964) believed. Demonstrations of the alleged virtues of the new must be supplemented by forms of persuasion likely to induce conversion. One might, for example, endeavor to make the older framework seem altogether unreasonable. Such modes for challenging and destabilizing brand loyalty may have been operative in Kohut's (1984) starkly contrasting traditional analysis's "commitment to a scientific objectivity that typifies the nineteenth century" (p. 111) with self psychology's superior, up-to-date "commitment to a scientific objectivity that incorporates the breakthroughs of our own century" (p. 111).

Kohut regarded Freud as the Newton of analysis (Kirsner, 1982). This appellation was, no doubt, honorific. It may also have been slightly derogatory, implying the founder might be yesterday's man. In contradistinction, Ernest Wolf regarded Kohut as the Einstein of analysis. More modestly, Kohut (in Kirsner, 1982) likened himself to Max Planck, the Nobel Prize-winning creator of quantum physics. He believed self psychology had accomplished a similarly crucial scientific shift from macropsychology to micropsychology (Kirsner, 1982). One could continue toiling at last year's crude macrolevel or elect to join the innovative, refined, cutting-edge thinkers of the microelite.

Whether Kohut is a kindred spirit of Einstein, Planck, or someone else, few would want to hitch their wagons to an outdated, 19th-century scientific canon as our field struggles to navigate the challenges of the 21st century. Kohut's skillful rhetoric may have influenced some to accept his conclusions about his paradigm's superiority without fully exploring the evidential base for these claims. Scrutiny of the data supporting some of his assertions (chapter I) suggested a different conclusion. The methodology I use in this book is not likely to induce dramatic conversions. It may, however, help encourage critical thought, fostering more judicious weighing of the relative merits of the traditional and the innovative in this and other instances.

The deepest flaw in *How Does Analysis Cure?*—Kohut's (1984) book in which the chapter under consideration appeared, was, according to Bollas (1986), that at times, "It reads like a commercial advertisement for self psychology" (p. 433). What Bollas viewed as a defect might relate to the need Polyani identified to induce conversion, and to our concerns about the dangerously persuasive power of rhetoric.

In our culture's zest for the new, we have "come a long way" (to borrow a notorious advertising slogan) from traditional societies in which only revered elders were considered to have attained sufficient experience and expertise to qualify them to transmit wisdom to the younger generation. One would not want to idolize tradition nor glorify concepts aged far too long in leaky barrels. Such ritualistic worship can be tantamount to echoing the reactionary sentiment that what's new in the latest is not good, and what's good in it is not new. That aphorism is a surefire recipe for rigor mortis. It would, however, be equally misguided to respond to any perceived hardening of conceptual arteries in the old system by taking manic flight from associated depressive anxieties. A more balanced response is required.

Dialectical Resolution

Must innovation devalue, displace, and destroy tradition? Can one eliminate or dialyze aging professional bath water without endangering the evolving conceptual corpus? One answer to these questions, contrary to the position of the authors like Goldberg, Kuhn, and others cited previously, derives from dialectics (Hegel, 1807/1910; Adorno, 1966/1973; Carveth, 1994). This theory posits that thought evolves through conflict. A thesis gives rise to an apparently contradictory antithesis. Rather than the latter annihilating the former, conflict is eventually reconciled on a higher level of truth via synthesis. That integration constitutes a fresh thesis, inevitably evoking a new antithesis, leading to yet another synthesis, and so on in interminable progression.

From this point of view, Freud's impressive thesis inspired Kohut's provocative antithesis. Initially, self psychological propositions were seen as an addition to analytic knowledge—valuable mineral salts invigorating the bath. Later, this new model came to be regarded more as an alternative theory, a replacement. Although Kohut did not eject the entire Freudian corpus, he did cast aspersions on its potency, creating an impression of a rather pale, aging body of knowledge and technique. Pitting his bold antithesis against this enervated Freudian thesis, he claimed victory for his version of the truth.

In the broader field of psychology that houses psychoanalysis, one sees increasing indications of dialectical thinking. For example, the first formal meeting between cultural and evolutionary psychologists—two groups that have historically had little to say to each other—recently took place at the University of British Columbia. Cultural psychologists made presentations the first day. The following day, evolutionary psychologists spoke. The third day, speakers presented research synthesizing the two approaches. To the extent that one can hope for greater conversations between the general field of psychology and our subdiscipline, such manner of dialogue bodes well for the future.

Centrifugal and Centripetal Thrusts

Like all creative scientists, Kohut was a daringly divergent thinker. These pioneers reject old solutions, striking out in new directions. Their divergent thrust is crucial for disciplinary development. They may, however, undervalue equally essential, convergent thinking (Kuhn, 1977).

Championing convergence, Edelson (1988) averred that

> The best explanation is one that is simple, not necessarily by any logical criteria, but in that it draws on established knowledge, upon what is already known or familiar. In other words, it makes use of a model, about which a great deal is already securely known. (p. 363)

Drawing on the established knowledge base, one need not be limited by it. One can improve the framework or create a different model/submodel.

Convergent and divergent modes inevitably conflict; the tension between them can become unbearable (Kuhn, 1977). The capacity to support such strain is prerequisite for the best research: "The successful scientist must simultaneously display the characteristics of the traditionalist and of the iconoclast" (Kuhn, 1977, p. 127). Kohut sometimes seemed to have had difficulty sustaining an optimal dialectic between convergent and divergent thinking. His research may have occasionally suffered somewhat from this imbalance.

I am not arguing against Kohut's divergences. I am simply drawing attention to his sometimes insufficient attention to convergence. Rather than classical inferences being superior or inferior, Freudian and self psychological perspectives may be complementary, like the theory of scientific progress Kohut articulated and my obverse theorem. This integrative viewpoint differs from those who believe these schools are simply incommensurable. A more combinatory stance, in contrast, resonates with Gedo and Goldberg's (1973) blunt assertion that "No single theory is fully sufficient to order even one set of clinical observations" (p. 172).

In consolidating the antithetical (divergent) status of self psychology, movement toward a more encompassing integration has been prevented or delayed. Greater openness to synthesis could hold more of the valuable, Freudian corpus together with self psychological insights in an expanded theoretical container. Such an enriched framework fashioned through a selective, dialectical process, might merit the title: comparative-integrative psychoanalysis. Whatever this more embracing framework is called, it needs to be sufficiently large, robust, and flexible to include the best of all streams of analytic thought. Paraphrasing one of the more acceptable, educational slogans of the younger Bush (Leave no child behind), one might say that no school should be left (completely) behind.

Returning briefly to the principle of complementarity, recall how physicists moved toward resolving their conflict as to whether light was essentially composed of waves or particles. They cleverly coined the appealing neologism, "wavicle," to capture the idea of an entity possessing both properties. Analysts might do well to emulate their practice, creating more flexibly encompassing formulations for our data. Might one imagine an analyst referring to him or herself as a Freudian self psychologist?

Psychoanalytic method can be conceptualized as a process of dialectical deconstruction (Barratt, 1994) aimed at revealing the repressed complementarity of opposing terms (Carveth, 1994). This methodology can also be applied toward comprehending and resolving disciplinary conflicts. For example, in hypercathecting self psychology, although inadvertently countercathecting or decathecting significant aspects of classical theory, Kohut lost touch with important elements of psychoanalysis. His thinking, clinical formulations, and interventions were sometimes weakened by the losses entailed in these cathectic dynamics. Revealing "repressed" Freudian meanings in his data, I am suggesting there can be far more complementarity and enrichment between classical and self psychological perspectives than Kohut and some of his colleagues might have led one to believe. Approaching our controversies with a comparative-integrative attitude can create a far more adequate container for conflicting ideas than can the more common path fostering premature, repressive resolution.

In a different context pertaining to paradigm shift (abandonment of seduction theory), Laplanche (1987/1989) noted the impact of similar cathectic dynamics on the evolution of analytic thought:

> These acts of repression, these defenses—which, like any defense, often destroy much more than they are intended to destroy and do away with whole segments of reality, in this case a whole segment of the reality of thought—include a sort of cataclysm to which we have yet to come to terms, which we have not yet worked through adequately. (p. 15)

As like-minded collaborators coalesced around Kohut's way of seeing (and not seeing) things, yet another cataclysm was created. As with most of our splits, we have not yet succeeded in working through that schism adequately. Comparative-integrative analysis can build bridges over the troubled waters roiling at the bottom of these conceptual chasms.

CONCLUSION

Although I focused on an example from Kohut's work to illustrate certain problems in the evolution of psychoanalytic thought, my intent was not to single out or criticize his or any other particular orientation. The illustration could have been drawn from a different school that, although perhaps less prominent in contemporary debates, would otherwise have served my purposes equally well.

Authors must inspire readers to want and perhaps to actually carry out additional tests on their hypotheses (Edelson, 1985). In this heuristic regard, Kohut succeeded. His general thesis concerning scientific progress and his particular thesis concerning the Oedipal complex evoked my antitheses and stimulated cogitation concerning possibilities for synthesis. Ironically, his material lent itself to challenging his assertion about the absence of phallic-oedipal dynamics. His illustration also proved suitable for demonstrating the broader contention that excessive attachment to the new, and to innovation, can impede scientific progress as assuredly as unyielding commitment to the old.

Rather than privileging either orthodoxy or innovation, I endorse the more encompassing perspective that thesis and antithesis may be largely complementary. The explanatory power of their integration will usually exceed that of either component. This combinatory advantage holds with regard to the macroelucidation of general factors that facilitate or impede scientific progress as well as for the microillumination of specific clinical data.

Contrasting classical and self psychological formulation, I have not proclaimed the former to be inherently better. I simply suggested, contra Kohut, that certain classical inferences appear strongly justified by his data. Both perspectives can contribute to comprehension. Just as it would be futile to debate whether length or width contributes more to area, it might similarly be meaningless to argue whether one point of view contributes more than another to the portrait of a patient or to our field in general.

Another reason for underscoring potential complementarity of perspectives as opposed to valorizing incommensurability is awareness of how acutely sensitive parties to such dialogue can be. Commenting on the work of two self psychologists, Richards (1992) suggested that although some of his ego-psychological speculations may have proved unproductive if they had been used in their case, others may have supplemented, without supplanting, their focus. Acknowledging that classical analysis may not have served their patient well, he stated he did not mean to imply intersubjectivity was wrong or that another approach was superior. Despite Richards's assertions of both/and intent, Stolorow and Trop (1992) clearly believed his aim was either/or, "transparently ideological and political," or designed to "persuade the reader that analysts informed by self psychology and intersubjectivity theory do not do real analysis" (p. 467). They were sure his goal was "to demonstrate the superiority of his explanatory framework over ours" (p. 467).

The self psychologists, no doubt, had their historical reasons for responding as they did. These reasons would not, however, be immediately obvious to someone reading their respective contributions to the symposium. Something else would, however, be abundantly clear, namely, that it can be difficult and dangerous to dare discuss not only religion and politics but also schools of psychoanalytic thought. The latter associations are all too often freighted with some of the worst features of faith and the machinations of power.

I would be chagrined if the ideas in these first two chapters were taken as reflecting opposition to the contributions of self psychology. At certain stages in conflictual dialogue, there can be a powerful tendency to perceive all participants as either for or against an innovative (or traditional) point of view. It is often healthier and more productive to be both for and against a new (or old) model.

Instead, one often reacts more like Freud (1911/1958b) described in his classic paper on the two principles of mental functioning. He believed infants' first act of judgment occurred on the tip of their tongues, namely, whether to swallow or spit something out. All too frequently, we make similar snap judgments when we attend to colleagues' presentations. If something does not taste quite right and familiar, we are inclined to reject it. On the other hand, if it is easily recognized, we may swallow it without any further critical thought.

There can be no question Kohut's ideas are important and deserving of further study and debate, Goldberg (1984a) asserted. Like Kohut before him (Kirsner, 1982), he implored these activities be undertaken less in a spirit of dissent than one of exploration, to find out whether they allow us to see more than before. Although this stance sounds eminently reasonable, our investigation led to the rather startling conclusion that valuable new ideas, like Kohut's, may have the inadvertent effect of allowing us to see both more and less than before. If we are not exceedingly careful, scientific gains may be cancelled by complementary losses. Such calculus may give new meaning to the concept of the null hypothesis. It is therefore crucial to have both differential and integral calculus.

Sadly, psychoanalytic findings are repeatedly eroded by waves of fashion (Gill, 1979) and the return of the repression, that is, retreat by analysts from insights they had once reached (Lewy, 1941). Gill believed only systematic, controlled research could counteract these deleterious tendencies and generate a secure body of knowledge. Although valuing empirical research, my contribution embodies a different (complementary) conviction that rigorous research of another (dialectical) sort can also counteract the erosion of knowledge. Experimental studies are neither the only nor necessarily always the best route to this desideratum.

One friendly critic, Paul Meehl (1993), believed psychoanalysis exhibits symptoms of a "degenerating research program" (p. 321). In his view, "The divergences in theory and technique among therapists in a broadly 'psychoanalytic' tradition are vast, increasing, and show little or no signs of the sort of cumulative, self-corrective, convergent development characteristic of post-Galilean science" (p. 321). A dialectical approach welcomes rather than regrets divergence. It realizes, however, that it is essential to balance divergence with convergence, thereby nurturing dialogue and encouraging transcendent synthesis. This comparative-integrative attitude promotes a profoundly generative research agenda far removed from the dreaded, degenerative processes that troubled Meehl.

Discussing Kohut's oeuvre in terms of the extraordinary impact of a set of new ideas on a scientific community, Goldberg (1984a) described this as a story that remains to be told. Although my thesis is not restricted to any single development's impact on the analytic world, it might be seen as a component in that saga. Goldberg characterized Kohut's final tome as one chapter in the evolution of psychoanalytic ideas. My contribution might be viewed as a cautionary footnote, admonishing analysts to learn from the history of disjunctive evolution in our field so that future development of analytic thought may become more integrative, with decreased tendencies toward splitting, both conceptually and organizationally. The desirability of authentic cohesion applies as much to a body of knowledge and to a profession as to the self.

Completing his final opus, Kohut expressed hope that colleagues, especially younger ones, would research issues he raised. He also wished his thoughts would stimulate them to formulate and pursue their own questions, thereby advancing psychoanalytic science (Elizabeth Kohut, 1984). My contribution might be viewed as honoring his generative desire, in a dialectical spirit, promoting detailed, critical examination of ideas and clinical material and vigorous debate between perspectives, all in the service of ultimately achieving a more comprehensive, enriched, valid, and clinically useful body of psychoanalytic knowledge.

3

Mangy Mongrels or Marvelous Mutts?
The Question of Mixed Models

Oh, East is East, and West is West, and never the twain shall meet,
Till Earth and Sky stand presently at God's great Judgement Seat.

—**Rudyard Kipling,** *The Ballad of East and West*

Delving deeply into many key contributions to psychoanalysis, comparing each with respect to certain core criteria, Greenberg and Mitchell (1983) performed an invaluable service for our field. They approached their broad task in terms of the challenge to the original, Freudian, drive/structure model posed by later, relational/structure models. With respect to the vital question of whether it is possible to combine these two frameworks, Greenberg and Mitchell concluded that integration cannot be accomplished because the models are based on "fundamentally incompatible … irreconcilable claims concerning the human condition" (pp. 403–404). Repeatedly they stressed their deep conviction that there is "an intrinsic incompatibility between the drive/structure and relational/structure models, one which can be neither overcome nor circumvented" (p. 378).

Greenberg and Mitchell's critique of model mixing was clear, strong, useful, and influential. It merits careful consideration. Their conclusion may seem to reflect a perspective diametrically opposed to the more integrative thrust I began to espouse in the previous chapters. I, however, argue that despite the definitive, uncompromising stance they took in 1983, there were actually seeds in that landmark text "calling for" a more integrative position.

LEANING TOWERS OF BABEL

Due to their reasoned conviction about the incompatibility of drive and relational models, Greenberg and Mitchell believed attempts to combine them were inherently unstable. Such endeavors inevitably collapse toward one side or the other, they argued.

Kohut's initial attempt to integrate his emerging psychology of the self with ego psychology provided them with a particularly clear case in point. Once the founder of self psychology had come to view drive as a breakdown product following empathic failure, he had embraced the fundamental premise of the relational model, they pointed out. By then, his allegiance to the principle of complementarity had become mere homage to a forsaken model.

Furthermore, they noted, Kohut believed self psychology was conceptually unintegratable with virtually all other psychoanalytic theorizing including the developmental approaches of Mahler (1972), Winnicott, and other authors writing within the traditions of ego psychology and British object relations. The fact that Kohut made such claims would seem to support Greenberg and Mitchell's assertion that his continuing statements concerning complementarity between self and ego psychology lacked substance.

There may, however, be another way of comprehending Kohut's seemingly contradictory views. He may have had an appreciation not only for the antithetical nature of these psychologies but also for their possible complementarity. Unable to resolve this contradiction in his thinking, he may nonetheless have been unwilling to consistently and totally deny its existence. Later, I argue that Greenberg and Mitchell held a similarly contradictory position. Although we are inclined to idolize consistency, it may not always be all it is characteristically cracked up to be. For an idol to have clay feet may not be a sin.

An author's shifting beliefs about complementarity and irreconcilability may sometimes have more to do with personal and political investment in his or her project than about any true impossibility of integration. For example, late in his career, Kohut was able to contemplate a more integrative stance (Mitchell, 1988). In contrast, at the time Greenberg and Mitchell wrote, Kohut was in the thick of developing his antithesis. He needed to propound a provocative, vigorous version of it to make space for his argument in the largely inhospitable environment in which he labored. Only toward the end of his life, after he had secured a hearing for his viewpoint and had acquired an affirming following, could he consider contemplating the next phase in the dialectic, namely, synthesis.

Although Greenberg and Mitchell (1983) made a compelling case for instability in Kohut's original attempt to blend self psychology with traditional analysis, they did not seem to feel all integrative efforts were quite as unstable. For example, they seemed slightly less unhappy with Edith Jacobson's model mixing (see, for example, Greenberg & Mitchell, p. 362). Nonetheless, Greenberg and Mitchell clearly believed hybrids were intrinsically inclined to topple and therefore not a good idea.

One could argue that such instability is not unique to hybrids; it also characterizes purebred models. Freud, for example, began with a theory of neurosogenesis based on relational traumata inducing problems of affect regulation that,

Greenberg and Mitchell emphasized, was remarkably similar to contemporary relational models. Several years later, Freud proposed a dramatically different framework emphasizing drives, endogenous oedipal fantasies, and psychic reality. His original, predominantly relational model had thus proved unstable. It now tilted strongly in the opposite direction.

In subsequent years, although Freud's new drive theory continued to be very important in his understanding of pathogenesis, he gradually moved toward a more integrative (accommodative) stance. Thus, his second framework, which Greenberg and Mitchell called the purest version of the drive/structure model, also proved unstable. It did not collapse, but it leaned in a more relational direction. Greenberg and Mitchell saw that shift as reflecting a clever strategy for accommodating critiques. Whatever its precise nature and motives, it reflects the instability of any model that places undue emphasis on either side of the dialectic.

In our drive to comprehend our world, we attempt to capture aspects of it with a thesis. Reality tends eventually to let us know that our achievement was incomplete. It confronts us with an antithesis, challenging us to come to grips with this greater complexity. As part of the process of responding to this challenge, we may ultimately envision a synthesis.

Instability and change are characteristics of life. Consequently, not only mixed models but also pure ones are likely to be unstable, at least in the long run. Any thesis eventually evokes an antithesis. The struggle between the two may ultimately lead to some form of synthesis that simultaneously constitutes a new thesis, provoking a new antithesis, and so on in endless evolution.

WARRIORS AND ACCOMMODATORS

For adherents of drive theory, Greenberg and Mitchell opined, the strategy of accommodation comes naturally; for relationalists, the strategy of radical alternative is natural (Greenberg & Mitchell, 1983). In my opinion, such sharp differences only hold true at certain points in the dialectical struggle.

After Freud had established his predominantly drive/structure model, Greenberg and Mitchell contended that for the duration of his career, he engaged in an ongoing, dialogic process, modulating this model to accommodate relational critiques. Their discussion of his deployment of this tactic is persuasive. With respect to that phase in the evolution of his thinking, their understanding of who accommodates versus who poses a radical alternative seems sound. If, however, we go back to the point where Freud switched from his originally more relational model to his drive/structure framework, the picture is different. At that point, his new drive theory constituted a radical alternative to his own relational model.

The drive/structure model can, therefore, be (and initially was) a radical alternative to a more relational model.

In his shift to a more drive/structure model, Freud was accommodating to critiques from colleagues who did not find it easy to believe that sexual abuse was as widespread as his original theory required. He also took into account protests of patients (including himself as his own analysand), prompting him to appreciate fantasies as a more important factor in neurosis than he had previously realized. He proposed a radical alternative to his originally highly relational model because he perceived it to be inadequate to encompass the clinical realities he was observing, endeavoring to comprehend, and treat.

In Freud's time and our own, it was and is essential for both drive theorists and relationalists to use both strategies, radical alternative (divergent, comparative psychoanalysis) and accommodation (convergent, integrative psychoanalysis), to achieve ever more accurate models. These two thrusts combined can create a more comprehensive, comparative-integrative psychoanalysis that can begin to do justice to the complexities of life. There is a time for war and a time for peace, a time to separate and a time to unite.

APPARENTLY PARADOXICAL

Like Greenberg and Mitchell (1983), Modell (1984) believed drive and relational models belong to "two different conceptual realms" (p. 257). Modell must, however, have sensed some instability in such a "do not mix" stance, for he soon added that, on the other hand, there was a "possibility that these two apparently irreconcilable contexts ... will at some later time be brought into a new synthesis" (p. 257). With this openness to integration, he must still have felt on uncertain terrain, for he quickly considered that, on the other other hand, "It is also possible that the existence of insoluble paradoxes may reflect an intrinsic quality of the human mind" (p. 258).

Being closed, open, perplexed, certain, unsure—sometimes sequentially—seem to be common positions adopted by those struggling toward comprehending complex conundra. Perhaps we need to learn to be more comfortable standing squarely in the spaces between these various positions rather than cementing our clay feet to any one island of pseudocertainty in the seas of controversy.

Modell's third option (insoluble paradoxes) suggests a willingness to consider a combined strategy, simultaneously mixing and/or not mixing. What appears paradoxical at a certain point in our evolution may, however, succumb to more straightforward synthesis at a later time. Apparent paradoxes may only be temporarily irresolvable. In such instances, Modell's third option would fold into his second.

Mitchell (2000) tended to be suspicious of such receptivity to model mixing. No doubt he had good reasons for his reserve: He believed blending would most likely lead to mere "juxtaposition of the models rather than a real integration of them" (p. 57). I regard such openness as more promising than dangerous. It may establish a necessary, healthy holding environment for seemingly incompatible entities. Over time, such a conceptual container can facilitate maturation from juxtaposition or paradox to true synthesis.

Winnicott's most wonderful gift to psychoanalysis may have been his concept of transitional space. In this creative zone, one can playfully hold, combine, separate, reintegrate, and otherwise experiment with ideas. To Winnicott's concept, I would add the notion of transitional time. The comparative-integrative framework provides a space that over time affords opportunities for creative synthesis.

EAST MEETS WEST

Greenberg and Mitchell (1983) powerfully buttressed their organization of the psychoanalytic field into incompatible domains by situating these dichotomous frameworks within the larger setting of divergent theories about human nature that have characterized the Western philosophical tradition. Viewed in this wider context, debate between drive and relational models mirrors the overarching discourse between individualism and collectivism. They were undoubtedly correct that this broader, intellectual/cultural picture constitutes a potent factor for comprehending both the durability of divergent psychoanalytic models and the difficulties encountered by those who have tried to transcend the conceptual chasm separating them.

Many analysts accepted Greenberg and Mitchell's articulate grounding of psychoanalysis' conflict in Western civilization's larger dilemma as the coup de grace for integrative endeavors. Despite their powerful, useful contextualization, one should not necessarily take it as the death knell for integrative pursuits. Nor, surely, did they intend their thesis to forever inhibit such intellectual efforts.

No matter how persuasive their portrait of the Western philosophical tradition may be, it need not stand as the final word for the West. Indeed, one might plead for some deity to please have mercy on us if the West does not seek and find a way to transcend its traditional modus operandi. Apart from fervent prayer and futurity, the very mention of the West should surely serve not as a conversation stopper but as impetus to cast an eye eastward.

At the first conference of cultural and evolutionary psychology (referred to earlier), the head of the University of Michigan's Culture and Cognition Program, Richard Nisbett (Snibbe, 2004) speculated that East–West differences in thought originated in the soils of ancient Greece and China. Mountainous Greece, unable to support much farming, gave rise to competitive, individualistic businessmen. China, in contrast, with better soil and irrigation, favored cooperative, collectivistic agriculturists. Heirs to these two traditions still differ not only in social relations but also in how they distribute attention, explain events, and reason about contradictions. For example, Occidentals try to ascertain which of two conflicting arguments is right. In contrast, people from the Orient try to figure out how to reconcile conflicting positions.

Translating Nisbett's findings into comparative-integrative language, it appears that in their struggle to survive and thrive, Occidentals have tended to emphasize the first phase of the dialectic (thesis vs. antithesis). Those from the Orient, in contrast, have focused more on the second part of the process (synthesis).

The Western philosophical tradition may not simply be the way things are or are meant to be. This larger context may, itself, need to be placed in a still larger context. It may constitute a problem that can be elucidated and at least partially resolved by bringing it into relation with Eastern traditions.

As we move from a globe of villages to McLuhan and Powers's (1989) global village, we will have increasing opportunities and requirements to blend Oriental and Occidental modes of thought. Taking advantage of such occasions, we can advance the comparative-integrative project in our discipline and elsewhere.

MAGNIFICENT MULATTOS OR MERELY MIXED MARRIAGES?

Despite Greenberg and Mitchell's (1983) insistence that each model "is a complete account" (p. 403) based on incompatible, underlying premises and that one must choose which side one is on, at other moments Greenberg and Mitchell seemed aware that the situation might not be so simple. Their appreciation of a less dichotomous perspective was embodied in statements such as "Human life reflects a paradox—we are inescapably individual creatures; we are inescapably social creatures" (p. 403). Their realization of this greater complexity seemed to exist alongside, rather than integrated with, their stronger view on the fundamental incompatibility of these two perspectives.

At the conclusion of their classic account, they proposed two possible outcomes of perspectival clash. The drive/structure model might prove compelling and resilient enough to incorporate all data and concepts generated by the study of object relationships. Relational/structure models would then wither away, having served a useful purpose, provoking a necessary expansion of the drive model. Alternatively, relational models could prove increasingly compelling, expanding and combining to provide a more encompassing, enticing framework for theory and practice. The drive model would then lose adherents, continuing mainly as an elegant, no longer functional antique.

From the overall force of their predominant argument, one might imagine that they would have had a clear preference with respect to those two possible outcomes. Instead, Greenberg and Mitchell concluded that phase of their sojourn in the tower of comparative analysis by declining to throw all their eggs into one basket. They shared their suspicion that neither scenario would come to pass. Neither model would achieve complete victory. "The paradox of man's dual nature as a highly individual yet social being runs too deep and is too entrenched within our civilization to be capable of simple resolution in one direction or the other" (p. 408). It seemed more likely to them that both models would persist. Each would undergo continual revision, and the rich interplay between them would continue to generate creative dialogue.

PERSPECTIVES ON PARADOX

Greenberg and Mitchell (1983) did not feel one integrative view could ever contain, let alone resolve, the antithetical tension between the two psychoanalytic models. Instead, they believed it was necessarily the case that "Any dialogue between their adherents, although useful in forcing a fuller articulation of the two models, ultimately falls short of a meaningful resolution" (p. 404).

Greenberg and Mitchell did not believe this sort of conversation and its outcome were simply thorny problems is search of solution. Rather, this status quo seemed simply to be how reality is and likely will always be. Inevitably, both sides "think in terms of a set of premises presumed to be fundamental and true and attempt to reconcile old and new ideas, old and new data, in terms of what they already know" (p. 383). The twain may meet, but will not meld. This modus operandi did not seem lamentable, merely how it is in a discourse in which crafty accommodation and radical alternative are, now and forever, likely the only options.

In contrast to their certainty about the incompatibility of the models, Modell (1984), as I noted, believed it might (or, then again, might not) be possible to synthesize the two perspectives. His attitude, in its more affirmative mode, fits mine.

Benjamin's (1998) view of paradox seemed in line with Modell's and my openness to higher level containment and potential synthesis. Splitting, Benjamin believed, is a regrettable breakdown of valuable tension between tendencies. Such disintegration leads to unfortunate adherence to one or the other side of the polarity. In harmony with the comparative-integrative approach, she favored striving to "undo repudiation (p. 6) ... transforming complementarities into dialectical tension, into tolerable paradox, instead of antinomies that compel dangerous choices" (p. 24).

E'ER THE TWAIN SHALL MEET AND PART

Dangerous or not, Greenberg and Mitchell (1983) felt those choices Benjamin (1998) abhorred were absolutely necessary. Splitting from his collaborative effort with Mitchell and Greenberg (1991), in his subsequent solo book, seemed to move toward choosing the first of the three options from their 1983 treatise, namely, that drive theory could prove sufficiently resilient to incorporate all data and ideas emanating from the study of object relations. He gave more weight to the idea that relationality itself reflected an attachment drive. The question for him became more about the nature of motivation rather than whether drives existed and constituted essential elements of comprehensive theorizing.

Greenberg announced his intention to confront the claims of relational theorists that they had created a drive-free psychoanalysis. He was convinced they had not. "Their formulations mask an implicit drive theory that explains why the relationships exist in the first place" (p. 70). Later, he reiterated that contention:

> Whether theorists are explicit about it or not, they are always working with some pre-experiential tendency that gives shape to relational experience. Relational theorists differ from Freud in the sorts of drives they have substituted for libido and aggression, and in their failure to specify the nature of these drives. (p. 88)

True to the belief Greenberg (1991) shared with Mitchell that one must choose sides, Greenberg hitched his wagon to the opposite track from his former coauthor. Realizing classical drive theory was far from sufficient, he regarded it as still having something important to offer to a comprehensive theory: "The interpretive system embodied in Freud's libido/aggression theory has enormous power to illuminate the hidden recesses of psychic life. It also has great limitations" (p. 67). Convinced of the necessity of a motivational concept-like drive, he developed his own, dual-drive theory based on a safety drive that moves one closer to people and an effectance drive that propels one toward autonomy.

Rather than continuing the belief Greenberg had held with Mitchell that the two models would likely continue forever, challenging and prodding each other to revise and improve themselves, Greenberg seemed to have moved toward his own resolution of the conflict under the aegis of drive theory. In Greenberg's modified framework, relationality (and its opposite) were drives. Similarly, drives were both relational and antirelational.

Despite my sense that Greenberg had resolved for himself the tension between the competing models by folding them into his new, improved, dual-drive theory, he did not seem to feel comfortably settled with this solution. On the first page of Greenberg's preface, he reiterated the previous position he held with Mitchell. The two frameworks reflect "ancient and irreconcilably alternative visions" (p. vii). Underscoring his allegedly continuing devotion to their former credo, he declared that he continued to believe "the two models are incompatible and that diversity is our best guarantee of vitality" (p. vii).

The supposedly irreducible nature of this dichotomy nonetheless generated "vexing questions" (p. vii) for him. Greenberg's clinical experience highlighted the fact that the analytic situation is constantly both social and personal/private. This "paradox illuminates both the power and the limits of each psychoanalytic model" (p. vii).

The subtle shifts in Greenberg's position resemble what I characterized as Modell's on one hand, on the other hand, then on the other other hand approach. Modell was acutely aware of the three positions he was delineating. It is not clear that Greenberg realized he was shifting between these options.

In any event, faced with what he perceived to be the shortcomings of both frameworks, Greenberg declared that he would "extract from each of them what fits best with my understanding of people" (p. viii). Although he believed this was not committing the sin of combining models, one might consider that he was doing just that. I would, of course, see this as virtuous.

In Mitchell's (1988) subsequent solo book, he moved from their (1983) dichotomizing position to a more accommodating one. "The two theoretical perspectives are not discretely dichotomous—they overlap considerably" (Mitchell, 1988, p. 4). Viewing the different traditions as partly compatible, although in some areas mutually exclusive, he thought it possible to achieve "selective integration" (p. viii). He found it feasible to bring together contributions of such diverse thinkers as Sullivan, Fromm, Fairbairn, Winnicott, Kohut, Bowlby, and Loewald. Mitchell's "critical eclecticism" (L. Aron, personal communication, 2005) has much in common with the comparative-integrative perspective.

Despite his increasing interest in synthesis, Mitchell continued to view drive theory as "outdated" (p. viii). Attempts to shore it up and maintain it by somehow fitting innovative thinking around it were undesirable, something that "inhibits and distorts innovation." There were, in his opinion, definite limits to what "critical integration" (p. viii) could achieve. "Although all psychoanalytic theories contain both monadic and dyadic features," he allowed, "each theory necessarily breaks on one side or the other of this dichotomy in assigning the source of structuralization of experience, the shaping of meaning, and this choice is fundamental" (p. 5).

CRITICAL, CREATIVE PARADOXICALISM

Like Benjamin (1998), Hoffman (1998) held a more permeable view of paradox and dialectics than Greenberg and Mitchell. Greenberg and Mitchell continued to believe (most of the time) in the necessity of choosing between models. In contrast, Hoffman usefully and bluntly declared that "The great divide in psychoanalysis is between dichotomous and dialectical thinking" (p. 26). Making it clear which side of the Grand Canyon he preferred, Hoffman warned that "In our zeal to correct overemphasis in classical theory on the individual dimension, it is important that we not swing to an overemphasis on the relational dimension, thereby isolating each from the other" (p. 103). Instead, a true solution "requires a synthesis of the two perspectives with appropriate redefinitions of each in the light of their interdependence." In a comparative-integrative spirit, he was convinced of the need to replace fragmented, dichotomous thinking "with an integrative sense of the interdependence of apparent opposites" (p. 223).

To understand some of the differences between dichotomous and dialectical thinking, it is useful to return to the research of Nisbett and his colleagues at University of Michigan's Culture and Cognition Program (Winerman, 2006). They presented pictures to Chinese and American subjects. The Chinese tended to move their eyes back and forth more between the foreground object and the background. The Chinese also looked at the background longer than Americans did.

The researchers also asked their subjects to describe an animated underwater vignette that included three big fish as focal objects and background features like rocks, seaweed, and bubbles. Americans were more likely to commence by recalling the focal fish. Japanese were more inclined to describe the whole scene, saying something like, "It was a lake or pond." Later, the Japanese recalled more details about the background objects than did the Americans. In short, Americans tended to zoom in more quickly on foreground objects, whereas Orientals paid more attention to context.

Cognitive differences between Westerners and Asians showed up in other ways as well. Americans are more likely to group items based on individual features they have in common. For example, they will say a cow and a chicken go together because they are animals. Asians, in contrast, are more likely to group items based on relationships. For example, a cow and grass might go together because a cow eats grass.

These studies supported the researchers view that Asians, whose more collectivist culture promotes group harmony and contextual understanding, think in a more holistic way. They pay attention to all elements in a situation, to the overall context, and to the relationships between items. The idea that culture can shape the way people perceive and think at these deep levels is a departure for psychology, which traditionally assumed such basic processes were inborn and universal.

Returning to Hoffman's (1998) integrative outlook, he wittily paraphrased Freud's famous dictum about the therapeutic action of psychoanalysis. Hoffman proposed that "Where id [and superego were, split off from each other] there ego shall be [mediating their dialectical relationship]" (p. 223). I, in turn, think it useful to paraphrase Hoffman's aphorism as follows: Where separate drive and relational theories once were, there comparative-integrative psychoanalysis shall be, mediating their dialectical relationship.

OM AND OMELETS

"Ultimately all fruitful theory is self-extinguishing because it generates the data that lead to its demise," Greenberg (1991, p. viii) asserted. Although he clearly understood transience and certain functions of theory, he may only have been partly correct. In the dialectical model I favor, the old thesis lives on, at least partially, in the new synthesis. This epigenetic theory concerning construction of knowledge parallels biological succession. Parents die, but their genes continue in altered arrangements in the next generation. Parental essence is also passed along on the psychic plane via introjection, identification, and other modes of cultural transmission.

Like the Hindu godhead, Hegelian dialectics entail a trinity: creation, preservation, and destruction. From this vantage point, fruitful theory is neither completely self-extinguishing nor absolutely other annihilating. In the encounter between theories, a process of creative destruction is involved, simultaneously generating, negating, and preserving.

In a more mundane metaphor, transforming eggs into divine omelets obliterates neither ova nor other ingredients. Enshrining the principle of creative destruction, culinary metamorphosis suggests a suitable analogue for integrating the diverse, delectable tendencies currently found on the kitchen table of psychoanalysis.

COMPARATIVE-INTEGRATIVE CREATIVITY

The psychoanalytic field remained largely divided into the camps Greenberg and Mitchell skillfully delineated for several more years after they had performed this valuable service for us. To a considerable extent, it continues much that way today.

In 1992, a significant event in psychoanalytic publishing occurred. Despite its direct bearing on our disciplinary divide, this event has not yet been fully masticated, digested, and absorbed. Drawing on evolutionary biology, Slavin and

Kriegman (1992) located a powerful position outside of psychoanalysis proper from which they could deconstruct and then pull together the essence of the seemingly irreconcilable narratives that had hitherto been such uncomfortable, quarrelsome cohabiters in the psychoanalytic, semidetached abode. Reminiscent of Archimedes famously asserting that if he could have an appropriate fulcrum away from planet Earth on which to plant his lever, he could move the world, Slavin and Kriegman found just such a place, sufficiently removed from our earthy quarrels. In that fortuitous domain, their fulcrum furnished adequate leverage with which they could move the psychoanalytic debate forward.

Fortified with insights from contemporary biology, they forged a model of the adaptive design of the human psyche that accommodated, indeed required, both the narcissistic (biological) nature of drive theory and the more altruistic (social psychological) thrust of relational theory. Rather than necessitating a choice between incompatible models, their framework encourages, actually demands, we choose both. Their dual-track theory exemplifies comparative-integrative thinking.

From the perspective of evolutionary biology, something is adaptive if it maximizes the pursuit of ends advantageous to underlying genes. This outlook is not simply survival of the fittest individual; the going-on-being of *genes* is the more powerful motivator. Genetic material survives better in offspring, for individual death is simply a matter of time. By the criterion of "inclusive fitness" (Hamilton, 1964), perpetuation of one's genes in others (and in the resultant gene pool for the species) is the measure of evolutionary success. Natural selection favors organisms that maximize their inclusive fitness.

Genes of parent and child embody identity and difference. From the "gene's eye view" (p. 50), self and other in kinship relationship are partly overlapping, partly distinct. Both common and divergent interests are built in at a fundamental, biological level to all organisms that reproduce sexually. Mutuality and conflict between generations are therefore inevitable.

Focusing on the genetically distinct part of each person, classical theory developed an individualistic bias. Focusing on the genetic commonality between parent and offspring, relational theories have assumed far greater overlap of interests than is warranted.

Each individual pursues its particular path to maximize inclusive fitness. Its aims bring it into conflict with other family members pursuing their paths. To reduce overt conflict with parents whose maximal investment is required, children draw on "deep psychodynamic structures" analogous to the inborn, linguistic structures (Chomsky, 1972) infants utilize to rapidly learn language. For example, a built-in capacity for repression allows them to withdraw conscious awareness from certain wishes, aims, affects, and images of self and other that would otherwise be disruptive in the family.

Unlike simple forgetting, what has been dynamically repressed does not disappear. Instead, a censored ("false") self is established for everyday living, whereas other potentials ("true self") are sequestered, awaiting the day when changed relational conditions might favor their being recontacted (adaptive regression) and reintegrated into a different, expanded sense of self. These innate psychodynamic structures (repression, false self, true self, adaptive regression, etc.) have been selected over millennia to facilitate survival in a complex social milieu on which we are highly dependent for a long time, but from which we must eventually emerge to function in new environments. For example, adolescents separating from their families may draw on their inborn capacities for regression to access repressed aims that can now be utilized in expanding, extrafamilial circles.

More than the pleasure principle, adaptive advantage guides individuals in deciding whether to repress or express. This perspective enhances our understanding of the phenomenon Freud referred to as the return of the repressed. It expands his mostly monadic concept, making it very social, embedded in the changing subcultural milieu and the context of evolutionary adaptiveness.

In the asocial, selfish drives of classical theory, Slavin and Kriegman detected an important mechanism guaranteeing access to motives dedicated to the promotion of individual interests. Endogenous drives protect against one's genetic self-interest being usurped by those who serve as important models for introjection, identification, impulse control, and other functions (e.g., superego formation). With increasing recognition of relational drives, they believed, it is important not to discount the continuing significance of the more selfish ones that classical theory has emphasized, albeit in a one-sided manner.

Slavin and Kriegman (1992) argued persuasively that contemporary evolutionary theory represents a substantive philosophical revision of the individualist/collectivist dichotomy that has characterized [plagued?] Western thought. Locating psychoanalysis within the broader context of modern biology provides a framework promoting synthesis with respect to the classical/relational dialectic that was grounded in that longstanding schism. Humans can now be seen neither as self-centered as the classical model envisioned nor as social as the relational model suggested. We are, instead, "semisocial beings" (p. 69), inherently divided between conflicting individual and collective aims.

Psychoanalytic thought evolved rapidly from Greenberg and Mitchell's (1983) outstanding comparative psychoanalysis to Slavin and Kriegman's (1992) comparative-integrative endeavor. This impressive progress supports the element of truth in Greenberg's (1991) conviction that "Ultimately all fruitful theory is self-extinguishing because it generates the data that lead to its demise" (p. viii). His work with Mitchell (and their subsequent solo efforts) organized the field to a point where Slavin and Kriegman could, from the neutral terrain of a neighboring discipline, understand and advance our discourse substantially.

The intellectual fervor ignited by Greenberg and Mitchell's landmark contribution has by no means been extinguished. Some theorists have, however, begun to move beyond their clarifying view of an unbridgeable schism between psychoanalytic models based on what they called the longstanding, "deeper divergence" in Western thought as a whole. At the leading edge of analytic discourse, a more hopeful, useful, comparative-integrative outlook is coming into being. This new perspective has the virtue of being consistent with evolutionary theory's relatively recent transcendence of the old individual/collective dichotomy. In tune with biology's breakthrough, we are now in a position to appreciate the possibility of a *deeper convergence* between formerly nonmixable models.

DOUBLE HELIX

In the same year that Greenberg and Mitchell launched their seminal text, Blatt and Shichman (1983) penned their important article, "Two Primary Configurations of Psychopathology." They delineated two essential dimensions of psychic life: self-definition and relatedness. These variables correlate conceptually with the dichotomous domains described by Greenberg and Mitchell; and, subsequently, the dual drives at the core of Greenberg's model; and, still later, the selfish and altruistic motives intertwined in Slavin and Kriegman's dual-track model.

Like the self psychologists Slavin and Kriegman, but coming from a different tradition, ego psychology, Blatt and Shichman regarded these twin thrusts as simultaneously present throughout life. Taking a creative view of Erikson's important work on the life cycle, they viewed it as implicitly supporting their idea that normal personality maturation involves the ongoing, mutually facilitating development of these two variables.

Erikson's psychosocial stages correspond closely to Freud's psychosexual developmental line. For example, Erikson's inaugural stage concerns the establishment of basic trust versus mistrust (orality). This foundation is followed by a focus on autonomy versus shame and doubt (anality), initiative versus guilt (phallic-urethral), industry versus inferiority (latency), and identity versus role diffusion (adolescence). Going further than Freud, Erikson spelled out key challenges of later life: intimacy versus isolation (young adulthood), generativity versus stagnation (middle age), and integrity versus despair (old age).

Blatt and Shichman believed it necessary to insert one additional stage, mutuality versus alienation (oedipal) into Erikson's scheme. Blatt and Shichman believed this issue to be phase dominant from about 4 to 6 years of age. At that time, cooperative peer play commences along with initial resolution of the oedipal crisis. With this modification, Erikson's epigenetic model neatly illustrates a developmental process alternating between relatedness and self-definition.

In a dialectical dance, individuals cycle between these two foci in a recurring, one-two pattern. Infants focus on relatedness (trust/mistrust). Growing toddlers emphasize self-definition (autonomy/shame, then initiative/guilt). Oedipal children shift back to relatedness (mutuality/alienation). Youngsters then embark on two more stages of self-definition (industry/inferiority and then identity/role diffusion) as they progress through latency and adolescence. In young adulthood, they return to relatedness (intimacy/isolation) followed by two more self-definitional stages (generativity/stagnation and integrity/despair) as they advance through middle age to senior citizenship.

Evolving capacities along these two developmental lines are normally coordinated. For example, if one is fortunate enough to have established a solid sense of basic trust (relational), one is much better equipped to assert autonomy (self-definition) in opposition to primary objects in the subsequent stage. That autonomy and ensuing initiative (self-definition) in turn facilitate collaborative relationships with others (mutuality vs. alienation) and so forth.

Interacting through the life cycle, these two tracks are more independent in the beginning. Around 6 years of age, when children become capable of concrete operational thought (Piaget, 1955), these agendas can be more easily integrated. This cognitive advance corresponds to the shift from dyadic to triadic object relations. Thinking is no longer so immediate, direct, literal, and restricted to simple contrasts (such as pleasure–pain or issues of power, control, and autonomy) that characterize dyadic relationships. Youngsters can now regard relationships in more comparative terms. They can reflect on and contrast the type of relationship they have with each parent and that their parents have with each other.

Greater blending of individuality and relatedness accompanying resolution of the oedipal crisis is expressed in an emerging sense of "we." The child understands himself increasingly as both separate and part of something larger.

In the second half of this book, I emphasize that dialectic development involves progression from comparative to integrative processes. This important trajectory is reflected in Blatt and Shichman's model.

Emergence of formal operational thought in adolescence facilitates further coordination of these developmental lines. The sense of individuality resulting from the acquisition of autonomy, initiative, and industry is now paired with growing desire to participate in social groups based on prior establishment of trust, mutuality, and cooperation. In favorable circumstances, one appreciates what one has to both contribute and gain from participation in the collective, unencumbered by excessive fears of losing individuality and values. This capacity to integrate self-definition and relatedness becomes ever more sophisticated as one works one's way through the challenges of later life cycle stages.

Blatt and Shichman's dual-track model preceded Slavin and Kriegman's evolutionary biological framework. Despite differences, they have significant similarities. Both portray an inherent complexity in the adaptive design of the human psyche that integrates equally necessary individualistic and collectivist elements. In Blatt and Shichman's model, this point is implicit. In Slavin and Kriegman's, it is explicit. It is heartening to see such convergence in state-of-the-art theorizing from disparate traditions.

The work of these self and ego psychologists has much in common with Greenberg's dual-drive and Mitchell's relational-conflict model. The powerful double helix image can help capture the intimate interplay of the two essential, complementary motives all these theorists have incorporated into their models. The twin spiral simultaneously suggests that this adaptive design of the human psyche is of such fundamental importance that it has been built right into humans' DNA.

TEXTUAL COMPLEXITY

In Mitchell's later writings, there are indications that he was keenly aware of the integrative, both/and approaches emphasized by Slavin and Kriegman (and Blatt and Shichman, 1983). Interestingly, Mitchell never cited their work. Mitchell's consciousness of the interconnectedness between these two tracks seemed to coexist with rather than achieve consistent, full integration with the primary thrust of his more dichotomous train of thought. For example, in Mitchell's (1988) book, he spoke of the "struggle to maintain our ties to others *and to differentiate* [italics added] ourselves from them" (p. 3). Later, Mitchell reiterated the individual's endeavor "to make contact *and* [italics added] to articulate himself" (p. 3). Despite this attunement to what Greenberg (1991) called "the problem of separation" (p. 90), Mitchell generally gave more weight to the "struggle to establish and maintain connections with others" (p. 4).

In that 1988 book, Mitchell argued that bodily experiences and events are evoked potentials that derive meaning from the way they become patterned in interaction. What is inherent, he emphasized, "does not push and shape experience, but is itself shaped by the relational context" (p. 4). From a more integrative sensibility, one might put the matter a little differently: The inherent *does* push and shape experience and is itself shaped by the relational context.

In contradistinction to his generally dichotomous stance, Mitchell manifested his appreciation of a more dialectical, integrative, paradoxical position in his selection of Escher's *Drawing Hands* as frontispiece for *Relational Concepts in Psychoanalysis: An Integration*. In this remarkable picture, the artist portrayed a hand drawing a hand. One cannot discern which one is drawing versus which is being drawn. Mitchell commented that Escher "vividly captures the nature of such a cycle of mutual influence. Each hand is both the product and the creator of the other. Human biology and human relatedness both *generate* [italics added] and are the creation of each other" (p. 5). One could hardly articulate a more integrative sensibility.

Contemplating Escher's drawing draws one into an almost irresistible engagement. This involvement is simultaneously fascinating, disturbing, paradoxical, and confusing. Finally one may feel one "gets it" and laugh. One may, for example, realize there is no hand drawing or being drawn by another. The whole dance is an illusion. The hand that really draws is not in the picture. That third hand is attached to Escher's body. Similarly, there is, in a sense, no "human biology and human relatedness" to generate each other. These entities are creations of human minds, convenient divisions that can become puzzling and divisive if one loses sight of their source.

As with Escher's etchings, we may have a similarly fascinating, disequilibrating experience trying to wrap our minds around the simultaneously bivalent nature of the human psyche. It may not then be so surprising to find that on the very page on which Mitchell extolled the virtues embodied in Escher's paradoxical sensibility and, especially, its validity with respect to the nature–nurture question, he proceeded to declare the exact opposite: "Either interaction is viewed in the context of the expression of preformed forces or pressures, *or* mental content is viewed as expressed and shaped in the context of the establishment and maintenance of connections with others" (p. 5). In the subsequent sentence, he reiterated this mutually exclusive stance: "Psychological meaning is either regarded as inherent and brought to the relational field, *or* as negotiated through interaction" (p. 5). As in Mitchell's book with Greenberg, he was very cognizant of paradoxical, both/and thinking but tended, perhaps almost in spite of himself, to favor a more dichotomous position.

Later, Mitchell (1988) pronounced similarly that "Meaning is not provided a priori, but derives from the relational matrix" (p. 19). In contrast, in Bion's (1962b) model of thinking, an inherent preconception encounters a realization, giving rise to a conception. That is, an a priori template provides a basis for seeking and mating with something external, making for a meaningful encounter. For example, an infant's inborn readiness to root toward a breast encounters mother's actual tit, giving rise to a sensorimotor representation of the good (and bad) breast. Meaning, thought, and living are made possible by creative mating between the innate and the actual. Cognition is preceded by recognition.

Beyond such primal encounters, from a Piagetian perspective, perception and thought involve ongoing processes balancing assimilation to what is already inside and accommodation to what one finds. In Winnicottian terms, it is difficult to distinguish what is found from what is created. There is always some merger between internal and external. Meaning is partly provided a priori *and* significantly forged in the relational matrix.

A footnote in Greenberg's book mentioned that a middle road in the philosophical debate between empiricists and rationalists was championed by Kant. Agreeing that all knowledge begins with perception, that Germanic philosopher also stressed that the perceptions themselves are conditioned by certain characteristics of the human mind. Kant's position is integrative, giving weight to both the innate and the environmental.

In his subsequent book, Mitchell (2000) moved toward an even more integrative position. Simultaneously, however, he maintained loyalty to his longstanding, mutually exclusive position. At times, he sounds just like Blatt and Shichman and Slavin and Kriegman (though again, he does not cite them). For example,

> Being a self with others entails a constant dialectic between attachment and self-definition, between connection and differentiation, a continual negotiation between one's wishes and will and the will of others, between one's own subjective reality and a consensual reality of others with whom one lives. (Mitchell, 2000, p. 149)

This profoundly dialectical sensitivity balances needs for attachment and individuation. It contrasts with Mitchell's often seemingly more one-sided account. For example, "People are constructed in such a fashion that they are inevitably and powerfully drawn together ... wired for intense and persistent involvements" (p. 21).

Later in Mitchell's book, he again wrote in the same spirit as Blatt and Shichman and Slavin and Kriegman. Elegantly articulating his relational-conflict model, he declared that "Intimacy necessarily entails accommodation which, no matter how freely and willingly undertaken, inevitably generates a push toward a reclaiming of the self" (p. 106). Intimate relationships "always entail an active tension and conflict between openness to the other and self-definition, between responsiveness to the other's claims and a need for boundaries" (Mitchell, 2000, p. 106). Referring to Winnicott's (1963/1972) paradoxical musings on the need to be found and not found, Mitchell noted that "each of us needs to remain in some sense 'incognito' as the ground for recapturing a sense of personal experience and a renewed capacity for intimacy. *Conflict is inherent in relatedness*" (Mitchell, 2000, p. 160).

This appreciation of Escherian, paradoxical sensibility and integrative thinking contrasts with other statements in that same text. For example, from his more usual, polarizing position, Mitchell espoused that "Trying to locate the innate in the relational model is impossible, because it takes a term which is central to one paradigm and tries to locate it within another, in which it necessarily has a very different meaning" (p. 61). Nonetheless, trying to make some room for the inborn, he allowed that "The very establishment of the relational matrix is innate, and human development can perhaps be best characterized as a 'continuous unfolding of an intrinsically determined social nature' (Stern, 1985, p. 234)" (p. 61). Slavin and Kriegman's view of humans as biologically designed to be semi-social, simultaneously social and selfish rather than continuously relational, seemed slightly less appealing to Mitchell than Stern's more unambiguously pro-social outlook.

FREUD AND MITCHELL

> But there is neither East nor West, Border, nor Breed, nor Birth,
> When two strong men stand face to face, though they come from
> the ends of the earth!

—Rudyard Kipling, The Ballad of East and West

What are we to make of these seeming contradictions in Mitchell's oeuvre? On one hand, they illustrate a tendency in the evolution of psychoanalytic thought to take a few steps forward followed by taking some back. Given that Mitchell wrote so insightfully about adhesive and conflicting loyalties, it is easy to imagine that such factors may have played a role in the development of his thinking in a broadly human and perhaps personal manner.

Throughout Freud's writing, "He presented a series of psychoanalytic axioms that he promptly undermined, often within the same paragraph, invariably within the same text" (Reisner, 1992, p. 287). Mitchell's contradictions might be considered evidence of a similar authorial style. This challenging proclivity in Freud's manner of explication has been termed auto-deconstruction. When a text auto-deconstructs, it complicates or qualifies itself in such a way as to put into question a thesis already announced expressly in the same text" (Casey, 1990, p. 234). This same dynamic may be observed in Mitchell's writing.

Contemplating this style favored by innovative authors like Freud and Mitchell, one might say that brilliant, truth-seeking minds are keenly aware that no statement can fully capture the abundant intricacies of reality. Every idea such writers propound inevitably gives rise to new questions in their minds and in those of their imagined audiences. Living in the dialectic, these authors are constantly involved in conversations with themselves, their readers, and their subject matter. Surfing the wave of evolutionary advance with dazzling aplomb, an element of creative instability characterizes their work. This dynamic enshrines crucial features of the life force in their text. Creation, destruction, and preservation jostle for expression. With less of these ingredients, their work might seem more stable and consistent. It would, however, be less vital, less throbbing with the complexity of truth, less suitable for attracting and engaging others, pointing toward desirable future creative development.

Comparable commentary on contradictions in Mitchell's evolving thought appeared in a recent review essay on two of his books by Jacobson (2003). Noting that Mitchell made a strong claim for his relational model and that its concordance with current wisdom in other fields might seem like reasonable support, Jacobson nonetheless believed Mitchell's rejection of hybrid theorizing was scientistic. Treating drive as if it could only belong in the individual model was, for Jacobson, underestimating the changes in intellectual climate and in psychoanalysis that Mitchell had been part of and, in some measure, led. Two irreconcilable worldviews of human fulfillment and meaning and drive's membership in only one of them by 2003 seemed less persuasive and plausible. "The claim of irreconcilability implies that the models are claiming an absoluteness to which we are not likely to give credence" (pp. 518–519).

Despite his disagreement with aspects of Mitchell's work, Jacobson (2003) shared a similar feeling to mine about Mitchell's manner of thinking/writing:

> Part of the liveliness of Mitchell, his fruitfulness and his generosity, was that he was always in excess of his theory, which is another way to account for his return to interesting questions even when they seemed to have been dismissed a while ago. (p. 529)

Mitchell appreciated that what he had discarded in those who had gone before him might be something beyond what was yet thinkable in his own theorizing. "Declining to be ruled by ancestors, he was willing to be haunted" (p. 529).

Looking through a Winnicottian window, one might say Mitchell engaged in a spirited attack on certain postulates of Freudian theory that captured his attention to discover which ones would survive. Those that endured his aggressive assault would be able to provide sufficiently solid support for future theory formation. Prizing reality over omnipotence, the objective object over the subjective object, he did not need to feel he had always and forever defeated his noble adversary. He could allow something vital in the opposing argument to survive, granting it a certain haunting presence and power in the background of his work. Rather than laying it to rest once and for all time, Mitchell permitted something of the specter of drive theory to cohabit corners of his oeuvre. The presence of this poltergeist was apparent in the enigmatic power permeating his Escherian frontispiece.

Pondering Mitchell's choice of Escher's *Drawing Hands* to introduce his book dedicated to (selective) integration, one might imagine he felt it necessary and desirable to delve into the transitional domain of art to capture an image sufficiently potent to portray the complex interaction between nurture and nature. Left brain linguistics could convey the dynamic relationship between the inherent and the relational and sometimes did in Mitchell's writing. Right brain intuition and creativity were, however, better suited for truly enshrining the intimate relationship between these essential dimensions. Like an ancestral coat of arms, Escher's drawing could serve as an inspirational, heraldic device, linking past and future generations of psychoanalytic thinkers, uniting theorists emphasizing biology with those stressing human relatedness in a larger picture portraying a more complex cycle of mutual influence. Only a work of art could be counted on to portray so essential a message in such an unforgettable way. Words, by contrast, could not yet articulate this wisdom in a sufficiently consistent, compelling, and memorable manner.

EROS DENIED?

In a stimulating article, "Eros Reclaimed," subtitled "Recovering Freud's Relational Theory," Reisner (1992) noted that throughout Freud's career, one can observe a progressive rebalancing of two essential aspects of human motivation. On one hand, endogenous forces seek discharge or transformation. Alongside this pressure, another thrust derives from the vicissitudes of relationship. Freud found enough challenge in this state of affairs to preoccupy much of his thinking throughout his life; so did some other authors I have discussed in this chapter, including Mitchell in his own way.

Early on, Freud posited a struggle between ego instincts (concerned with the survival of the individual) and sexual instincts (survival of the species). Initial infant–mother connection was not explained by libidinal needs; rather, it served ego instincts, Greenberg (1991) noted. Unlike the sexual drive that can be satisfied autoerotically from the start, and through fantasy, ego instincts require an external object. Pleasure needs permit delay in object choice and support wide latitude in object selection. In contrast, self-preservative needs bring the infant quickly and specifically to the mother. "Ego-strivings from the beginning are directed at object[s]" (Freud, 1915/1987, p. 11).

Freud's final instinct theory portrayed the fundamental conflict as being between Eros and the death instinct. Contrary to common opinion, Reisner and some others such as Loewald (1988) and Laplanche (1989) believed the radical idea in Freud's (1920/1955b) revision of drive theory was not the death instinct, but Eros. Thanatos served as repository for Freud's longstanding ideas about the organismic aim to reduce tension. In contrast, Eros's goal was different and new, namely, to "hold up the falling level and introduce fresh tensions" (1920/1955b, p. 47). These latter qualities provided a radically revised view on the nature of instinct.

Instead of physical impulses seeking discharge, in his mature theory of motivation, Freud talked much more psychologically. Whereas Thanatos strives to "undo connections and so to destroy things" (1940/1964, p. 148), libido "coincides with the Eros of the poets and philosophers which holds all living things together" (1920/1955b, p. 50). Much as Klein shifted from her devotion to a death instinct needing redirection and release to focus on more recognizably human feelings such as envy, hate, love, reparation, and gratitude, so Freud gravitated toward his new "instinct of love" (p. 209). Rather than discharge, this motive promotes psychic tension and interrelationship. Its purpose, Freud declared grandly, "is to combine single human individuals, and after that families, then races, peoples and nations into one great unity, the unity of mankind" (p. 122). This aim clearly differed from the simpler, hydraulic discharge model that, as Holt (1976) opined, best describes the ebb and flow of urinary tension.

Throughout Freud's oeuvre, particularly during what has been termed the height of his classical drive period (1905–1915), Reisner noted a profound corrective to his discharge paradigm. In "Three Essays on the Theory of Sexuality" (Freud, 1905/1953b)—alongside the prominent representation of drive as endogenously derived, independent of its object, seeking reduction of tension—close examination reveals a contrary view of sexual impulses that challenges and enriches that classical view. In this alternative perspective, sexuality is brought into existence by the mother (anaclisis), especially by her absence, stimulating longings for her return. Sexuality here is tension producing, not solely tension reducing. Furthermore, perception of this tension is pleasurable.

This alternative view ultimately emerged as the dominant force in Freud's theory of Eros, the love that binds. For the duration of Freud's career, Reisner argued, Eros was irreducibly object seeking rather than pleasure seeking. Symbolizing the drive toward relationship, Eros works to "establish greater unities among living things" (Freud, 1940/1964a, p. 148). "The core of his being, his purpose" is "making one out of more than one" (1930/1961, p. 108). Human motivation was henceforth viewed as the conflictual interaction between strivings for relationships with all their inherent tensions and the longing to be relieved of such contacts to eliminate the tensions stemming from such interaction.

Primary identification, Freud realized, was an extremely important phase and mode of relationship preceding more differentiated forms. Loewald, too, placed much emphasis on that concept and utilized it as the foundation for some of his most creative contributions. Mitchell believed Freud did not know how to incorporate this construct into drive theory but allowed it to coexist. As a kernel of auto-deconstruction, it enriched and complexified but did not make Freud's model implode. It rested in his theoretical abode until investigators such as Loewald and Mitchell roused it, elucidating its importance. The concept of primary identification fits well with Reisner's fruitful description of Freud's blossoming attunement to primary object seeking and the role of Eros.

In his project to reclaim Freud's relational theory, Reisner was critical of both the classical/ego-psychological group and the emergent, relational one. Reisner believed that in neglecting Eros, both associations ignored not just the core concept of Freud's last 20 years but a major portion of the canon that preceded it. In editing out Freud's relational contribution, classical theorists have deprived their psychoanalysis of the creative internal tension that inspired and propelled the founder to some of his most profound theoretical insights. In accepting this distortion of Freud's theory, relational and self psychologists deprived him of his rightful place as originator of many key concepts in contemporary psychoanalysis.

SUMMARY

Purebreds, mangy mongrels, marvelous mutts, and dogs of diverse pedigree play happily in the park. You cannot mix models, Greenberg and Mitchell proclaimed persuasively. Canines cavort blissfully oblivious to that canon. Their masters may, however, try to enforce the separation principle. Notwithstanding their nixing mixing, Greenberg and Mitchell sometimes indulged in that activity and embraced contradiction and paradox. Despite their forays into the forbidden zone, they never achieved a comfortable, satisfying, full integration of the divergent models their comparative analysis had so carefully delineated. Other theorists, such as Reisner and especially Slavin and Kriegman, have been able to build on Greenberg and Mitchell's work to make substantive contributions enabling us to progress beyond antithesis toward synthesis. Championing diversity, conflict, and reconciliation, the comparative-integrative perspective embodies the spirit of Freud's final instinct theory, particularly the role of Eros in its function of bringing things together and sustaining and promoting transformative relationships.

II

THE COMPARATIVE-INTEGRATIVE POINT OF VIEW

The best lack all convictions, while the worst
Are full of passionate intensity.
Surely some revelation is at hand.

—Yeats, "The Second Coming"

4

Implications for Psychoanalytic Theory (and Organizations)

The Skylark School
Argues with the Frog School
Each with its song.

—Shoha, 19th Century

ONE PSYCHOANALYSIS OR MANY?

Diverse psychoanalytic paradigms possess similarities as well as distinctive perspectives on psychic development, derangement, and treatment. Recently, there has been increasing interest in our multiple models of mind. Those welcoming this expansive atmosphere have preferred pluralism to the hegemony of a constricting, monolithic perspective (e.g., Benjamin, 1995; Bollas, 1989; Fast, 1998; Kligerman as cited in Wallerstein, 1993; Pine, 1990). For them, the hallowed concept of neutrality has increasingly come to mean an "openness to new perspectives" including a commitment to taking them seriously, refusing to believe any interpretation complete and any meaning exhaustive (Aron, 1996, p. 28).

Others lament or rage against the growing strength of what they have perceived to be misguided deviations. For them, "mindless eclecticism" threatens the very survival of psychoanalysis. Countering these latter charges, ecumenicists have chastised those adhering rigidly to "the sacred rituals of thoughtless traditionalism" (Gedo, 1994). Stimulated by heterodoxy, they have looked askance at those forever content to "stagnate in the lowlands of orthodoxy" (Schafer, 1976, p. 57). From the highlands, they have looked down on traditionalists living in a "self-imposed jailhouse," forging their own bars, their "own unique escape from freedom" (Goldberg, 1990, p. 5). Lively debate between the orthodox and the ecumenicists has generated both heat and light. These are interesting times.

Diversity in psychoanalysis is not new. Only recently, however, have we collectively come "to experience it as a major problematic … and we have barely begun to explore its scientific and professional implications" (Wallerstein, 1992,

p. 5). Considering this matter of paramount importance for the evolution of our discipline, Wallerstein (1988) made it the subject of his presidential address to the Montreal Congress of the International Psychoanalytic Association (IPA) in his seminal presentation "One Psychoanalysis or Many?" Reflecting on that talk, Wallerstein (1990) noted that no paper of his had ever provoked such intense reaction, both positive and negative. That dramatic response attested to the significance, passion, acrimony, and vitality associated with this debate.

Two years later, concurring with Wallerstein's assessment of the topic's timeliness, the Rome Congress adopted "The Search for Common Ground" as the theme for that next conference. At the same time, the IPA inaugurated a monograph series, distributed to all members, presenting Freudian classics with commentaries by analysts of diverse persuasions—another manifestation of the growing desire to foster familiarity with multiple points of view.

Five years before the Montreal Congress, Schafer (1983) published a tome he hoped would prove useful "in developing the foundations of a modern epistemology for psychoanalysis and, in tandem with that, developing a much needed discipline of comparative psychoanalysis" (p. x). Although characterizing the latter endeavor as "a virtually undeveloped intellectual pursuit" (p. 282), he acknowledged that some efforts toward comparative analysis had been made, such as Munroe's (1955) book. In every case, however, "the result has been no more than a first approximation of the necessary form and content of this endeavor" (Schafer, p. 282).

In addition to those Congresses and Schafer and Munroe's work, there have been several other noteworthy contributions to the developing comparative literature (e.g., Gedo, 1984; Greenberg & Mitchell, 1983; V. Hamilton, 1996; Pulver, 1987; Slavin & Kriegman, 1992). Although Schafer's judgment about comparative analysis being in its infancy remains almost as true today as it was two decades ago, the time is increasingly propitious for significant advances to be made in developing this vitally needed aspect of our discipline. The ripeness of the moment, its suitability for bringing germinating seeds to fruition, can be attributed to favorable climatic conditions within our discipline and in the broader intellectual/sociocultural context in which psychoanalysis exists, be it in splendid or dreadful isolation or fructifying dialogue.

Although supporting the call for comparative analysis, I advocate going a significant step further. Understanding similarities and differences is necessary and insufficient. Beyond tolerating or embracing diversity, we must also understand and ultimately transcend it. For these reasons, I favor a comparative-integrative attitude. (Although not using precisely this term, some others have written in a manner that has definitely promoted this spirit, e.g., Gedo & Goldberg [1973], Mitchell [1988], Pine [1990], and Slavin & Kriegman [1992].)

In this chapter, I emphasize the importance of a comparative-integrative methodology for theory building (and for the construction, deconstruction, and reconstruction of psychoanalytic organizations). In ensuing chapters, I explicate the need for this point of view in relation to clinical practice and pedagogy.

TRANSCENDENTAL DECONSTRUCTION OF THE MYTHIC

The heated, personalized debates, the militantly maintained divisions, the seemingly irreconcilable differences, the peculiar failure of the field to heal its theoretical splits except by one side casting out the other and claiming to be "chosen," the way Cain and Ishmael and Leah were cast into the wilderness … and the way Napoleon crowned himself, are more or less the same today as they were in the past. (Kuspit, 1994, p. 885)

Comparative-integrative analysis addresses this "peculiar failure" of our field head-on. Like comparative analysis, it promotes realization that no school has a monopoly on truth. Perspectives are not pure revelations of reality but rather collections of hypothetical constructs. Partially derived from data, they also determine which data will be attended to or disregarded.

Referring to these constructs as fictions, Schafer (1983) described schools of thought as loosely integrated, changing bodies of fictions. When this aspect of their nature is forgotten, fictions tend to become myths—ultimate, unchangeable assertions about reality. Like primitive religious beliefs, he noted, they are not open to challenge. Alternative conceptions are simply dismissed.

In belonging to a school, Schafer contended, one works within a more or less closed system. An increasingly audible chorus views such impermeability as enervating. "A closed system is a dead one," Lussier (1991, p. 57) opined. "To the extent that we isolate ourselves from a portion of the discourse, we are deadened," Ogden (1986, p. 3) asserted. One wastes away on the restricted diet afforded by a shut-in system.

Like being locked into a particular culture or period of history, Schafer (1983) noted, theoretical embeddedness is largely unconscious. Challenging sequestered thinking, comparative-integrative analysis helps transform unconscious embeddedness into conscious reflection. Evaluating and endeavoring to integrate previously unavailable contents, this approach fosters "retrieval of the alienated" (Ogden, 1986, p. 3), enriching and revitalizing our discipline. Such resuscitation and expansion is increasingly needed in an era when one increasingly encounters articles, even entire books, bearing titles such as *The Prison House of Psychoanalysis* (Goldberg, 1990), *The Death of Psychoanalysis* (Prince, 1999), and so forth.

If the aim of a system is to create an outside where you can put things you don't want, then we have to look at what that system disposes of—its rubbish—to understand it, to get a picture of how it sees itself and wants to be seen. (Phillips, 1995, p. 19)

Diamonds may be discovered in the trash—gems for which no place could be found in the original setting, the inner circle, the sacred ring. Such scavenging is not new for our field. We are "accustomed to divine concealed things from despised or unnoticed features, from the rubbish-heap, as it were, of our observations" (Freud 1914/1955e, p. 222).

Proscribed vocabulary in any theory is as telling as the recommended one (Phillips, 1995, p. 19). We need to pay special attention to forbidden words and ideas (cf. Willock, Bohm, & Curtis, in press). The degree to which we outlaw them suggests they have dangerous power. We had better explore that manna and come to understand it. Too often, we react to such terms, instead, the way bees do when a member of their species that does not belong to the hive enters, performing an unfamiliar dance. We, too, are prone to respond to communications from different schools with stinging attack. Our ofttimes venomous reaction is interesting but surely not the best we can do when experiencing systemic discomfort.

Elucidation has always been central to psychoanalysis. The comparative-integrative approach extends this aim beyond the traditional realm of individual psychopathology (including the psychopathology of everyday life) to the newer, equally exciting realm of our discipline's unconscious and its quotidian pathology.

Some find this critical, complex, provisional, demanding attitude toward ourselves—our theories, our organizations, and our practices—liberating; others experience it as burdensome and disquieting. Surely, it is both. The vehement, venomous, vital passions fomented by Wallerstein's plenary addresses suggest the health and integrity of our science requires and is crying out for this new approach. A growing number of analysts appear ready to take on this exciting project.

The science and philosophy of the 20th century has comprised serial attacks on all but the most pragmatic, provisional, contingent doctrines of realism, Barratt (1994) noted. Many analysts nonetheless continue cheerily oblivious to these developments. Venturing beyond Schafer's (1983) portrayal of *The Analytic Attitude,* Barratt suggested every school has an attitude. Each theory establishes illusions and boundaries of designation exempt from questioning and critique. These attitudes resist our responsibility to interrogate everything we do, including theorizing.

In the zone of unquestioned myth, analysts indulge in inferential leaps that are usually inoffensive, even invisible to their close colleagues. These pirouettes are part of the acceptable dance in every hive of analytic activity. In contrast, these cognitive vaults leave analysts who dance in other companies spinning with epistemological dizziness and disbelief.

Mythic mentation is reminiscent of Snakes and Ladders. That enduringly popular board game embodies tensions between cooperative and competitive strivings, rule commitment, and earlier developmental wishes and fears. Longing to enact omnipotent flying fantasies, to hurdle tall obstacles in single leaps (the ladders), aficionados are simultaneously attuned to contrary feelings about thwarting, treacherous aspects of reality (the serpents). In mythic mode, analysts bypass grounded, one-step-at-a-time approaches to data and thought. They take handy shortcuts, magical ladders to divine destinations. To proponents of other perspectives, these logical leaps up linguistic ladders suggest wild analysis (Freud, 1910/1957; Schafer, 1985). They fear these flights of fantasy are simply seductive snake rides down slippery slopes of regressive, magical, or just plain sloppy thinking.

The need to recognize incoherence, inconsistency, and incompleteness in our positions, stemming from unexamined presuppositions and indefensible leaps of faith, was stressed by Schafer (1990). Schwaber (e.g., 1987, 1990), too, has criticized theory-driven, inferential jumps and has advocated more careful listening and questioning. Barratt (1994) suggested a different analytic attitude based on privileging free association in a manner akin to deconstructionism. Realizing theorizing is always operative, he advocated it be treated with suspicion. Rather than utilizing it to enhance identity, security, and certainty, theory should serve as impetus to radicalize the analyst's free associative interrogation. That, for Barratt, is the sine qua non of the psychoanalytic odyssey.

I certainly endorse more careful listening, questioning, and the provisional, skeptical attitude toward formulations that have been urged by Schafer, Schwaber, Barratt, and others. I believe, however, that a more powerful safeguard against becoming or remaining trapped in a closed system suffused with mythic mentation is a comparative-integrative attitude. This critical approach guarantees the careful attention, querying, and tentative attitude that those authors have rightly implored us to embrace.

The necessity of moving beyond our cherished tribal simplicities, narcissistic investments, and aggressive indulgences is increasingly apparent in the (post)modern world. If one has lived in more than one culture or delved into more than one religion, one is likely to have a more open mind. Similarly, familiarity with multiple theoretical systems protects one against falling too easily into the illusion/delusion that any single manner of formulating/intervening is the only or necessarily the best way. Increasingly, it is recognized that it is no longer a luxury but rather "essential to try out radically different conceptual models" (Schafer, 1976, p. 59).

Tolerance should not be considered a lack of intellectual ability but an active, energizing ideal, Roazen (2002) counseled: "Not being too sure that one is right is a mark of having a civilized intelligence" (p. 284). He looked favorably on Erikson's (1950) model that views people in terms of how many contradictions and tensions they are capable of unifying constructively. The opposite of this tolerance of ambiguity, uncertainty, and paradox is what Erikson (1975) termed "the human propensity to bolster one's own inner mastery by bunching together and prejudging whole classes of people" (p. 175). Huddled in exclusive schools of thought, psychoanalysts have excelled at this human proclivity.

Unfortunately, even now "It is difficult to find any psychoanalyst who is really deeply conversant with more than one approach" (Mitchell & Black, 1995, p. 207). Only rare individuals, such as Grotstein, can boast fluency in several analytic languages, even if, as he put it, he speaks some with a heavy accent.

This state of affairs is regrettable for, as Donnel Stern (2003) put it, you do not really understand your own theory unless you understand the alternatives. He went so far as to assert that one cannot really have a viewpoint unless one can intelligently contrast it with another. ("He's as blind as he can be, Just sees what he wants to see ... Doesn't have a point of view, Knows not where he's going to, Isn't he a bit like you and me?"—Lennon & McCartney, "Nowhere Man.")

Investment in primary transitional (illusory) objects is eventually withdrawn and spread across the entire cultural field (e.g., religion). Such phenomena should never be questioned, Winnicott (1952/1971b) advised. There is merit in this considerate, respectful stance. It can, nonetheless, be argued that it is essential to query even our most sacrosanct domains, including each psychoanalytic subculture's conceptual inner sanctum. Otherwise, credos become "unquestioned myths" (Schafer, 1983), security blankets to wrap ourselves in, sanctuaries for untested dogma. The issue must therefore become not whether to question our beliefs and those of our neighbors but how to do so.

A New Analytic Attitude

Can one honor a tradition *and* question it? To critique and revise Freud's theory—even radically—is our prerogative as well as our way of being determined by it, wrote Jessica Benjamin (1995). Furthermore, "To acknowledge as well as oppose this determination by a discourse is a critical form of gratitude—to kiss as well as bite the hand that feeds you" (p. 4). This challenging conversation provides a way, she suggested, "to satisfy the need to be located in history, in tradition, without feeling that you have simply been enlisted into it: to accept that you have not created yourself without being deprived of creativity" (p. 4).

From a comparative-integrative point of view, discourse as critical gratitude is a useful metaphor for examining not only Freudian fundamentals but all analytic belief systems, all hallowed hypotheses, so we can respect and value but not be unduly constrained by them.

Fish are not conscious that water constitutes their environment, one terrestrial pundit opined. They would need to leave their aqueous milieu to develop an "analytic attitude" toward it. Like schools of fish, we students of analysis need to voyage from the psychoanalytic ponds in which we were born and bred to swim in different pools to get perspective. From there, we might be able to "kiss as well as bite" our alma mater (Latin, literally, our nourishing, dear mother).

Fusing aggression with libidinal attachment to our school of thought enlivens our relationship to it. The combined drives facilitate healthy separation individuation. They enable us to progress beyond blissful, illusory, primary identification without losing all aliment emanating from such primal sources.

Infants, in Grotstein's (2000) view, experience themselves as "incompletely separated from a mythical object behind them, their background presence, their object of tradition, which rears them and sends them forth" (p. 17). He believed this presence was the phantasied, mythical counterpart of Erikson's (1959) concepts of epigenesis, sense of tradition, and cultural and racial identity. "We feel a sense of comfort that someone stands behind us in our effort to face the world" (Grotstein, 2000, p. 18). For analysts trained in any of our limited schools, there are liabilities as well as pleasures to staying in or straying from one's background object of tradition.

Comparative-integrative analysis does not endorse leaping from some supposedly outdated paradigm to some revolutionary, new, improved model. Such simplistic solutions to theoretical/clinical conundra risk our sautéing ourselves from frying pan into the flames. I delineated the problematic nature of such switches (e.g., rejecting ego psychology for self psychology) in chapters 1 and 2. Instead, a very different kind of shift is necessary—from a uniparadigmatic to a multiparadigmatic, dialectical perspective. This latter outlook is consistent with and goes beyond Luria's (1968) assertion that scientific observation's "main goal is to view an event from as many perspectives as possible" (cited in Alvarez, 1992, p. 184).

Comparative analysis, an increasingly popular endeavor, at least in principle if not in practice, cannot be the final requirement, the summum bonum, for the evolution of analytic thought. Like motherhood and apple strudel, it is only a piece of what is needed. Comparative-integrative analysis, on the other hand, provides a suitable banner highlighting the direction in which and the method by which our discipline must advance. Familiarizing, comparing, and contrasting become even more valuable activities when viewed as providing necessary groundwork for further, essential development (synthesis) toward an increasingly inclusive, rich, complex discipline.

This approach does not simply advocate accepting what common ground might be more or less readily agreed on such as that delineated by clinical as opposed to general theory (Wallerstein, 1990). That attitude risks settling for lowest common denominator ground. It tends to "underestimate grossly the role that theory plays in practice" (Gill, 1994, p. 149).

Rather than perpetuating the battle for which school shall rule all disputed conceptual territory, erecting walls against unruly elements, the comparative-integrative approach enables psychoanalysts to reclaim vast lands pertaining to both theory and technique from current seas of controversy. This reclamation project will provide fertile soil for our discipline's growth.

In his controversial article "The Impending Death of Psychoanalysis," Bornstein (2001) declared, "If psychoanalysis is to flourish in the 21st Century, the prevailing theoretical frameworks must be discarded and replaced with a single integrative model … A new paradigm for psychoanalysis must emerge or the theory will perish" (p. 12). Although I cannot agree with everything Bornstein asserted in his article, his call for an integrative model is obviously a point of concord.

Bornstein (2001) was more concerned with the schism between psychoanalysis and mainstream psychology/psychiatry. My focus is on divisions within psychoanalysis. One can, however, strive to improve relationships in one's home while also working toward better relations with neighbors. Comparative-integrative methodology provides tools for working on both fronts.

More than a decade before Bornstein's provocative article, Laplanche (1987/1989) proclaimed that "Psychoanalysis is in a state of crisis because it has no sense of where it is going" (p. 154). Comparative-integrative analysis sheds light on this confusional state. It affords a direction, goal, and means for getting us out of this longstanding morass to a far better place.

PSYCHOANALYTIC HISTORY

> Everybody's talking at me / I don't hear a word they're saying / Only the echoes of my mind.

Fred Neil, "Everybody's Talkin'"

Reflecting on the intellectual ambience in which he was raised, Schafer (1999) remarked that the followers of Hartmann, Kris, and Loewenstein developed "a very strict orthodoxy" (p. 351). Furthermore, "It was professionally perilous to question publicly this orthodoxy" (p. 351). The same sad situation, no doubt, holds true for all other analytic orthodoxies, past, present, and future. Threats to one's professional survival and advancement can be powerful motivators and potent inhibitory forces.

Examining analytic orthodoxy, Bergmann (1997) queried, "What then is the role of the historian?" Immediately, he answered, "Certainly not to re-fight old battles." He concluded that "The task is to supply a wider frame of reference than was available to those who created this history" (p. 84).

Congruent with Santayana's famous aphorism ("If we do not learn from history we shall be doomed to repeat it"), Rubin (1998) warned:

> Psychoanalysis does not have a future if it fails to come to terms with or remains bound to its past. Psychoanalysis has to do with itself what it recommends for patients, namely, assimilate its past so that it can understand its present and enliven its future. (p. 198)

Concurring with Bergmann, Santayana, and Rubin, I examine some wars that enlivened and disrupted the analytic landscape. My purpose is to offer a more comprehensive (comparative-integrative) framework for viewing/handling those conflicts.

At a simpler (perhaps simplified) time in the history of our discipline, ego psychology's triumvirate averred that

> Progress in psychoanalytic theory has led to a better integration, an ever closer connection, of its various parts. It is this very feature in its development that makes the emphasis on the interrelatedness of its hypotheses and also, particularly, on the "hierarchy of propositions" so essential a part of any evaluation and appropriate use of theory in psychoanalysis. (Hartmann et al., 1953, p. 143)

Although agreeing wholeheartedly with the importance of connecting the diverse parts of analytic theory, I, like Kuspit (1994), am less sanguine about this being the status quo then or now.

In contrast to the relatively rosy, tidy view espoused by the North American mainstream's trinity, Kuhn (1970) observed that science is "a rather ramshackle structure with little coherence among its various parts" (p. 49). His characterization applies to psychoanalysis. This less neat portrait was endorsed by Loewald (1978): "Let us admit that psychoanalysis, for the time being, is a rather untidy discipline, still feeling its way" (p. 5). The comparative-integrative point of view provides a compass to orient us in this quest.

With respect to coherence, analytic theory currently approximates the situation immortalized by the blind fellows who encountered a representative of the family Elephantidae. Where each chap stood informed and limited his understanding in a major way. Touching the trunk, one described the creature as serpentine. The leg man proclaimed the animal resembled a tree trunk. Individual theories may have severe limitations; conglomerated, they can provide a more comprehensive portrait of the elusive beast.

In the unconscious, the *pars pro toto* principle (part standing for the whole) holds considerable sway. From the perspective of secondary process, however, a component may not convey an accurate picture of an entity. Psychoanalytic theory building has too often teetered toward "a group of partial truths in danger of being elevated to whole fictions" (Silverman, 1987, p. 280). In contrast, a comparative-integrative approach creates a climate of understanding and a methodology wherein it would be unthinkable to try to constitute a complete discipline by selecting a few of the available parts and ignoring other, crucial components.

Not one to shy away from sacred elephants, Mitchell (1988) dared challenge the wisdom enshrined in the preceding folk tale. Some investigators, he believed, could be exploring giraffes rather than elephants. Integrative efforts might then portray a creature having four long legs, mammoth ears, and a long neck and trunk.

Rather than the possibility of creating such a chimera being a fatal argument against the desirability of a more encompassing model, I see Mitchell's warning as speaking to the error of premature synthesis (Aron, 1995). This mistake is modeled on the combined parent figure, the infantile fusion of interacting maternal and paternal presences. This amalgam provides the basis for children's monsters, nightmares, and other persecutory delusions (Segal, 1964), and Mitchell's "*giraphant*" (my term).

Contraries coexist in the unconscious (Freud, 1940/1964). They do not influence each other or, if they do, "no decision is reached, but a compromise comes about which is nonsensical since it embraces mutually incompatible details" (p. 169). The giraphant exemplifies such a whimsical combination. These fusions are not useless, for they attract attention, stimulating associations and alternative formulations.

It is equally important to avoid the opposite error, splitting off contradictions and ambiguities, separating them from each other, Aron noted. This mistake is modeled on attacks on the primal scene, the advanced version of the combined parent, based on defensive attempts to keep the parents apart so they cannot interact.

In healthy development, the primal scene symbolizes two contrasting ideas that can be held together in the mind. The individual concepts can interact without either becoming fused (as in the combined parent) or fractured.

Affirmative aspects of splitting provide order and control chaos until such a time as integration is possible, Aron noted. I believe Greenberg and Mitchell utilized such splitting to good effect to separate drive from relational theories. When they wrote, the time was not yet ripe for synthesis. It remained for others, such as Slavin and Kriegman, to create a bed capable of holding these two grand narratives.

Comparative-integrative psychoanalysis welcomes conflicting conceptualizations rather than fearing, resenting, attacking, or neglecting them. "Each of these conceptual schemata encodes one or the other of the primary meanings implicit in human existence—unfortunately often to the exclusion of all other meanings" (Gedo, 1984, p. 159). Whereas scientific paradigms suppress observations that might be subversive to their commitments (Kuhn, 1970), the comparative-integrative approach leads one to be intrigued by different models, to struggle to appreciate what they might add to a more comprehensive view of the elephantine phenomena we seek to understand and perchance transform.

The correspondence theory of truth posits that reality is impossible to know in its entirety, but one can achieve better understanding through a cumulative process of reality testing (Hanly, 1990). The fabled, blind wallahs remind us that we need multiple perspectives and, one might add, multiple modes of probing reality. In clinical practice, we use eyes, ears, minds, countertransference, empathy, and diverse theories to accumulate the necessary components for comprehending patients. We abide by the methodology articulated a few hundred years ago by the Japanese poet, Onitsura: "To finally know / the plum, use the whole heart too / and your own nose."

To construct adequate theory, draw on diverse ego functions, for example: attention (vs. selective inattention to different perspectives), comprehension (as opposed to dismissing foreign theories with little attempt to understand them), discrimination (between different theories), and judgment (of their relative merits). Particularly important for the comparative-integrative perspective is the ego's synthetic function.

Ego psychologists are not the only ones to have appreciated the synthetic function. Slavin and Kriegman (1992) noted that the cost of the human strategy for structuring the self in a provisional fashion around a sometimes precarious federation of self/other schemas is the ever-present risk of disintegration, fragmentation, and identity diffusion. Their understanding could be extrapolated to psychoanalytic pluralism in which fragmentation and identity diffusion have been fully realized. "The maintenance of self-cohesion, as the self psychologists contend, should then be one of the most central, ongoing activities of the psyche—possibly the most central or superordinate principle of human psychic activity" (p. 205). Their conclusion applies not only to the psyche but also the discipline.

Aron underscored the idea that we need identity and multiplicity. The former involves continuity, constancy, and synthesis. People need a cohesive, integrated sense of self. They also need to accept their own internal differences, tolerating and even enjoying confusion, contradiction, flux, lack of integration, and even chaos in their sense of who they are. The paranoid-schizoid (PS) position contributes the capacity for multiplicity, difference, and discontinuity. The depressive (D) position provides integration and identity. Both positions are as essential for disciplinary development as for individual maturation.

By drawing on affirmative aspects of PS and D, the comparative-integrative approach facilitates advancement of our science. In contrast, "Argument by authority stands directly in the way of the benefits, zealously guarded since the Renaissance, of an adversarial, critical, and dialectical tradition of investigation" (Spence, 1994, p. 3). Outside closed systems, theses evoke antitheses. "Without disagreement psychoanalytic theory would be dead" (J. Sandler, 1983, p. 41). Controversy should be courted, not condemned.

Notwithstanding Hartmann et al.'s (1953) optimistic assertion about our discipline's progressive integration, due to Napoleonic tendencies manifested by various schools, our field has actually been in a prolonged, presynthetic state. Progressive dialectic movement has been stalled. States of strain, turbulence, and denial are seen in individuals, organizations, and our discipline as a whole.

SPLITTING PROCESSES IN PSYCHOANALYTIC THEORY AND ORGANIZATIONS

> And we are here as on a darkling plain
> Swept with confused alarms of struggle and flight,
> Where ignorant armies clash by night.
>
> —**Matthew Arnold**, *Dover Beach*

Wars of Words, Sounds of Silence

Closed-minded, mutually antagonistic theoretical systems suggest fixation in paranoid-schizoid mentational modes. All that is good, true, beautiful, and trustworthy is believed to be ensconced within one's orientation; that which is bad, false, inelegant, and dangerous resides in someone else's. Each school needs to be vigilant lest its systems and people become contaminated by unsavory, foreign ideas.

We have a tradition of handling unwelcome dissent (stranger anxiety) with surgical splitting. Paranoid anxiety permeates psychoanalytic institutes (Kernberg, 1986). Professional insecurities foster intolerance of diversity and dysfunctional organizational defenses (Eisold, 1994). Establishing a climate for conversing about these problems is a precondition for working our way out of these constrictions on thought, activity, and association.

Excessive splitting characterizes an immature stage in everyone's life and perhaps in the life of a discipline. Unable to integrate affectively diverse experiences, infants utilize splitting and allied mechanisms to establish some sense of order and safety. At first such separations happen relatively passively, providing a simple mode for organizing emotionally diverse experiences. Later, when the ego is stronger, the preverbal set deploys these processes more actively for defense, stringently separating good from bad self-representations and object representations, preventing contamination. In the course of its development, our discipline has utilized both active and passive forms of splitting to segregate the sacred from the scary.

Our field has suffered from what Kleinians refer to, in primitive syndromes, as a relative weakness of the life instinct, that is, the force that binds, seeks connections and unity, and counteracts disruption. In less instinctual language, Freud (1933/1964a) asserted that the ego is characterized by synthetic tendencies that are lacking in the id. Our discipline has been more like id than ego, more unconscious than conscious. Opposing tendencies have dwelt side by side, unable to effect synthesis, analogous to the situation ontologically prior to the predominance of integrative abilities.

The key to the requisite ego strength (ability to reduce tensions, mediate, reconcile contradictions) resides in the synthetic function (Nunberg, 1938). We have not done very well at maturely settling conflicts. We have frequently resorted to strategies, more primitive than sophisticated, more defensive than adaptive. Stridency reflected rigidity, not strength. Greater use of our integrative function is essential for developing our collective ego strength, something we need to confront contemporary challenges.

Our active splitting began with Freud's efforts to guard against antianalytic tendencies. Freud feared deviations might dilute and destroy his conceptual baby. As his wobbly body of science struggled to come of age in what he perceived to be a hostile milieu, he aggressively defended his creation. Adopting a stance toward dissension that he said the ego used in relation to internal dangers, that is, treating them as if they were external, he extruded dissidents beyond the boundary of his cherished "movement" (Freud, 1914/1957). Currying his benevolent regard, like-minded followers joined forces to keep the barbarians outside the gates. These centripetal processes resemble the modus operandi of the purified pleasure ego (Freud, 1915/1957a) that establishes narcissistic boundaries to foster the feeling that all good is securely within one's own self (or group self), whereas all bad has been pushed into some other, undesirable self (or movement).

Since the early extrusions (e.g., Jung, Adler), many other developments exceeded our integrative capacities. Expulsions, defections, and schisms ensued. Peaceful or antagonistic coexistence obtained. Each faction tended to dismiss alternatives as wrongheaded, simpleminded, old-fashioned, crazy, or dangerous. In these derogations, one recognizes processes akin to borderline defenses (devaluation coupled with idealization). Analysts indulging in such processes need not have prominent narcissistic or borderline features, but such diagnostic descriptors may capture aspects of our discipline's discourse and evolution, or lack thereof, as pugilistic partisans spar on the borderline between competing schools.

"With each split there is a lost opportunity" (Casement, in Astor, 1998, p. 709). If our discipline is finally ready to progress beyond the sorry state of having left a few too many troops behind (in the upper trenches of PS), we will have to adopt more mature, ambivalent attitudes toward both our favorite and devalued schools. We will need to tolerate more complexity and internal conflict in ourselves, our theories, and our organizations. The easy rewards attached to a simplifying, externalizing stance will have to be surrendered. It may also be necessary to work through guilt and shame for previously excessive aggression toward enemies now reclassified as friends.

This greater capacity for ambivalence and ambiguity will reflect and promote our advance into a more salubrious, "depressive" position. Development entails a mixture of confusion, gratification, anxiety, and excitement. Fortunately, when the maturational moment is ripe, there is usually more pleasure than pain in the affective balance.

Historical Position

The time has come, Ogden (1986) suggested, to rename the depressive position. The established term captures the loss of simplicity, boldness, absolutism, and satisfyingly self-righteous, black-and-white thinking characteristic of the earlier, PS perspective. Emphasizing affect, it hints at what is feared and defended against by those embedded in rigid, antithetical, paranoid-schizoid functioning. Ogden's preferred term, *historical* position, highlights the more sophisticated commitment to complexity inherent in D. Rather than just living in the moment, Ogden's (1986) phrase implies one must sustain a sense of temporal flow, understanding how the past operates in the present. Eschewing disavowal, this perspective struggles against dissociative tendencies. It rejects attempts to reinstate purity and simplicity by denying or otherwise annihilating contradictory streams of thought.

Applying Ogden's term to disciplinary development promotes understanding that we are constructing a complex, conflictual, evolving science. Committed to considering seemingly contradictory positions from different epochs, geographical regions, authors, and institutions, we endeavor to integrate these perspectives rather than dismiss unwelcome aspects of the dialectic. The historical position is the appropriate place for comparative-integrative psychoanalysis.

Paralleling personal development, our discipline needs to strive for a more optimal, progressive balance between PS and D. Augmenting what we might call H (the historical position) and lessening our reliance on modi operandi rooted in PS, including attacks on linking (Bion, 1959), will make us a more healthy, cohesive, robust discipline. Exchanging rigid pseudostrength for truer, more flexible, adaptive power, we will become a less borderline science.

Container, Contained, Incontinent

Bionic alpha function contrasts with anti-alpha (Sandler, 1997) that attacks transience, a quality Freud (1916) described as characterizing life. Anti-alpha interferes with accessing truth through tolerating paradox, uncertainty, and the unknown—painful qualities from the pleasure principle's point of view. Anti-alpha represents unwillingness or inability to attain D and to freely experience movement between PS and D (PS<—> D). It freezes the <—> part. Alpha's relationship to anti-alpha can be summarized as alive, animate <—> dead, inanimate.

Although focused on individual functioning, Sandler noted that "Psychoanalytic theories can become concrete, taking on for their proponents the quality of absolute truth" (p. 50). This crystallization of fictions into myths (Schafer, 1983) is illuminated by Sandler's conceptualization. Anti-alpha mitigates against the invigorating balance between PS and D. Hostile to the historical position, it grimly reaps our discipline's vitality, replacing it with stifling rigidity and suffocating indoctrination in analytic training (Lussier, in Wallerstein, 1993).

In contrast to anti-alpha's desire to deanimate, Winnicott (1988) was intrigued by the opposite "state of the human individual as the being emerges out of the not being" (p. 131) as "living arises and establishes itself out of non-living" (Winnicott, 1963/1972, p. 191). Winnicott (1988) viewed aloneness as transitional between "unaliveness" (p. 132) and aliveness (Sandler's space between inanimate and alive.)

As a school of thought comes into being, it may want to exist for a time as an "isolate" (Winnicott, 1963/1972). This aloneness should, however, be transitional. To become fully alive means entering into differentiated object relating. Discourse with other subjectivities, other perspectives, is essential. Resisting this progression, an orientation can only oscillate between isolation and unaliveness.

Infants, like borderlines (Kernberg, 1975), separate good and bad representations to avoid confusion and panic. In our discipline, similarly, there has been angst that integration would lead to disorder. This fear has nurtured hopes of safety through segregation. Dividing our worlds promotes a state in which "Our most intense erotic attachments are to our categories. "We hold ourselves together by keeping things apart" (Phillips, 1995, p. 123). Freud's (1909/1955a) insight that "All knowledge is patchwork" (p. 100) would seem dangerously untidy to seasoned segregationists.

In the debate over one psychoanalysis or many, protagonists fear our discipline will degenerate into either chaos or petrifaction (Wallerstein, 1993).

Isolation risks ossification. Dialogue could entail chaos. Some disorganization might, however, be fructifying. The primal scene may be petrifyingly chaotic to a child but otherwise to the developmentally more advanced. With adult wisdom, Loewald (1973/1980d) advocated "disorganization in the service of the ego" (p. 340). He believed creative dissolution was required to arrive at novel resolutions manifesting higher levels of organization. He was discussing individuals, but his principle holds for larger systems.

Can one navigate between stony Scylla and chaotic Charybdis, between aloneness in the presence of the other (Winnicott, 1958a) and active relating? The answer depends on alpha. Petrifaction reflects anti-alpha. Chaos indicates insufficient alpha to contain and transform beta elements into manageable, meaningful units that can be stored in memory and utilized to promote thought. When adequate alpha is available, ideas that seemed antagonistic can be synthesized. The optimal vehicle for receiving and transmuting the charged beta elements characterizing diverse orientations is comparative-integrative analysis.

Edenic Controversy

Adherents of each perspective tend to derogate all others. There is, nonetheless, one thing on which they all agree, Shane (1987) noted. That common ground is the shared sentiment that mixed-model theorists confuse apples with oranges, inevitably composing sloppy, inelegant, unappetizing, fruit salads. In comparative-integrative cuisine, however, if one selects a good balance of ingredients, cutting off coarse and overripe spots, one can create a delicious, nutritious dish. A mixed model need not be a mixed-up model.

Our discipline now has sufficient ego strength to progress beyond cognition excessively imbued with splitting and repression. We can allow different ideas to coexist without being seized by irresistible impulses to destroy, devalue, or disregard. Increasingly, we can tolerate diverse bodies of thought, allowing them to commingle. Theoretical apartheid is on the wane. Intercourse, even marriage, between different constructs is no longer a cardinal sin in all quarters. In fact, some are beginning to suspect closed systems may be the sinful, incestuous ones. "In house" schools of thought, journals, and conferences, whatever their merits, inadvertently encourage members to love ideas selected on a narcissistic basis rather than promoting more mature levels of object choice.

One cannot mix apples and oranges. Despite universal knowledge of this law, many superb fruit salads contain both and more. What about combining more disparate entities, say apples and sex? *Genesis* contained these elements and then some. Although chaos and petrifaction were well within Yahweh's repertoire, his primal couple avoided these fates despite having transgressed the law of the isolate, naughtily mixing with forbidden fruit and serpents. They were allowed to go forth and multiply via lively object relating, mingling genitals and genes to their hearts' content. It can be likewise in the epigenesis of analysis. Freud, Klein, Kohut, and others can attend the same party rather than separating along party lines. At this party to end all parties, all may boogey to the beat of Bob Marley's "One Love," singing "Let's get together and feel all right."

The healthier disciplinary climate that is emerging suggests we are developing a more secure base (Bowlby, 1979) from which to explore new possibilities. We need not cling forever to our original Eden, the theoretical matrix into which we happened to have been born. We do not have to be so uptight, inhibited by stranger anxiety, basic mistrust, and authoritarian dictates. We can enjoy apples and oranges, pomegranates and persimmons. Breathing more easily, we can ascend the developmental scale, individually and as a discipline.

DEVELOPMENTAL ARREST

Modern science begins with synthesis.

— **Gaston Bachelard,** *The New Scientific Spirit*

Paraphilia

Polarities such as negation versus recognition and dominance versus intersubjectivity have been elucidated by relational psychoanalysts (e.g., Benjamin, 1995). These propensities pertain not only to individuals but also groups. Negation and dominance, as opposed to recognition and intersubjectivity, have been all too apparent in interactions between analytic organizations.

Perverse sexuality is excellently centered (Freud, 1916–1917/1963):

> All its actions are directed to an aim. … One component instinct has gained the upper hand in it and … has subjected the others to its purposes. In that respect there is no distinction between perverse and normal sexuality other than the fact that their dominating component instincts and consequently their sexual aims are different. In both of them, one might say, a well organized tyranny has been established, but in each of the two a different family has seized the reins of power. (pp. 322–323)

Freud was discussing infantile psychosexuality. One might speak analogously with respect to our polymorphous models of the mind. When a partial theory has gained the upper hand, it may make it virtually impossible for subjects to see, or find interest, let alone excitement, in what turns on members of other schools. When a component theory has "seized the reins of power," a "well organized tyranny" (Freud, 1916–1917/1963, pp. 322–323) results. The intellectually perverse features of perspectival bondage can be gratifying, reassuring, inhibitory, and oppressive.

Warning of the danger of "perverting the psychoanalytic attitude through idealization of analytic theories and thinkers," Joyce McDougall (1995, p. 235), an expert on paraphilia asked, "Is not our leading perversion, then, the belief that we hold the key to truth?" (p. 234). She lamented the fact that the beliefs of psychoanalytic sects prevent their converts from benefiting from each other's discoveries.

In his book *The Language of Perversion and the Language of Love,* Bach (1994) noted that people with perversions have difficulty dealing with the ambiguity of human relationships. They have not developed the transitional psychic space that would allow them to contain a paradox, making it difficult for them to recognize the reality and legitimacy of multiple points of view. His observations seem applicable to the arrested development of psychoanalytic discourse.

"The development and application of any systematic language for psychoanalytic interpretation implies some kind of colonization" (Schafer, 1976, p. 363). The question is the imperial flag under which this colonization "will be carried out, which is to say the regime that will create the most favorable conditions for enlightened and enlightening development" (p. 363). From the comparative-integrative point of view, flags of competing states need to be subsumed under a new banner belonging to a superordinate league of nations. Such associations do not appeal to groups with imperialistic aims unless they can see a way, as Freud said, of seizing the reins of power. Nonetheless, this ideal is increasingly relevant as we realize the problems of psychoanalytic colonialism.

Repression and Perversion

As Vienna's most infamous son bombed Britain, bitter battles raged below between adherents to the banners of Anna Freud and Melanie Klein. Some Viennese defended Freud's writings to the letter because they believed Klein's ideas "open the door to a perversion of psychoanalysis and the loss of their professional identities as psychoanalysts" (Steiner, 1985, p. 58).

Fear of the perversity of otherness, with consequent need to repress the ego alien, was discussed by Breuer and Freud (1895/1955) a half century earlier: "The basis for repression itself can only be a feeling of unpleasure, the incompatibility between the single idea that is to be repressed and the dominant mass of ideas constituting the ego" (p. 116). Although Breuer and Freud were referring to individual psychopathology, their idea can be extrapolated to group pathology. When members of a school believe a new concept does not fit their dominant ideational mass, they may feel displeasure and extrude the misfit.

There are, of course, different types of groups (Bion, 1961). Excommunicative tendencies would be especially pronounced in groups organized around principles of fight and flight. An association dedicated to comparative-integrative principles would not favor banishment. It would, therefore, be closer to Bion's ideal, the working group.

A decade after his important publication with Breuer, Freud (1905/1953) continued to explore related ideas. Abandoned impulses would seem

> perverse—that is, to arise from … zones … which, in view of the direction of the subject's development, can only arouse unpleasureable feelings. They consequently evoke opposing mental forces … which, in order to suppress this unpleasure effectively, build up the mental dams. (p. 178)

Freud's insightful words bring to mind his own aggressive reaction to Ferenczi's (1949) article, "The Confusion of Tongues between Adult and Child." The reason for his agitated response appeared to have been that his supposed disciple had abandoned the colonial flag that Freud was convinced provided the "most favorable conditions for enlightened and enlightening development" (Schafer, 1976, p. 363). Ferenczi drew on concepts of interpersonal trauma as opposed to intrapsychic forces to explain pathogenesis—principles Freud had "abandoned." In view of the direction of Freud's development, Ferenczi's paper aroused unpleasure. He therefore erected a mental dam against these threatening ideas. Ferenczi was soon damned as mentally deranged.

Contributing his diagnostic acumen to shed darkness on this situation, Jones (1957) declared that Ferenczi "developed psychotic manifestations that revealed themselves, among other ways, in a turning away from Freud and his doctrines" (p. 47). Theoretical disloyalty was considered so delusional and perverse it had to be quarantined. As editor of *The International Journal of Psycho-Analysis,* Jones was able to construct a dam to keep Ferenczi's paper out of the mainstream for 16 years.

Totalitarianism

Exploring tyranny, Bollas (1992) valued Arendt's insight that its roots lie in ideologies. Claiming total explanation, ideologues divorce themselves from experience from which they learn nothing new because their operating logic orders all facts to support their axiom. "Something almost banal in its ordinariness—namely our cohering of life into ideologies and theories—is the seed of the Fascist state of mind when such ideology must (for whatever reason) become total" (p. 200).

To achieve totality, the mind or group must entertain no doubt. Equated with weakness, uncertainty is expelled. This excommunication is accompanied by special acts of binding around ideological signs, Bollas noted. The mind ceases to be complex, as maxims, oaths, and mental icons fill the gap previously occupied by the polysemousness of the symbolic order. In contrast to such simplicity, when the mind entertains the various parts of the self and representatives of the outside world in democratic order, it participates freely in a "multifaceted movement of many ideas" (p. 201).

Although Bollas was not writing about psychoanalytic politics, one can see parallels. Later, for example, I consider Rangell's "total composite psychoanalytic theory." His totalizing could be seen to exemplify Bollas's depiction of something "banal in its ordinariness." Rangell was, no doubt, simply articulating maxims and icons of his ego-psychological heritage. He seemed unconcerned that "The authoritarian quality of Hartmann and his group was enormous" (Kernberg, in Bergmann, 2000, p. 228), or and that "The authoritarianism was really quite devastating," as Ostow put it (p. 232).

Totalitarian hatred of difference accords with Chasseguet-Smirgel's (1984) viewing perversion as based on denial of difference. Conformity, negation, dominance, and rigidity are preferred over the "multifaceted movement of many ideas." They desire to eliminate those who would initiate such cacophony. Advocating for a more democratic psychoanalysis, Phillips (2002) decried this fear and hatred of conflict.

The word *perversion* is derived from a Latin root meaning to turn. Totalitarians like to march full speed ahead, despising deviations from the straight, narrow, and true path. *Pervert* originally meant to overturn, upset, ruin. Although that meaning is now considered obsolete, it is still what totalitarians fear. Deviations to them are intolerable, evil, revolutionary acts. Nowadays, to pervert means to deviate from truth, right, rectitude, and a regular course, to violate, corrupt, and derange. In keeping with those dreaded meanings, one begins to comprehend why Ferenczi was deemed demented after penning unpopular prose.

In contrast to the sweet simplicity craved by ideologues, many cutting-edge thinkers no longer feel nurtured by closed systems. They embrace new paradigms based on multiplicity, complexity, and contradiction. Like Winnicott (1952/1971b), they view the capacity to tolerate ambiguity and paradox as developmental achievements. They prize reflecting on one's perspective, accepting that paradoxes may arise on embracing more than one point of view. Paradoxes are valued for their capacity to "contain rather than resolve contradictions, to sustain tension between elements heretofore defined as antithetical" (Benjamin, 1995, p. 10).

Comfort with ambiguity and incoherence enables one to avoid premature closure, covering unease with a false self. Categorical thought is increasingly regarded as a resistance to, or collapse of, paradoxical thought. "With the preservation of paradox lies the necessity for an ongoing process of negotiation" (Pizer,

1998, p. 5). Not enamored with negotiation, totalitarians prefer other means for "resolving" conflict.

What need, wish, or susceptibility leads individuals to exchange distributive dimensionality for a pigeonhole? Pizer wondered. What group qualities militate toward the allotment of individual complexity into reductive roles? Is a "false-self" the price of membership? Do conservative constraints operate through individuals who have gravitated "upward" to positions of power? Do these restrictions reflect limitations in mutual recognition as an evolved competence with the attendant reification of unitary identities? Are we witnessing the relief individuals find on surrendering internal complexity, conflict, and contradiction to the group structure? Pizer's penetrating questions recall Fromm's (1941) analysis of fascism's allure in his classic, *Escape from Freedom*.

Fixation

In Freud's system, fixation represents a particularly close attachment of instinct to object. Sometimes we fixate on theoretical perspectives. Such addictions, Goldberg (1990) believed, fill structural deficits.

Fixation, Freud (1915/1957a) wrote, "frequently occurs at very early periods of the development of an instinct and puts an end to its mobility through its intense opposition to detachment" (p. 123). Fixation on a theoretical model often occurs early in one's professional development, ending mobility of thought. Fixation is favorable to fascistic tendencies. Invitations to defixate frequently meet fierce resistance, as Freud (1915/1957a) described.

Shifting from id toward ego psychology, Freud's observations about the healthy (nonfixated) ego came to parallel the comparative-integrative perspective concerning thinking and disciplinary structure and Bollas's description of the democratic mind. The ego is an organization, Freud (1926/1959a) wrote,

> based on the maintenance of free intercourse and of the possibility of reciprocal influence between all its parts. Its desexualized energy still shows traces of its origins in its impulsion to bind together and unify, and this necessity to synthesize grows stronger in proportion as the strength of the ego increases. (p. 98)

Discussing the near impossibility of candidates maintaining a capacity for independent thought, Glover (1942/1991) had fixation in mind:

> I had all along been one of those who held that candidates are not or should not be sucking infants—that they should be able to stand up to differences of opinion and method existing amongst their teachers and that they should learn to form their own opinions on controversial matters. (King & Steiner, 1991, p. 146)

Presumably, he was differentiating his position from those who continued to believe candidates should be sucklings. Eventually he decided he had been wrong. "Experience has taught me, however, that this is too much to expect from any but the most superior candidates." During the Controversial Discussions, he lamented that

> Even well-balanced candidates are unfavorably affected by the situation … are in a welter of confusion, bafflement, and bewilderment. Nor is it possible for the candidates to escape—for his transferences once established will handcuff him securely to his analytic father or mother.

With these words, Glover portrayed a powerful pedagogical perversion: bondage between students and teachers/analysts. This outcome was inevitable, he believed. Perhaps it was in a milieu where those charged with establishing the frame had difficulty comfortably containing controversy in a manner that was flexible, reassuring, and exciting rather than rigid, anxious, and confusing. Glover eventually quit the British Society, feeling he could no longer contain himself in such a milieu.

Fear and Fetish

When analysts believe they know beforehand what is developmentally and therapeutically important, theory might be termed "phobic," Rubin (1998) averred. Such theory serves to delimit the field of conceptual possibilities, restricting where one can travel intellectually. Similarly, when analysts endow a less threatening theoretical phenomenon with special significance so as to ward off danger unconsciously associated with other things, then theory might be "fetishistic" (p. 165).

In his work on analysts' metaphors, Carveth (1984) was similarly concerned with fetishistic flight from incompleteness and otherness. Fixed images can defend against infantile dangers. Their deliteralization and relativization may arouse anxiety and depression and hence, resistance. On the phallic level, for example, believing our metaphor is omnipotent, we feel in possession of the phallus, he wrote. We therefore defend our metaphor phallus furiously against competing tropes that by implying insufficiency or inadequacy of our fetish, risk reopening the question (the wound), stimulating castration anxiety.

Contra Kohut's concept of the coherent self, Loewald (1973/1980a) averred that individuals exhibit "powerful resistance against … integration" (p. 348). Integration anxiety suspends individuals between unintegrated experiences and the integration ones that might come if development were allowed, Gaddini (1982) noted. This precarious equilibrium is preferred because of the fear that evolution might open the door to a new version of a prior traumatic separation. Loewald and Gaddini were discussing individual psychopathology, but their views are useful for understanding resistance to theoretical integration.

In their still interesting work on dissociative phenomena in hysteria, Breuer and Freud (1895/1955) discussed something akin to integration anxiety. "The incompatible idea, which, together with its concomitants, is later excluded and forms a separate psychical group, must originally have been in communication with the main stream of thought," they wrote. "Otherwise the conflict which led to their exclusion could not have taken place. It is these moments, then, that are to be described as 'traumatic'" (p. 167). One can extrapolate to the organizational domain. When dialogue with dissidents breaks down, separate psychoanalytic societies are formed. These moments are typically traumatic.

The decision to terminate such trauma by dissociative mechanisms, although intended to solve a problem, inevitably gives rise to difficulties. Interpersonal and relational analysts have done much to preserve and develop the concept of dissociation. For example, Stern (1997) noted this defense is designed to avoid the possibility that full-bodied meaning will occur, providing a story that "accounts for what it addresses but tells us nothing we don't already know" (p. 98). Such processes have a stultifying effect on disciplinary development.

THE DISCIPLINE'S UNCERTAIN STEPS TOWARD (AND AWAY FROM) A COMPARATIVE-INTEGRATIVE POINT OF VIEW

Imagine no religions.

—John Lennon, *"Imagine"*

Endorsing the Witch

In the North American, ego-psychological milieu, Kernberg (1975) was one of the first mainstreamers to go against received wisdom by daring to draw on Melanie Klein's oeuvre. He usefully incorporated some of her ideas into his theory of borderline conditions and pathological narcissism. His ability to effect such a synthesis may have been facilitated by his having traversed multiple cultures during his lifetime. Born in Vienna, raised in Argentina, he came to professional maturity in the United States. His endorsement of Kleinian concepts made it possible for other ego psychologists to be less closed to these heretofore despised ideas.

One of the few native North Americans to seriously consider Kleinian thought was Ogden (1986). That one must understand Freud to comprehend Klein sounds reasonable. Ogden advanced the less obvious proposition that one cannot fathom Freud without knowing Klein. Melanie Klein's investigations drew attention to strands in Freud's work that might otherwise have been missed. Ogden's position illustrates the principle that dialogue between orientations is necessary and mutually beneficial. Seemingly incompatible schools may turn out to be complementary and reciprocally enriching.

Another North American scrutinized the contributions of contemporary London Kleinians (Schafer, 1994a, 1994b, 1997a). Reminiscent of Cohen's poetic proposal, "Let Us Compare Mythologies," Schafer suggested comparing ego psychologies. Kleinian and Freudian schools each have distinctive ones, centered on object relations, Schafer concluded. He had come a long way from the critical tone he conveyed in earlier statements, for example, "Klein and her so-called English school ... carried the reifications of metapsychology to a grotesque extreme" (p. 3). In Schafer's later years, he realized he had been "indoctrinated to consider Kleinian analysis ... as a mythology or demonology" and that "dutifully, I went even further" (1997a, p. 427).

In contrast to Schafer's evolved position, his mentor (Rapaport, 1959/1967a) declared that "The 'theory' of object relations evolved by Melanie Klein and her followers is not an ego-psychology but an id mythology" (p. 750, footnote). Reflecting ego-psychological prejudice, that stance would discourage comparative investigation and make integration unthinkable.

Bearing in mind Schafer's warning that schools of thought are collections of hypothetical constructs that easily devolve to mythic status, one could argue that Rapaport's commentary was not completely inaccurate but suffered from epigrammatic concision. His remark might have been less likely to generate animus if he could have acknowledged that his own system may also have crystallized into mythology. Rather than simply rejecting his pithy observation, we might recognize it as having greater generalizability than he realized.

More than some Freudians, Freud recognized the capacity of constructs to morph into myths. Characterizing his mental topography as "fiction" (1933/1964c, p. 95), he cautioned against undue attachment to it: "The theory of instincts is ... our mythology" (1933/1964c, p. 95), he confessed. It was "a working hypothesis to be retained only so long as it proves useful" (1915/1957a, p. 124). He referred playfully to his metapsychology as a witch, "the most dispensable part of the whole scheme" (p. 225).

Mythification can, however, be difficult to undo. Potent myths do not relish being reclassified as simple working hypotheses. Guardians of myth may fight fervently against their deconstruction.

When heavyweights such as Schafer and Ogden added their muscle to Kernberg's powerful endorsement of certain Kleinian principles, the overwhelmingly negative view of the dark lady could no longer hold. Mythic Klein was gradually reduced to a collection of working hypotheses (in comparative circles, if not in all Kleinian quarters).

As in mythification, so too in salutary demythification, celebrity endorsements are a potent phenomenon. Social psychologists have studied the power of charismatic spokespersons to influence public voting and buying habits. Similar processes operate in our field far more than we might like to believe. In treatment, Freud struggled valiantly against suggestion and favored real thinking. In psychoanalytic theorizing, however, suggestion never stopped playing a profound role.

Two Steps Forward, One Step Back

Long an advocate of comparative analysis, Schafer may be moving toward a comparative-integrative perspective. He now considers contemporary London Kleinians to be "Kleinian Freudians," related to, integrated with, and not alien from "Traditional Freudians."

Although his term is clearly comparative-integrative, he may not see himself that way. At IPA's Rome Congress, he (1990) argued against searching for common ground. Four years later, he maintained that position: "I do not believe that common ground can be found," he declared. Instead, "It is best to regard the two approaches [Freudian and Kleinian] as incommensurable" (1994a, p. 474).

His conclusion is particularly intriguing for having appeared in the very article in which he documented previously underappreciated kinship between contemporary Freudians and Kleinians, thereby contributing to their rapprochement. Why, then, would he deplore the quest for common ground? That search, he believed, implies differences are regrettable, something to be leveled in the pursuit of "a single master text" (p. 52). He advocated that we should, instead, celebrate distinctions. Ongoing conflict will lead each school to improve itself by recognizing and then working on its incoherence, inconsistency, and incompleteness. Sublimated aggression, he pointed out, has wonderful uses.

Schafer's stance deals nicely with the initial phase of the dialectic (thesis vs. antithesis). There, his exuberant cry, "Vive la différence," makes sense. His position is less suitable for the subsequent stage (synthesis). The first phase is the appropriate arena for the play of sublimated aggression. The second movement requires a shift toward a phase dominance by Eros, the tendency toward union.

The sublimated aggression of comparative analysis is necessary but insufficient. It must be coupled with the sublimated Eros of integrative analysis, which has equally delightful uses. Fusing the two drive derivatives permits us to create a superior, comparative-integrative psychoanalysis.

Novel Resolutions

Conflict may best be "resolved" by creating conceptual containers capable of allowing for the tensions of diversity. It can, for example, "be useful to think of ourselves as multiple personalities, and of our internal worlds as more like a novel than a monologue," Phillips (1994) remarked. Each character, or part of ourselves, has different projects. Some of these voices become muted. Genuine conflict resolution requires "forging of incompatibles." The art of psychotherapy involves "turning what feel like contradictions—incompatibilities—into paradoxes." This process does not "entail ironing out the conflicts" (p. 50). Similarly, Rivera (1989) stated that personality integration involves not silencing voices but rather growing ability to call all voices "I," disidentifying with any one as the whole story.

Phillips's and Schafer's interest in literary analogues is shared by an increasing number. For example, Hanly and Hanly (1999) proposed that "Good analysts should do, with explanatory hypotheses and the interpretations they suggest, what writers do when they hold in mind the interplay of several narrative perspectives" (p. 15).

Advocating forging incompatibles, Phillips followed Freud's footsteps, for the founder's monumental achievement in intellectual history was fusing science and the humanities (Gedo & Pollock, 1976). Esteeming the relationship between truth and fiction, Freud (in Mahoney, 1982) shared that "In my mind I always construct novels" (p. 11).

Extending Phillips's cogitations to the state of our discipline might assuage Schafer's fear of fascistic leveling under the weight of a single master text. Bringing together the multiple analytic monologues, giving expression to voices that have been muted, allowing them to interact in a novel format, and forging incompatibles need not entail destructive flattening. It can lead, instead, to a diversified, enriched topography. It is autocratic relationships, not democratic ones, that squash diversity, compressing, flattening, ironing, and deadening a discipline.

Fear of flattening was addressed by Fast (1998). Contributing to self-theory, she noted that integration of self-states does not result in a "bland uniformity of experience, an 'averaging' that loses the exhilaration of difference" (p. 62). On the contrary, "It is through the integration of I-schemes that we achieve richness" (p. 62). As with self, so with the discipline of analysis: Integration enriches, isolation impoverishes.

Psychotherapeutic art, as Phillips envisioned it (transmuting contradictions into paradoxes), may be just the prescription the field of analysis requires. "Technique consists of intervening from time to time to make sure that each voice is heard, that each one of the protagonists in the inner debate has his say in turn and does not overwhelm and totally obscure the other participants" (Arlow, 1985,

p. 24). How productive it might be to apply such updated versions of the classical concepts of equidistance and neutrality to our theoretical debates.

Controversial Discussions

Over a half century ago, the British capital hosted the historic battle between the Anna Freudian thesis and the Kleinian antithesis. Rather than killing off one voice or the other, that Institute restructured itself to allow three streams of thought to coexist. Continued debate was thereby assured. Potential for synthesis was represented by members of the nonaligned, independent, middle group.

Even before those discussions, Kleinian views had influenced the Viennese belief system. For example, Anna Freud considered reparation, a linchpin of Kleinian theory, as "indisputable" and "accepted as an integral part of current psychoanalytic theory" (Isaacs, in Steiner, 1985, p. 49).

Through decades of pluralism, each side influenced the other (Hayman, 1994; Pulver, 1993; Schafer, 1994a, 1994b; Steiner, 1985). Freudians became more aware of the primitive origins of object relations, phantasy, aggression, defense, transference, and the multiple functions of projective identification and countertransference. Kleinians became more cognizant of the mature Oedipal complex, ego psychology, and the historical and ongoing role of reality. Each camp moved toward a more comprehensive, integrative position. Thanks to these conversations, London Kleinians evolved more than their European (Paniagua, 1995) and South American (Schafer, 1994a, 1994b) kin.

Kleinians never sought to be a "separate psychical group." During the discussions, Isaacs (in Steiner, 1985) expressed the desirability that "all this nonsense about 'Kleinians' and 'Freudians' be given up" (p. 49). Similarly, when asked if he was Kleinian, Bion retorted, "Heavens no! I'm no more Kleinian than Melanie was. She always thought of herself as Freudian, but Anna (Freud) saw to it that she would be labeled 'Kleinian'" (Grotstein, 1983, p. 31). Grotstein (1983) believed Bion's position was "Once Kleinian or once Freudian, it's no longer psychoanalysis" (p. 31). Limiting oneself to a single school is opting for an impoverished science and profession.

Fortunately, Kleinians are now being welcomed back into the fold. Desegregation benefits both sides. Kleinian constructs are no longer deemed deranged and dangerous. They are now merely different. The former hardening of the antitheses is softening, paving the way for synthesis.

At the growing tip of the Kleinian development, one no longer sees died-in-the-wool Kleinians but, blessedly, Kleinian Freudians. Although Schafer contrasted them with traditional Freudians, it might be more valid to say that at the cutting edge of ego psychology dwells a new creature, the dialectically transformed, "Contemporary Freudian" (a British term) or post-ego-psychological or contemporary structural conflict theorist (American descriptors). The dialectic between A. Freudians and M. Kleinians has progressed to one between contemporary Freudians and Kleinian Freudians. Calling oneself traditional Freudian or pure Kleinian will increasingly serve mostly to indicate that one has not kept up with the dialogue.

In time, it will be undesirable to identify with any pole of the current dialectic. Terms such as Kleinian Freudian, contemporary Freudian, and self psychologist will only have historical meaning. As incompatibles are forged, fragmented states of incompatibility will wither away. Heirs of pugilistic partisans will mothball ancestral coats of arms. They will simply be analysts, belonging to a more integrated, complex, mature discipline. Beneficiaries of past desegregationist struggles, they will no longer misunderstand patients or other people so frequently or profoundly. Where stultifying anti-alpha was, transformative alpha function shall be.

Deconstructing "Total Composite Psychoanalytic Theory"

Although British arrangements "prevented further splintering or growing apart, more needs to be done … to effect reliable unification" (Rangell, 1988, p. 334). Actually, the British did more than impede alienation. They created a dialogic container fostering decreasing differences. Their once vehemently opposed groups enriched one another, thereby growing closer. Rangell was, however, correct to assert that more must be done do achieve greater unity.

Espousing theory building by accretion, Rangell's motto was retain the enduring, add the new. Although this strategy sounds reasonable, he seemed more wary of innovation than his credo might lead one to suspect: "It is not what any of the new alternative theories adds which creates a problem, but what each of them, without exception eliminates" (p. 326), he declared.

This provocative opinion has some merit. In Part I, I shared my similar concern that Kohut, for one, lost quite a bit as he forged his brave new psychoanalysis.

It is less easy to concur with Rangell's (1988) sweeping assertions about what each new school eliminated. "Kleinian analysis discards the oedipal; the interpersonal and derivative object relations schools turn away from the intrapsychic" (p. 326). His declarations may apply to some Kleinians, interpersonalists, and object relational theorists. As generalizations, however, his characterizations appear extreme rather than being even-handed, comparative analytic conclusions.

Contrary to Rangell's assertions, relational thinkers such as Benjamin (1995) have emphasized that intrapsychic and intersubjectivity theory are complementary. Without the intrapsychic concept of the unconscious, she asserted, intersubjectivity theory becomes woefully one-dimensional.

Rangell's term, "total composite psychoanalytic theory" (p. 316) sounds laudable. One would want to embrace it wholeheartedly. Serious concerns arise, however, if one examines what Rangell (1988) viewed as suitable for this "continuous cumulative theory" (p. 335):

> The straight line of theoretical progression I consider as having preserved advances and built upon them includes—the line is skeletal, but will convey the nature of the thinking—from Freud, to Anna Freud, Rapaport, Hartmann, Fenichel, Kris, Waelder, Jacobson, Spitz, Greenacre, Mahler ... Stone, Arlow, Brenner, Blum. (p. 329)

This lineage does, indeed, "convey the nature of the thinking." A heritage omitting Klein, Fairbairn, Winnicott, Balint, Kernberg, Kohut—to mention just a few giants in our field—is impoverished. Its narrowness recalls Wallerstein's (1992) description of the constricted literature his training cohort was exposed to during the 1950s; yet Rangell articulated his ideal line at the end of the 1980s. Being so partial, the path he favored clashes with his concept of total composite psychoanalytic theory.

All new facts can be accommodated by total composite psychoanalytic theory, Rangell proclaimed. No doubt they could be, in principle. In actuality, his chosen lineage prefers to disregard many highly significant facts (e.g., the Kleinian development, British object relations theory, self psychology, interpersonal psychoanalysis). Kuspit's (1994) warning seems apposite: "The urge to totalize indicates that the limits of a particular avenue of approach to the psyche are being approached ... as though psyche is warning us that only a both/and approach can begin to do it justice" (p. 857).

Total psychoanalytic theory encompasses "diversity in unity" (Rangell, 1990, p. 862). Again, this value sounds most admirable. Rangell (1990) proceeded to clarify what sort of diversity he had in mind: "That is why ... there are multiple, not one but five or six, points of view within metapsychology, and why the principles of multiple function (Waelder, 1930) and overdetermination (Freud, 1900 [/1953a]) play central roles in assessing all psychic phenomena" (p. 862). His notion of multiplicity betrays a distressing dearth of diversity. Rangell's (1990) restrictive unity seems like stifling homogeneity achieved by gross exclusion.

In the final paragraph of his clearly written article, Rangell (1988) coined the variant "straight-line cumulative theory" (p. 338) to characterize his position. Like its Greek equivalent, *orthos*, straight, meaning upright and correct, as in orthodox, more accurately describes his perspective than his better known term, "total composite psychoanalytic theory." The linear cognition enshrined in his straight and narrow approach cannot suffice for a field in "considerable intellectual disarray" (Gedo, 1999, p. xv).

Rangell's recommendations neither reflect nor foster creative, dialectic inter-change between the various branches of the Freudian family tree. They would, on the contrary, consolidate the "parochialism" and "cultishness" (Gedo, p. xv) that plague our discipline.

Like Schafer's fear of leveling, Rangell worried that the new invariably elimi-nates valuable insights. Having explored the relationship between innovation and tradition in Part I, we are keenly aware of that danger, but that investigation reached a more optimistic conclusion.

A more adequate, encompassing, comparative-integrative epistemology might enable people adhering to Rangell's ideal to embrace something more complex, interesting, and enlivening than "straight-line cumulative theory," thereby achieving a truly total composite psychoanalytic theory worthy of the name. I would like to think Rangell's group might ultimately come to value this perspective given our deeply shared concern for preserving traditional treasures, integrating new findings, preventing further splintering, and achieving greater unification.

Protecting Analysts' Inheritance

Some analysts fret about straying too far, sojourning too long off the beaten path. "Some people say that if you venture into these uncharted lands, you may not find anything, and even if you do, it is doubtful whether it is worth risking our psychoanalysis for it," Balint (1968) noted. He, however, was "not so pessimistic" for, he reasoned, "Pure gold has the remarkable quality of withstanding any fire and even of being purified by it." He did not see any reason to be afraid for the essentials of our science: "Should any of its minor frills burn away, being not of pure gold, the better for future generations" (p. 103).

Unconsciously, our relationship is often not so much with theories but with figures representing them, in the transference sense, Bernardi (1992) believed. Accepting analysis as pluralistic implies renouncing a unitary, personalized ideal linked to the fantasy that an only heir (theory) corresponds to an only father (Freud). Diversity challenges that sense of specialness and entitlement.

Advocating a new language, Schafer (1976) realized, similarly, that he was posing a dual threat: object loss (the version of analysis one values and loves) and narcissistic loss (personal unity, worth, and satisfaction associated with thinking in familiar ways). "One cannot but fear, resent, and resist such a call for change" (p. 124).

Early analysts' primary concern was defending "an approach, a theory, a body of knowledge perceived to be in danger by dilution or contamination," Michels (1998, p. 5) noted. Some day there will be a "shift toward testing, developing, improving, and changing that early set of beliefs and theories rather than protect-ing them" (Michels, 1998, p. 5). Some analysts will resist this prophesized change, feeling the earlier need to ensure traditional beliefs do not become tainted. Others will embrace the idea that the best way to protect our golden heritage is to test, develop, alter, and ameliorate it. The comparative-integrative point of view provides a means for accomplishing these new goals.

Extension, Modification, Comparative Integration

"Extenders move psychoanalysis into unexplored areas," wrote Bergmann (1997). Their findings demand no revision of theory, evoking no enmity. They are universally appreciated. In contrast, modifiers threaten continuity, creating controversy. They also keep analysis alive and are a source of new ideas. "Modifiers demand that we give up the cherished belief that psychoanalysis is developing along a straight line, that every new generation merely adds to the finding of the previous one" (p. 82).

The group Rangell represented only seemed comfortable with extenders. Excommunicating troubling modifiers to preserve a cherished orthodox line enervates discourse, restricting disciplinary action to "mop-up work" (Kuhn, 1970).

A paradigm is initially a promise of success based on selected, still incomplete examples. Normal science consists in actualizing that hope by extending knowledge of facts the paradigm displays as particularly revealing, increasing the match between those facts and paradigm predictions, and further articulating the paradigm itself. "Few people who are not actually practitioners of a mature science realize how much mop-up work this sort of paradigm leaves to be done" (p. 23).

Kuhn was by no means contemptuous of mopping. He noted, however, that the "enterprise seems an attempt to force nature into the preformed and relatively inflexible box that the paradigm supplies" (p. 24). Nonetheless, he emphasized that few nonscientists can imagine "how fascinating such work can prove in execution" (p. 24). That this labor provides such gratification is fortunate, for "Mop-up operations are what engage most scientists throughout their careers" (p. 24). All mop-up work and no modification would, however, render a discipline more dour than need be.

Why do most of us confine our contributions to extension? Apart from the fact that such labor is important, there may be other reasons. Grounding his thinking in Rank's discussions of children breaking free from maternal embeddedness and artists struggling to solve mysteries of human existence, Spezzano (1993) asserted that establishing oneself as a subject rather than an object of another's subjectivity is the fundamental human task. Authorizing oneself to bring new meanings into the world, then carrying them into the subjectivity first of the mother, then later authorities, risks the security of the status quo. It engenders guilt for favoring one's own interest/excitement over the other's. These acts signify withdrawing love from mother, investing it in oneself.

Perceiving a possibility that varies from what is currently thought or done positions one for a Rankian creative moment. One must decide whether to endure the anxiety and guilt of disrupting the status quo—an act of violence to the symbolic mother even if one's intent is simply to act on enthusiastic interest, Spezzano believed. These separation affects hinder our leaving our various psychoanalytic matrices. Distaste for such dysphoria may influence us to restrict our focus to mop-up work, even preventing us from indulging in and benefiting from the audacious contributions of others who dared to modify.

Resistance is not simply avoidance of insight or fear of change, Bromberg (1998) believed. It is, instead, a dialectic between preservation and transformation, reflecting the need to maintain continuity of self-experience during growth to minimize the threat of traumatization. Sometimes self-preservation is accomplished at the expense of growth. The individual is then removed from full involvement in the here and now. Extending Bromberg's discussion, one could say some analysts and organizations have been so concerned with self-preservation that they have isolated themselves from the excitement and potential enrichment of broader discourse. This retreat has been detrimental to their personal/organizational growth and to their patients, students, and readers.

Astute on the nature of resistance, Bromberg was also optimistic about it: "The human personality possesses the extraordinary capacity to negotiate stability and change simultaneously, and it will do so under the right relational conditions" (p. 209). A comparative-integrative ambience furnishes those right conditions for our discipline to negotiate this important dialectic. Without this methodology, our field will remain marooned in the past or will surge precipitously into the future, crippled by premature jettisoning of valuable ideas.

Bergmann's dichotomy between extenders and modifiers was, itself, created by nondefensive, refined splitting. From the comparative-integrative perspective, even this useful split can be transcended. Ultimately, modifiers are extenders. Although they may appear to threaten continuity, in the long run, they ensure psychoanalysis' continued existence by nurturing its élan vital. Keeping the discipline lively, dissidents disrupt but ultimately extend its life, helping bring the field to its next stage. There is a dialectic between extension and modification.

Our discipline might be viewed as middle-aged, facing the maturational turbulence Erikson (1950) insightfully labeled "generativity versus stagnation." Modifiers assist us in creatively navigating such developmental impasses. Maximizing our chances of resolving our climacteric, they augment our likelihood of advancing to successfully cope with the final challenge, integrity versus despair. Integration is what the comparative-integrative perspective is about.

Toward Mature Genitality

The philosophy of science is ... in need of genuinely new principles. One such principle is the idea that the character of things may be essentially complementary.

—**Gaston Bachelard,** *The New Scientific Spirit*

"Winning is not everything; it is the only thing." Poking fun simultaneously at that cynical slogan and oedipal chauvinism, Benjamin (1995) suggested an alternative motto: "What I have is not everything, but it is the *only thing* (worth having)" (p. 65). She wrote eloquently of shortcomings of simple, mutually exclusive, derogatory attitudes toward gendered otherness frequently established during resolution of the oedipal crisis. Following Kohlberg's (1981) developmental distinction between conventional and postconventional thinking, she stressed the necessity of advancing beyond conventional, phallic-oedipal reasoning to post-oedipal possibilities.

The genital character, the apogee in Freud's developmental scheme is, in fortunate cases, formed during adolescence. At that time, as Piaget, Kohlberg, and others emphasized, capacities for abstract reasoning, symbolization, and taking the other's perspective become more available. In contrast to the infantile genital stage, mature genitality embraces the tension of opposites rather than splitting them.

Only when libido has reached the sixth (postambivalent) stage does the individual have full capacity for object love and adaptation to reality, Abraham (1924b) asserted. Only then is the object seen as whole. Prior to that time, "The genitals are more intensely cathected by narcissistic love than any other part of the subject's own body. Thus everything else in the other can be loved sooner than the genitals," he stated. On the level of the phallic organization of the libido,

The last great step in its development has obviously not yet been made. It is not made until the highest level of the libido—that which alone should be called the genital level—is attained. Thus we see that the attainment of the highest level of the organization of the libido goes hand in hand with the final step in the evolution of object-love. (p. 495)

A quarter of a century after Abraham, Balint (1955) wrote in a similar spirit that genital love "demands a collaboration from the object amounting to an almost complete identification with the subject" (p. 233). The capacity for truly genital love requires transcending earlier, gendered splitting to empathize with partners.

The infantile genital organization and its adult counterpart is comparative ("Show me yours and I'll show you mine. ... Girls suck. ... Boys are yucky. ...

Men are bastards. ... Women are bitches"). For those fortunate enough to consolidate identities in mature genitality, a comparative-integrative attitude gains phase dominance.

These ideas on the oedipal and postoedipal can illuminate analysts' understanding of the mutually exclusive, driven, devaluing attitudes toward different, competing theoretical orientations. Traditional analysis, espoused as a hard-line, dominant, rigid, overvalued paradigm, is excessively phallic-oedipal. To the extent one feels one's orientation embodies just about everything worth having, whereas other perspectives are not worth much ("They don't know dick"), characterized more by what they lack than what they have (castrated), one speaks from a less than optimally balanced, mature, genital position. Rather than having acquired the first and last word, one may be trapped in a closed system, akin to a rigid, defensive, conventional resolution of the phallic-oedipal stage. Debates about which orientation is better, more potent, or prettier (aesthetically and conceptually more elegant) mirror what used to be called the battle of the sexes.

Not until mature genitality can one be maximally creative and generative. At that level, one is not frightened of the other. Difference is no longer deficit. One seeks to know otherness in terms of what it is as opposed to what it is not, embracing and prizing it rather than conquering and subduing it. (That latter option is a step above the simpler wish to obliterate difference with unsublimated aggression.) Coming together can then be in attraction and love, without repulsion, repressed or overt. Getting to know the other, one learns about one's own nature, one's bisexuality. Ignorance and splitting yield to integration. Refined re-fusion replaces refusal. "Forging of incompatibles" through comparative-integrative processes promotes higher union.

Traditional analysis did not possess as many theoretical tools as we now have for comprehending these developments. Nonetheless, at its best, it understood these phenomena. Fenichel's (1945) classic text offers intimations of this grasp while also reflecting refreshing awareness of the limitations of available knowledge:

> One can speak of love only when consideration of the object goes so far that one's own satisfaction is impossible without satisfying the object, too. This kind of feeling oneself in union with the object has surely something to do with identification ... a kind of partial and temporary identification for empathic purposes. (p. 84)

With humility, he added:

> We know nothing about the specific nature of this identification. We can only say that the experience of a full and highly integrated satisfaction facilitates it, and that genital primacy (ability to have an adequate orgasm) is the prerequisite for it." (p. 84)

Fenichel elaborated that "The full capacity for love not only changes the relations toward other persons but also the relation toward one's own ego." That is, he linked growth of object love with transformations in narcissism:

> At the height of full genital satisfaction identification comes back on a higher level; a feeling of flowing together, of losing one's individuality, of achieving a desired reunion of the ego with something larger which has been outside the boundaries of the ego. (p. 85)

Fenichel noted that consideration of the object as a condition for the full development of object relationships was called the erotic sense of reality by Ferenczi (1925), who pointed out that full appreciation of reality is lacking in those who remain fixated at precursive stages of love. With appropriate modesty, Fenichel added, "The nature of the identification on a higher level which constitutes love is still obscure" (p. 86).

Prior to the phallic-oedipal phase, recent theories of psychosexual development have suggested boys and girls enjoy undifferentiation and overinclusivity (Fast, 1978). In this kindergarten of earthly delights, they can fantasize having/being it all. In imagination, they possess desirable qualities of both sexes. (What I have is everything.) Dionysian, both/and, polymorphous, sensuous philosophy appeals more than the severe, renunciative, Appolonian, either/or type. Pleasure before reason is the guide. Under the sway of wish-fulfilling, primary process, what later comes to be labeled mutually exclusive exists happily, side by side, in each psyche.

Over the course of the phallic-oedipal phase, most children largely abandon the aspiration to be more than one gender. Knowledge, logic, and rationality gain ascendancy over wish-fulfilling fantasy. Unconsciously, they may resist these losses, but consciously they tend to deny such longings. They may buttress disavowal by derogating the opposite sex and idealizing their own.

One's sense of masculinity or femininity results from constant citings and recitings of a culture's normative gender practices, Layton (1998) believed. Assuming a sexual and gender identity involves not only identifications that are permitted but also repudiations of those that lie outside the norm. Identity is based as much on disidentification as on identification.

Consolidating gender involves pathological processes, Goldner (1991) asserted. Incongruent thoughts, acts, impulses, moods, or traits must be disowned, displaced, misplaced (as in projective identification), or otherwise split off. What has been disavowed typically returns to haunt and threaten the subject.

Viewing gender as fundamentally and paradoxically indeterminate, Goldner challenged the assumption that internally consistent identity is possible or even desirable. Building on her work and that of other relational theorists, Pizer

(1998) described how normal processes of gender sorting entrap people in double binds that are inescapable, unnamable, and nonnegotiable. These unbridgeable paradoxes coerce mental foreclosure and dissociation. Far from being natural, cultural (or psychoanalytic) requirements of conforming to a singular role entail pathogenic collapse of the subjective paradox of coexistent psychic unity and multiplicity. In similar spirit, Benjamin (1995) advocated accepting the ambiguity and multiplicity of preoedipal cross-sex identifications, embracing the truth of gender incoherence rather than the false self-appearance of stability.

Beginning in adolescence, there are opportunities to rework (or reify) tenuous resolutions as one negotiates (or portages around) the mature genital phase. Freud (1919/1955d) may have been in an unusually optimistic mood when he proposed that "The great unity we call ... ego fits into itself all the instinctual impulses which before had been split off and held apart from it" (p. 161). Nonetheless, one appreciates the important synthesizing function he was admiring and promoting. At the very least, the ego has a chance of accomplishing what he described if it confronts the challenges of the mature genital stage.

In this developmental process, there is some regression in the service of the ego (Kris, 1952). De-differentiation allows the psyche to reestablish contact with previously abandoned ego states. Reactivating aspects of the overinclusive stage, the individual can cherish, identify, and empathize with the genital partner.

As our field faces the challenges of integration, those who derogate such efforts with epithets such as "mindless eclecticism" may be expressing their discomfort with elements of de-differentiation and regression involved in such reorganization. They may fail to grasp that comparative integration does not entail repetition of a primitive, overinclusive stage. It does not valorize a fluid, Dionysian outlook that may have obtained prior to the acquisition of Apollonian abstract operations. On the contrary, it promotes the flexible bridging of the mature genital stage, holding paradoxical elements, sustaining tension, and synthesizing where possible. Shunning overexclusiveness, it strives for an appropriate degree of inclusiveness.

Relevant to this problem of overinclusion/underinclusion, Carveth (1984) noted that cognitive "linkers" have a "feminine" bias toward similarity. Wanting everything to touch, merge, be the same, they have little tolerance for differences. "Separators," on the other hand, have a "masculine" preference for difference. Seeking to differentiate and keep things apart, they have little tolerance for similarity or merger. Neither bias, he concluded, to the extent that it entails a defensive repression of one or the other component of our bisexuality (Freud, 1905/1953b), can result in optimal psychic functioning.

Conceptual tools useful for transcending archaic resolutions of conflict were forged by Freud (1911/1958b). "The psychical apparatus had to decide to form a conception of the real circumstances in the external world," he stated.

> A new principle of mental functioning was thus introduced; what was presented in the mind was no longer what was agreeable but what was real, even if it happened to be disagreeable. This setting up of the *reality principle* proved to be a momentous step. (p. 219)

This step has not been taken by most schools of psychoanalytic thought. They content themselves and even prefer to function on the basis of an earlier principle of mental functioning, that of the purified pleasure ego.

As "a field that has progressed by the same inner conflict it discovers in individuals" (Kuspit, 1994, p. 885), psychoanalysis is similarly liable to bungled actions, deficits, compensatory structures, compromise formations, and other symptomatic manifestations. Traditional analysis, for example, appears to have experienced some degree of developmental arrest in the phallic-oedipal phase. Freud's theory best described the phallic-oedipal boy, and he usually treated other facets of development as variations on this theme, for better or for worse (Schafer, 1983).

This partial fixation of a significant portion of our field may be one reason the genital character is infrequently discussed. This summum bonum has also proved elusive in the structure of our associations. Mainstream analysis may have lost sight of the necessary, transitional steps from the infantile genital organization to the possibility of mature genitality. Comparative-integrative analysis provides a way to move beyond this developmental impasse, a tool enabling us to proceed from not looking (at other perspectives) to actively searching, seeing, contrasting, and, ultimately, synthesizing to become a more creative, genital enterprise.

Awareness of the difficulties inherent in querying the centrality of the Oedipus complex signifies maturation in our thinking, said Simon (1991). Realization of the obstacles to answering this question can provide groundwork for formulations richer and closer to the complex ambiguity of clinical practice. Unlike those who fear such debate means our discipline is dissolving into terminal chaos, he believed we are in "a time of fructifying confusion and disagreement" (p. 665). The alternative to this interrogation is that "We can have a neat and comfortable theory, but one that runs the danger of requiring that the analytic couch become a procrustean bed" (p. 666).

Procrustes was, of course, the mythological man who invited folks to his bed but did not make love to them in traditional ways. His was a more PS love. He could not enjoy and cherish them for what they were. He felt driven, instead, to stretch and mutilate them to fit his image of how they should be. Far from being a genital character, he was a perverse exemplar of a uniparadigmatic tradition.

The alternative to a procrustean bed is "an unwieldy and conglomerate theory, awkward to handle and not entirely smooth and consistent, but that allows greater freedom to analyst and patient in seeing and learning what is in fact there and operative" (Simon, p. 666). Such a couch (or consulting room) might be described as eclectic or, in more challenging, innovative, dynamic terms, comparative integrative.

Simon concluded that "Psychoanalysis has definitely entered its oedipal phase, and it is smack in the middle of an only very partially resolved Oedipus complex" (p. 666). The comparative-integrative perspective enables us to understand that partial resolution and envision how to elevate ourselves to a more fulfilling position.

Having traversed the sometimes rough ride from phallic-oedipal chauvinism to mature genitality, some analysts may be reluctant to contemplate going through a parallel process with respect to theoretical orientation and organizational identity. Children can find their way out of symbiosis with the help of objects of identificatory love (Benjamin, 1988). Something similar may be needed to liberate us from theoretical/organizational embeddedness. The comparative-integrative point of view may serve as a suitable object with sufficient identificatory attraction to facilitate this maturational process.

CONCLUSION

Years ago, Freud (1916/1972) sounded a cautionary note. "I take the opportunity of warning you against taking sides in a quite unnecessary dispute," he began.

> In scientific matters people are fond of selecting one portion of the truth, putting it in place of the whole and of then disputing the rest, which is no less true, in favor of this one portion. In just this way a number of schools of opinion have already split off from the psycho-analytic movement." (p. 346)

Our field has not found it easy to heed this sage advice. Often we have, instead, taken sides, fostering splits rather than unification. Freud himself did not find it easy to adhere to this balanced position he advocated. He played a more active, aggressive role in organizational fragmentation than his phrase, "have already split off," would suggest. Whatever the allocation of responsibility and whether such disputes were unnecessary or inevitable, the rigidity, isolation, and hegemonic tendencies of competing schools have exacted a hefty toll on analytic thought.

Following Kuhn's (1970) counsel that historians must describe and explain the congeries of error, myth, and superstition that have inhibited the more rapid accumulation of the modern science text, in this chapter, I have examined how erroneous beliefs, limiting mentational modes, and calcification of constructs into myths impeded analytic progress. I proposed a comparative-integrative approach as a methodological remedy for these faults in the structure of our discipline. I identified tentative steps toward and away from this solution. I explore implications for practice and pedagogy in the next two chapters.

No longer in its infancy, the science of psychoanalysis is at least in its late adolescence. Notorious for Sturm und Drang, this developmental stage is a time of possibility and danger. To establish a coherent identity (versus one foreclosed to ward off confusion) and assume our rightful place in the pantheon of mature sciences, we must bring our seemingly contradictory theories together, subjecting them to all the formal operations (Piaget's term for the reasoning skills that come to fruition during adolescence) we have. Rising to the "historical position" (Ogden, 1986), we need to bring the synthetic function of our egos to bear on warring and incommunicado (cold warring) factions. If we fail, we will continue floundering fragmented, torn asunder by bellicose points of view. If we are successful, our discipline will become increasingly cohesive under the aegis of Eros, shining brightly among the advanced sciences.

As the Sphinx challenged Thebans with her life or death riddle, so Wallerstein (1988) posed his seemingly simple question to our community: "One psychoanalysis or many?" Our response will have, if not life or death consequences, vitalizing or stultifying implications for our discipline's health.

"The fate of psychoanalysis will stand or fall on the strength of its theory," proclaimed Rangell (1988, p. 314). Fragmented theory cannot be strong. The key to ego strength lies in reconciling "discontinuities and ambiguities" (Erikson, 1975, p. 19). This principle holds true for disciplinary strength. If we answer Wallerstein's query creatively and well, we may help repair a field riddled with contradictions. In so doing, we will forge A Psychoanalysis for Our Time (Rubin, 1998).

Many voices responded to Wallerstein in many keys. We continue, however, to be plagued by divisions and uncertainties as to what might constitute the optimal rejoinder, the best path to pursue. In this confusing, conflicted situation, the comparative-integrative perspective provides a solution that might be condensed as follows: Out of one psychoanalysis came many. Out of the many shall come one: e pluribus unum.

5

Significance for Psychoanalytic Practice

Forgive them, for they know not what they do.

—Luke 23:34

INTRODUCTION

In the previous chapter, I explored the pluralistic state of our discipline, only recently recognized as a major concern worthy of concentrated attention (Wallerstein, 1992). Although many prefer to ignore the unsettling implications of multiperspectivism, an ever growing number believe we must rise to the challenge. Although this issue has stimulated angst and acrimony, it simultaneously presents exciting opportunities for creating a more complex, cohesive, comprehensive, and useful science and profession.

I recommended a comparative-integrative response to Wallerstein's challenging question "One psychoanalysis or many?" Although supporting those who promoted comparative analysis, I advocated going further. I proposed working to understand how, when, where, and why new psychoanalytic conceptions arise and how they might not only contradict but also complement one another. Out of the many partial schools of thought can come an increasingly unified one.

With respect to pluralism, Wallerstein (1992) noted that "We have barely begun to explore its scientific and professional implications" (p. 5). I considered some of those in the previous chapter. In this chapter, I concentrate on the clinical relevance of the comparative-integrative point of view.

CLINICAL VERSUS GENERAL THEORY

Utilizing George Klein's (1976) distinction, Wallerstein (1988) concluded that at the general level of relatively abstract theorizing, there are many psychoanalyses. In contrast, in the more experience-near domain of clinical theory and practice, there was common ground. "Adherents of whatever theoretical position within psychoanalysis, all seem to do reasonably comparable clinical work and bring about reasonably comparable clinical change" (Wallerstein, 1988, p. 13).

Is his assertion true? Many believe so. Some have even articulated this position more strongly. For example, Furer, Nersessian, and Perri (1998) stated that "Although different schools ... are very different metapsychologically or in their general theories, they all center on transference, resistance, and conflict in practice, and are therefore clinically equivalent" (p. 31). Common ground implies considerable overlap. Clinical equivalence takes that idea much further. It asserts there are no practical differences; diversity only exists at the metapsychological level.

In contrast, Rangell (1988) felt differences exist as much in clinical as in general theory. Gedo (1984) believed largely unconscious values underlie deep divisions with respect to both clinical theory and metapsychology. Deeming our diversity "deplorable," Green (2000) believed "We are practicing psychoanalysis with the use of maps that give ... contradictory directions" (p. 447). Cooper (1985) admonished, "We should take the opportunity of this competition of theories to emphasize the *differences* in clinical work ... because only by understanding our differences can we begin to test different treatment methods" (p. 19). Pine (1998), likewise, underscored diversity in technique. Like myself, he has long extolled integrative efforts, but he felt this should be done "not at the level of general theory but at the level of clinical theory" (p. 37).

In Part I, I suggested theoretical frameworks can exert a major influence on what can and cannot be seen clinically. Not only illuminating but also blinding, theory can reduce or at least alter options for intervention. A broader, multifaceted framework expands one's visual field, augmenting possibilities for therapeutic work.

Even increasing from a one-dimensional to a two-dimensional theory can massively increase understanding and clinical efficacy. For example, in his recent book on contemporary London Kleinians, Schafer (1997a) announced his intention to reopen closed eyes and ears not only to a valuable body of analytic contributions but also to the rich, primitive world of object relational phantasy that "so many of our patients seem to require us to attend to and that doctrinaire ego psychological work so often encourages us to ignore" (p. 429). Like Schafer, I believe, "Theory is indeed a technical issue" (1981, p. 64).

Long ago, Balint (1968) noted that analysts of all schools have successes, difficult cases, and failures. Protagonists of particular schools succeed or fail with different patients, he believed, and the mode of failure or success might vary with different techniques. He sensed that analysts anxiously resist research in this area.

Latin American psychoanalysts have attributed recent burgeoning of analytic interest on their continent to their receptivity to the "confrontation and clash of every psychoanalytic perspective" (Wallerstein, 1990, p. 7). Wallerstein's perception of this Latin hunger to import points of view contrasts with older perceptions of South America as a dark, Kleinian continent. This enthusiastic, Latin discourse proved problematic for him. "Debating these general theoretical perspectives—may be chimerical and irresolvable, i.e., ultimately sterile" (p. 7), he warned.

Debate implies argument, at the end of which an adjudicative body may declare a winner. Wallerstein, like Schafer (1983), believed we are not sufficiently advanced to judge between the merits of different systems, certainly not by scientific experiment. From that point of view, debate may indeed be premature and pointless. From the comparative-integrative perspective, debate is by no means futile. It is, however, just the first phase in creative, dialectical discourse. It is the playground of sublimated aggression and need not terminate in traditional, binary judgment, victor taking all, vanquished driven from the field. This feisty, initial phase of conflict, thesis versus antithesis, must be followed by a stage in which sublimated Eros (the drive for unification) reigns supreme. The goal of comparative-integrative discourse is to advance the discussion to that level. The achieved synthesis will constitute a new thesis, evoking a fresh antithesis. *E unum duo; e duo unum*, and so on, in interminable progression.

Hopes that controlled experiments will ultimately decide between theories are likely illusory or exaggerated. Formal experiments have informative roles to play. It is, however, unrealistic, perhaps simplistic, to appeal solely to them for adjudication as to which theory is right. Waiting for that judgment day (when: there will be sufficient funding for researching the variables we value; psychoanalysis will be a powerful presence in academia; we will have enough data to decide delicate issues) can be a procrastinator's refuge.

Rather than patiently praying for such a divine day, we need to utilize currently available, noble ego functions (for example, perception, discrimination, judgment, and, especially, the synthetic function) to achieve more complex, multifaceted resolutions of our pluralistic dilemma. Such dialogic pursuits may generate more heat than cooler, statistically based, laboratory research. That warmth may, however, be essential to forge unity out of "incompatibles." With our full array of ego functions, we can ask in what ways one perspective illuminates data compared to another, with which patients, at what phases of treatment. Assuming each theory contains some truth, we need to consider how they might fit together to provide a more comprehensive picture of a patient, phenomenon, syndrome, or discipline.

Even though controversies between schools are still very much alive, we have the benefit of some historical distance (and a comparative-integrative perspective) that we can deploy to comprehend why dissidence arose, led to dissociations, influenced theoretical development, and so forth. For example, Schafer (1976) described how Hartmann was spurred on in his pioneering efforts by his recognition that neo-Freudian and Kleinian critiques had to be faced. These challenges owed their existence to defects in the Freudian framework (e.g., its neglect of a systematic consideration of adaptation, the environment, values, aggression, and the earliest phases of development including superego development).

Debate stuck in the arena of sublimated aggression will likely prove "ultimately sterile" whether the participants are clinicians, theoreticians, or researchers. Aggression can be energizing and pleasurable (Mitchell, 1993). On its own, however, it is nonproductive. For theoretical intercourse to be fruitful, different discourse is needed. Fructifying dialogue must include unificatory desire. This libidinal element in the vigorous coupling between thesis and antithesis optimizes the likelihood that the interaction will be creative, not infecund.

Whether the recent Latin American "confrontation and clash" will prove "chimerical, irresolvable, that is, ultimately sterile" depends on the balance between Eros and Thanatos in the discourse. In little over a decade, the South American presence in the International Psychoanalytic Association grew from distant third party to equal partner. This coming of age suggests a vigorous, libidinal drive. The new Latin appetite for incorporating diverse perspectives and their enthusiastic debates suggest a promising, creative fusion of drives rather than sterility.

In the next chapter, I examine a curriculum specifically designed to promote that very "confrontation and clash of every psychoanalytic perspective." The aim of this contentious course structure is to help create a more interesting, robust, integrated body of analytic theory and practice.

MEANINGFUL ENCOUNTER OR NONEVENT?

> Turning and turning in the widening gyre
> The falcon cannot hear the falconer;
> Things fall apart; the centre cannot hold.

Yeats, "The Second Coming"

Limitations of single-model thinking are frequently encountered in case presentations. In such fora, favored frameworks sometimes strike one as woefully inadequate for elucidating the complexity of the clinical material and the patient's condition.

A more charitable attitude was articulated by Wallerstein and Weinshel (1989). Each theoretical perspective is a "legitimate framework within which respected colleagues can organize the clinical encounters in their consulting rooms and interact therapeutically with their patients" (Wallerstein & Weinshel, 1989, p. 358). Wallerstein and Weinshel's stance certainly contains important truth. It is, however, arguably too tolerant. It unduly accepts a fragmented, limiting state of affairs that is far from ideal for optimal outcome with any individual let alone for the full spectrum of analysands.

In contrast to the excessive charity of common grounders, Gedo (1991) asserted that "The single most important factor impeding full exploration of the psyche is the rigid application of any preconceived conceptual schema to the clinical material" (p. 100). In such treatments, patient and analyst often talk "past each other, not making authentic connections" (Modell, 1987, p. 234). Rather than a "meeting of minds" (Aron, 1996), these encounters resemble ships passing in the night. This more hard-nosed perspective challenges the assumption that theoretical frameworks are relatively unimportant and that all clinicians do essentially similar work, yielding similar outcomes. This contentious stance raises the disquieting challenge that all may not be so well in our consulting rooms. Each perspective may not be quite as legitimate, respectable, and adequate as might be more comfortable to believe.

I am, of course, not suggesting any framework is completely invalid: far from it. The comparative-integrative perspective does, however, posit that it is no longer tenable to restrict oneself to any single paradigm.

Each isolated, inward-looking tradition "has its own evolutionary path" (Gedo, 1999). They do not inevitably remain completely stuck in their limited understanding. Unfortunately, in Gedo's opinion, apparent adaptability to challenges pertaining to their deficits is all too often "merely a grudging retreat from the indefensible positions each school espoused in the past" (p. xv).

Any depth psychology is, of course, an advance beyond mere descriptive psychiatry or behaviorism, providing a richer matrix for comprehending and ameliorating distress. We are, however, at a stage in the evolution of psychoanalytic thought in which, considering our wealth of paradigms, we would be offering those who seek our assistance an impoverished framework if we ignored insights from models other than the one we trained in or preferred for other, equally idiosyncratic reasons. Seeing patients through a single conceptual lens, we will miss a great deal, lending too much validity to Phillips's (1995) cautionary counsel that "The risk of psychoanalytic theories, of psychoanalytic expertise, is that it won't even meet the patient half-way" (p. 45).

The problem of partial theories was noticed long ago. When the Training Commission of the British Society asked prominent analysts for views on the effects of theoretical disagreements, Brierley (in Steiner, 1985) proffered that analysis should be eclectic, flexible: "I am more inclined to alter my preconceived notions to fit the patient's new pattern than to cut the pattern to fit my notions" (p. 42). Her sartorial statement recognized the need for balancing assimilative and accommodative proclivities, constantly questioning the adequacy of our receptive apparatus rather than being excessively embedded in our theories.

If the analyst does not have a flexible, questioning, comparative-integrative perspective and cannot shift out of limited model embeddedness, the likelihood of a healthy, analytic process unfolding is greatly reduced. "Doctrinaire misapplication of any of the perfectly serviceable clinical theories at our disposal will bring actual exploration of the analysand's individuality to a halt" (Gedo, 1991, p. 100). Similarly, although he acknowledged that Freudian theory has been responsible for significant advances in understanding human accomplishments and afflictions, Greenberg (1991) hastened to add that "It has also guided many analyses to a dead end" (p. 67).

No perspective provides "a complete clinical and theoretical approach all by itself. It is in the nature of each and every systematic approach that it sets limits on what is available to it" (Schafer, 1997b, p.12). With a comparative-integrative outlook, one will be far less constricted. One's free-floating attention will be at liberty to roam and resonate with insights from a wide range of contributors from diverse geographical locations and historical epochs.

THE MULTIFACETED PSYCHOANALYTIC SUBJECT

Each school polemicizes limited features of analytic life. Consequently, Bollas (1989) averred, "Each Freudian should also be a potential Kohutian, Kleinian, Winnicottian, Lacanian, and Bionian" (p. 99). Familiarity with multiple models maximizes clinicians' chances of achieving a meeting of minds, a broad, deep analytic process, and therefore, more positive outcomes, he believed.

Each approach provides the analysand with a different analytic object, Bollas (1989) asserted. Each object facilitates a particular use of the analyst, a particular category of psychic movement. The true self's unfolding depends on provision of these objects. For example, he wrote, an analyst who never speaks of castration but who only uses terms such as *annihilation* fails as an object of analysand use for experiencing and knowing the castration complex. Therefore,

> The contemporary analyst's task is to understand the many schools of analytic thought, as each represents a specific analytic function that needs inclusion in the psychoanalytic field. ... If the analyst can free himself from any freezing of his potential multiple functioning, then he can present the analysand with more usable objects. (p. 99)

When Bion (1970) advocated abnegation of memory and desire, Grotstein (1983) believed he was pointing to the desirability of desaturating ideas of dogma so the analytic container might be open for new possibilities. Rather than being completely imbued with Klein, Freud, Jung, or the like, the analytic object needs to be discovered and rediscovered from different vertices, Grotstein asserted.

The eclecticism articulated by Bollas and Grotstein was echoed by Pine (1998): "I have not come across a patient to whom the full panoply of psychic mechanisms and technical approaches was not relevant. There is no patient who needs, for example, a unitary 'self-psychological' approach, or a unitary any other approach" (p. 54).

Eclecticism has sometimes received poor press. In some quarters, it is a derogatory epithet much as the political designation *liberal* became a term of contempt in certain influential American circles, to the astonishment and dismay of many around the world. Similarly in South Africa, "It is hard to describe the detestation in which the words *liberal, liberalism, and liberalist* are held in white Pretoria" (Paton, 1953, p. 71). In Eissler's (1965) book *Medical Orthodoxy and the Future of Psychoanalysis,* he spoke of "the poison of eclecticism" (p. 84). In contrast, Pulver (1993) usefully reminded us that the eclectics were a respectable school of ancient Greek philosophers. Their point of view still has many virtues.

The comparative-integrative attitude welcomes the eclectic philosophical spirit. Beyond liberal tolerance of diversity, it encourages the "clash and confrontation" of different schools. With a constant eye toward integration, it seeks to create a more complex, multifaceted, useful, psychoanalytic object.

"All models of the mind are of equal importance," Gedo and Goldberg (1973) averred. However, "Because they are applicable to different levels of hierarchy, they are not comparably useful in organizing the understanding of a given problem" (p. 9). An analyst with a limited model may function well with some types of individuals or with certain features of various patients. She or he will not likely work optimally with a broad range of analysands or with issues that emerge in many cases that are not well accounted for in that analyst's model.

Patients whose analysts are constrained from tailoring formulations and interventions to fit their unique natures may still gain something from their analyst's limited perspective. They may also benefit from supportive aspects common to most therapies including learning to bring at least one additional perspective (the analyst's) to bear on the interpretation of experience. The particular gains that could be acquired through more accurate analytic comprehension and intervention do not, however, seem possible in such cases. Due to such considerations, the comparative-integrative perspective both supports and challenges Wallerstein's idea that we all do comparable clinical work producing comparable changes.

COLLECTIVE COUNTERTRANSFERENCE

Shortcomings in analytic comprehension may indicate countertransferential difficulties (Goldberg, 1987). Countertransference may not just be an individual matter; it may be common in a particular orientation (Modell, 1987). "Every metapsychology contains the seeds of an incipient counter-transference" (Levenson, 1992, p. 464). Choice of theory may conceal a countertransference predilection (Shane, 1987). The analyst is well advised to assume his or her theories have defensive functions, to "be alert to what exactly he uses them not to hear" (Phillips, 1995, p. 45).

It is common knowledge, other than to adherents of a theory, Shane (1987) quipped, that all Kleinians are crazy, full of rage; self psychologists cover fear of aggression with syrupy empathy; classical analysts mask fear of the primitive with rigid insistence on mature responsibility; and developmentalists dignify the banalities of the nursery out of a timid need to avoid oedipal passions.

Lively derision between schools notwithstanding, antagonists do actually agree on one thing, Shane noted. That common ground is the belief that all mixed-model theorists are obsessively, phobicly, or stupidly incapable of commitment. Contemptuous of the eclecticism, these pure souls are convinced one cannot (should not) commit to more than one framework. Idolizing their school, they believe one should not worship other gods. Those consorting with more than one model are guilty of polygamy and perversion, shamelessly harboring a harem of models. Pigging out in what Rangell (1988) referred to critically as a "cafeteria of paradigms" (p. 325), they lack discipline and discernment.

Feeling eclectics violate some basic taboo, purists resonate with Chasseguet-Smirgel's (1984) emphasis on the perverse inclination to abolish essential differences in the degenerative descent from sacred oedipal heights to profane anal depths. These critics feel one should engage one model—theirs—marry it, and remain forever faithful. Exploring beyond that conventional structure is tantamount to participating in a forbidden ménage à trois or à quatre, cinq, six ... "Liberalism denotes moral looseness and degeneracy" (Paton, 1953, p. 71).

In contrast to this fear of embracing diverse models, Bollas (1987) believed some theoretical differences we enjoy these days occur because different groups address themselves to different transference positions that imply corresponding countertransference dispositions that, in turn, have implications for technique. Although some especially disturbed analysands may live within only one position, "most analysands live through all the transference positions" (p. 241). A comparative-integrative model enables us to address a maximal range of these transference/countertransference dispositions.

To whatever extent the theories we embrace are determined by countertransferential factors, the narrow rigidity in our allegiances has long limited clinical acumen and efficacy. "Theoretical preconceptions determine how we conduct an analysis. What we focus on will have enormous influence on the unfolding of the psychoanalytic process" (Modell, 1987, p. 233). A narrow model shrinks our focus. A constricted outlook prevents the full unfolding of a transformative, analytic process.

PLENITUDE AND POVERTY IN PROFESSIONAL TRAINING

A senior analyst's work was characterized by Modell (1987) as constricted by classical education. That learning could be other than expansionary might surprise some. This disquieting position is not, however, just that of one disgruntled analyst. "Professionalization leads ... to an immense restriction of the scientist's vision and to a considerable resistance to paradigm change" (Kuhn, 1970, p. 64). Such training promotes assimilating data to framework rather than using discrepancies to challenge, alter, or expand the paradigm.

One would have little trouble finding work compromised by classical, self psychological, Kleinian, or any other monoparadigmatic training. Mistaking part of the truth for the whole is a problem to which partisans are prone. The pleasure principle's primary process prefers to believe our theory encompasses just about everything (*pars pro toto*). This comforting illusion keeps the less welcome reality principle at bay. It can be profoundly unsettling if the news seeps through that "No single theory is fully sufficient to order even one set of clinical observations" (Gedo & Goldberg, 1973, p. 172).

Analysts may feel not only stimulated but also overwhelmed by the constantly expanding professional discourse. Publicly, we applaud it. Privately, we may sometimes clap with one hand. The impressive growth of our literature, not to mention that in cognate disciplines, can be humbling and anxiety provoking. New ideas, organizations, journals, and schools of thought constantly emerge. Lamenting that it is becoming difficult to keep up nurtures the comforting illusion that we were once au courant and only recently fell behind.

Protection against stimuli may be more important than reception, Freud (1920/1955b) remarked with characteristic perspicacity. He hypothesized a protective shield preserving organismic integrity in face of the enormous stimulation in the external world. Such a barrier may be necessary throughout life. During our careers, this device may protect us from bombardment by books and journals we must read, conferences we ought to attend, Internet discussion groups we should join, ideas we need to grasp and better utilize, and so forth. Paradigms function as shields, insulating us with familiar ideas, encircling us with like-minded colleagues who agree on the irritating wrongness of others. These stimulus barriers help shut out annoying, ego-alien perspectives, protecting us from the anxiety that might flood us if all that stimulation were to penetrate.

The renowned humorist (and professor of political economy at McGill University) Stephen Leacock quipped that receiving a Ph.D. meant one had been filled with knowledge and there was no room for more. His wit may be relevant to many analytic trainings. A little knowledge is a dangerous thing, particularly when advertised and misperceived as being larger than it is. (I am reminded of the helpful graffito adorning the wall above the urinal in the Rackham School of Graduate Studies at the University of Michigan that cautioned, "Stand closer, it's shorter than you think.") Today, an exclusively classical, Kleinian, self psychological, or any other single model training constitutes treacherously little knowledge. Rather than overestimating the degree to which we have been filled up, we must make room for more.

We should not settle into any single, comfortable view of technique, Pine (1998) proclaimed: "There is no room for orthodoxy" (p. 7). Regrettably, there are still many training programs in which there is little space for heterodoxy.

RAPPROCHEMENT

Socratic humility (realizing the more we learn how much we still do not know) can be elusive. On his 90th birthday, Clifford Scott (Meloche, 1998) opined that ignorance, being infinite, is more impressive than knowledge. Elated by increased understanding, we may be loathe to face the deflating fact that there remains so much more to be learned. We might prefer scotomization. "What I don't see, other people don't, and indeed doesn't exist" (Isaacs, 1948/1952, p. 106). Blind spots become part of the protective shield against stimuli, against too much light.

Lack of awareness of the limitations of our knowledge fosters and is fostered by closed system thinking. Such unconsciousness may help sustain enthusiasm and grandiosity, albeit in a defensive, false form. Grandiosity derives partly from what Mahler (1972) called the practicing phase (approximately 10 to 18 months of age). Who can forget the awkwardness and excitement with which they acquired the skills to stroll the psychoanalytic path? Slowly but surely, with many a slip, we perfected our ability to walk the walk and talk the talk. Like Mahlerian toddlers pleased with our exciting, new, hard-won abilities, we may be blissfully oblivious to the fact that one day we may have to decenter from egocentrism and put our capacities, our sense of self and others, into very different perspective. A Mahlerian "rapprochement crisis" is necessary if we are to take the crucial developmental step of reconciling our cherished theory with the reality that there are other points of view at least as powerful and important as our own.

The current controversy with respect to pluralism presents us with just such a rapprochement opportunity. Isolationism no longer works. Although we may not know exactly what to do with multiplicity, "we are not free to evade it" (Eigen, 1993, p. xxiii). Marginalized voices have perforated our stimulus barriers. The time-honored psychoanalytic strategy for handling dissidents that Rachmann (1999) referred to as *todschweigen* (death by silence) no longer suffices to patch the holes in our conceptual envelope. We need a new theoretical wardrobe. We can no longer "make do" with the old one. Rapprochement is a troubled time. It is, nonetheless, essential for development.

TO SEE OR NOT TO SEE

Some analysts' familiarity with early development appears sketchy. They seem at a loss with problems rooted in these stages. They may try to comprehend such phenomena in terms of regression from oedipal conflict but demonstrate relatively little understanding of the domain of fixation, the basic fault (Balint, 1968) in which their patients are caught (cf. Gedo, 1980). They may rely on nonanalytic, even antianalytic models to explain the etiology, nature, and necessary treatment for disorders exceeding the scope of their narrow model.

A different group of analysts whose preferred theories are anchored earlier in the developmental spectrum may have a different problem. They may have insufficient knowledge of or feel for phallic-oedipal complexities. This shortcoming makes it difficult for them to comprehend and optimally assist patients presenting problems at that level. For example, believing Fairbairn focused excessively on dependency, Greenberg (1991) asserted that he "collapsed the richness of the oedipal period ... into a replay of the themes of earliest infancy ... an excellent example of what happens when an analyst is seduced by his theory" (p. 70).

Reflecting on his training at the oedipal end of the continuum, Schafer (1999) "realized how little room was left for—indeed, how little permission was tacitly given for—the study of the continuing force of early developmental stages in later life" (p. 342). Because this lack seemed at odds with what his patients appeared to need, he "began to read more widely, traveling through Winnicott to what were then considered to be the outrageous and implicitly taboo publications of the early Kleinians." His patients must have benefited greatly from his violating training taboos.

All patients require the full range of analytically informed interventions, from pacification of primitive states of overexcitement to interpretation of oedipal conflicts (Gedo, 1981).

> Every analytic patient will sooner or later present behaviors referable to the poorly resolved sequelae of each phase of development. Hence every analytic procedure must consist of the application of all possible modalities of treatment in various combinations. This point of view may seem novel, but in fact simply articulates the logical consequences of an epigenetic theory of psychological development. (p. 263)

When analysts' models are deficient at one level, their analysands will not receive the understanding and intervention they require.

Verbal interpretations work well at the oedipal level, but the therapeutic relationship is more important when working at the level of the basic fault, Balint (1968) believed. Addressing a similar matter, Winnicott (1971a) bravely shared that "It appalls me to think how much deep change I have prevented or delayed in patients *in a certain classification category* by my personal need to interpret" (p. 86).

Clinicians locked into perspectives are reminiscent of the gentleman whose sole implement was a hammer. Ensorcelled by the tool illusion, every conundrum resembled a nail and was treated accordingly. "A model is a tool, and one tool is no better than another, although in performing a specific task certain tools are more useful than others" (Gedo & Goldberg, 1973, p. 9). Practitioners need a variety of sophisticated implements. Many institutes still produce too many single instrument practitioners. One needs a fuller tool chest to get the job done. That container does not have to be perfectly organized at all times.

SERIAL ANALYSES

> It is theoretical oversights that we fear, for it is obvious that physicists and mathematicians don't forget anything—they simply leave things out.

> **—Gaston Bachelard,** *The New Scientific Spirit*

Recalling Pine's (1998) opinion that no patient needs a unitary self psychological or unitary any other approach, one might wonder what happens to the many analysands who nonetheless receive such treatments. Some do not lie quietly and patiently on the procrustean couch. They quit. There are analyses terminable, interminable, and preterm. Others continue to some sort of ending that may exude a whimper rather than a bang. They may give muted, mixed, or negative reviews of their analyses and of analysis in general. Some seek second and even more analyses. Others live with whatever they gained, knowledgeable or oblivious of the shortcomings.

A moving portrait of one who had two suboptimal analyses emerged from Rubin's (1998) study of one of the greats in our discipline, Donald Winnicott. He believed Winnicott's lifelong concerns with authenticity and relatedness arose from troubling experiences with a depressed, emotionally unavailable mother and an absent, puritanical father, topped off by lengthy experiences with two analysts who likewise "failed to make contact with him at a deep psychological level" (p. 82).

Winnicott (1969) described 10 years of analysis "at the hand of Strachey" (p. 129). Strachey "adhered to a classical technique in a cold-blooded way for which I have always been grateful," Winnicott claimed (in Rodman, 1987, p. 33). With these jarringly juxtaposed descriptors, it is not completely surprising to learn that Winnicott also believed this treatment "did not help him as much as it should have done" (cited in Rubin, 1998, p. 91).

Several years after his cold-blooded treatment, Winnicott had a shorter, 5-year analysis with the prominent Kleinian, Joan Riviere. In a letter to Melanie Klein, he stated, "Some of the patients that go to 'Kleinian enthusiasts' for analysis are not really allowed to grow or to create in the analysis and I am not basing this on loose fantasy" (as cited in Rodman, 1987, p. 37). Riviere's "analysis failed me" (p. 34), Winnicott bluntly stated. What was missing was "something which I could not get in either of my two long analyses" (p. 34).

Winnicott felt his analysts failed to meet his spontaneous gestures in a way he needed to facilitate the emergence of authenticity and aliveness, Rubin concluded. Instead, they participated in a reenactment of the "False Self" mode of living that had characterized his childhood. "It is possible to see analyses going on indefinitely because they are done on the basis of work with the False Self," Winnicott (1960, p. 151) stated. With wry wit, he observed that it is possible for an analysis to proceed for years without the analyst realizing he does not have a live patient on the couch. His sobering observation no doubt derived, at least partly, from his lengthy experience as a patient.

At least in retrospect, Winnicott seemed to have been acutely aware of and deeply disappointed by the limits of his analytical experiences. On the other side of the empathic divide, his analysts seemed to have been stuck in considerable countertransference. In letters to his wife (Meisel & Kendrick, 1985), Strachey discussed irritations with Winnicott including his wish to terminate him in mid-analysis. Strachey shared details of Winnicott's sexual life in derogatory terms. Riviere went further, making caustic remarks about Winnicott's personality during public meetings. Riviere (in Kahr, 1996) announced to the medical section of the British Psychological Society that Winnicott "just makes theory of his own sickness" (p. 62).

The poignancy of these less than completely stellar analytic relationships—with frustration and disappointment on one side, bitterness and contempt on the other—suggests that in important ways, these encounters were like ships passing rather than minds meeting. Phillips's (1995) remark that the risk of analytic theories and expertise is that it will not even meet the patient halfway seems painfully apposite.

Commenting on serial analyses that were ultimately successful, Stein (1991) noted that earlier, failed analyses were sometimes not due to deficiencies in the analyst's empathic/affective processes or personal dynamics but "resided in the theory, which soaked through cognitive, perceptual, and affective processes in the analyst" (p. 329). At the time Stein trained, had candidates confided that they felt confused in a session, unable to think, or that they were going mad, they would not have been allowed to continue training. Now such admissions are taken as signs of potency. Stein attributed these radical changes in reported countertransference to changed theories.

In keeping with Stein's observations, V. Hamilton (1996), based on her empirical investigation, noted that "If we consider the range of psychoanalysis' basic concepts, countertransference could be counted amongst those which have undergone a radical transformation and expansion" (p. 215). Undoubtedly, increasing dialogue between perspectives has contributed significantly to this improvement.

Areas of failure in Winnicott's analyses led him to make them the focus of his creative research, Rubin suggested. He placed the need to discover and express the true self at the heart of his oeuvre. Paradoxically, he also maintained that "each individual is an isolate, permanently non-communicating, permanently unknown" (p. 187). Far from lamenting this state (1963b), he maintained it was important that this "incommunicado element" (p. 187) not be found. He went so far as to proclaim it would be catastrophic if communication seeped through one's defenses to violate the self's core. At other times, he claimed it would be a disaster if the hidden self were not located. Rubin's (1998) research goes a long way toward elucidating this apparent paradox. Locating its roots in nonfacilitating aspects of Winnicott's childhood, and later his analyses, suggests limits on the eternal, universal nature of this conflicted sensitivity.

Winnicott (1949) seemed aware of the origins of his scientific interests: "Psycho-analytic research is perhaps always to some extent an attempt on the part of an analyst to carry the work of his own analysis further than the point to which his own analyst could get him" (p. 70). Through scholarly exploration and communication, he hoped to obtain something that was lacking in his analyses.

Following a scientific meeting, he wrote to Klein:

> What I was wanting on Friday undoubtedly was that there should be some move from your direction towards the gesture that I make in this paper. It is a creative gesture and I cannot make any relationship through the gesture except if someone came to meet it. I think that I was wanting something which I have no right to expect from your group, and it is really of the nature of a therapeutic act. (p. 34)

Sadly, what could not be received on the couch could not be responded to in the scientific forum either.

Kohut is another individual whose research was partly driven by the need to find things he could not reach in his initial treatment. His famous paper "The Two Analyses of Mr. Z" is now generally taken to be autobiographical, the second treatment being his self-analysis. Some readers concluded that Mr. Z finally found the appropriate analysis, the one he had always needed. I would be inclined to think Kohut, like most people, needed both classical and self psychological perspectives and perhaps a few others.

BEYOND MULTIPLE ANALYSES

Serial analyses are one way of trying to transcend the limitations of unitary approaches. From Winnicott's experience, one sees they do not always achieve what is hoped for. Therapeutic needs are more likely to be met if the limitations of "cold-blooded" classicists, "Kleinian enthusiasts," and other unitary practitioners are replaced by a more encompassing, comparative-integrative outlook open to engaging novel phenomena rather than relegating them prematurely to an established pigeonhole. Understanding that there are multiple perspectives on problems, some not yet formulated, some more useful than others in particular circumstances, helps one avoid becoming, or remaining, ensorcelled by one point of view, sure that patients or colleagues who disagree are simply making arguments or theory out of their sickness.

With a variety of theoretical gloves, one has a better chance of catching a wider range of spontaneous gestures. With a comparative-integrative mitt, less of our patients' efforts to communicate and relate will whiz past our ears. Our framework needs to include Freudian, Kleinian, and the middle school wisdom of Brierley (in Steiner, 1985) "more inclined to alter my preconceived notions to fit the patient's new pattern than to cut the pattern to fit my notions" (p. 42) and Kohut's (1984) wise counsel:

> If there is one lesson I have learned during my life as an analyst, it is the lesson that what my patients tell me is likely to be true—that many times when I believed that I was right and my patients were wrong, it turned out, though often only after a prolonged search, that my rightness was superficial whereas their *rightness* was profound. (p. 83)

Combining these frameworks provides expertise needed to meet patients at least halfway and make more authentic, transmuting connections.

Working with his model of the four psychologies of psychoanalysis, Pine (1990) was able to transcend his classical base to draw on contributions of Klein, Kohut, Winnicott, and others as the clinical situation warranted. With this integrative framework, he felt he was able to work much more effectively with patients. Similarly, with the multimodal model Gedo fashioned and refined over time, he found his results were better than those reported by others, not because he had superior clinical acumen, but due to his consistent application of his interpretive model of mental functioning and technique (p. 297). Summarizing his results with terminated cases in three separate publications (Gedo, 1979; 1984, chap. 2; 1991b, chap. 10), he concluded, "The variations of technique I have used have enhanced my ability to bring analyses to mutually agreed upon conclusions" (1994, p. 297).

SYNTHESIS

Necessary aspects of analytic functioning are currently split off from what should be a more cohesive core of knowledge and technique. Important ideas and modes of intervention are lodged in separate schools. These displaced fragments need to be drawn together into a more unified frame. This prospect might seem unwieldy. It is, however, parsimonious compared to the currently ungainly, fragmented, embarrassing nature of our discipline.

Payne believed analysis flourishes in an atmosphere of scientific controversy. Largely due to her influence, King and Steiner (1991) wrote there is only one psychoanalytical society in Britain today. That outcome may not be entirely desirable, but it is an interesting and in some ways impressive phenomenon. My concern is not the survival of any single society but with creating an ambience enabling the discipline to flourish, not only through welcoming controversy but also via creative attempts at synthesizing. In the next chapter, I present a curriculum designed to foster this goal along with a provisional evaluation of its effectiveness.

6

Significance for Psychoanalytic Education

And what rough beast, its hour come round at last,
Slouches towards Bethlehem to be born?

Yeats, "The Second Coming"

INTRODUCTION

After training in a lockstep paradigm, Wallerstein became interested in learning about the frameworks of his international colleagues. Based on these engagements, he formulated his famous query "One Psychoanalysis or Many?" He favored searching for common ground. In fact, he thought we already had it, at least in clinical practice. Believing we might never achieve theoretical unity, he thought struggling toward that goal might be a waste of time.

Along with some others whom I cited in the previous chapter, I felt there was not as much consensus at the clinical level as Wallerstein believed. In contrast to his optimism about the technical common ground and his pessimism about ever achieving much theoretical consensus, I advocated a comparative-integrative method for working toward increasing unity at all levels. Having explored scientific, professional, and clinical implications of this perspective, in this chapter, I concentrate on its educational significance.

THE THIRD LEG

A few leading educators have shared their disquieting opinion that our educational program has failed to keep abreast with the times. "Psychoanalytic education is at least in the doldrums, if not exactly in crisis," Holt (1992) opined. "Young people who wish to become psychoanalysts must go through a program that has not been changed in essential respects since the 1920's; not surprisingly, many of them are bored and restive" (p. 392).

Wallerstein and Weinshel (1989) also lamented that our educational system has remained essentially the same "despite the fact that the formal didactic seminar has been the object of unremitting criticism and has always been looked upon as the least essential component" (p.355) in the tripartite training model. In contrast to the neglected classroom, our discipline has "always taken the training analysis and supervised analyses with the utmost seriousness" (p. 356).

Having diagnosed the malaise, Holt posed the key question: "How can we improve psychoanalytic education, fostering intellectual independence, skepticism about dogma, and a zest for discovery through scientific method?" (p. 397). I address these concerns in this chapter.

WHERE TO BEGIN?

In the late 1980s, an enthusiastic group of colleagues assembled in Canada to create a new postgraduate educational body, the Toronto Institute for Contemporary Psychoanalysis. The Curriculum Committee was given the responsibility of devising a 4-year seminar program. After reflecting on the thorny pedagogic problems plaguing our field, we decided the most promising solution would be to adopt an explicitly comparative-integrative philosophy. Building on the work of those who have endorsed eclecticism (e.g., Bollas, 1989; Pine, 1994; Pulver, 1993), comparative analysis (e.g., Greenberg & Mitchell, 1983; Schafer, 1983), "ecumenicism" (Gedo, 1992), and "selective integration" (Mitchell, 1988, p. viii), we advocated examining and contrasting currently segregated models to foster dialectical synthesis to whatever degree possible.

Members of the Curriculum Committee knew each other at least to some extent. Amazingly, this diverse group (e.g., a dyed-in-the-wool Kleinian, an enthusiastic self psychologist, an articulate ego psychologist, an eclectic) found it fairly easy to come to consensus as to what would constitute an ideal curriculum. The congenial experience of this working group was repeated at the level of the Board of Directors who enthusiastically endorsed the Curriculum Committee's proposal.

Although I am sure some would have preferred us to have developed a Kleinian, self psychological, or other uniparadigmatic training, everyone seemed able to subordinate their idiosyncratic desires to the aggregate's interest. This accommodating spirit may have been due in part to the fact that most members of the group had earned doctorates in psychology and so were favorably inclined to the vitalizing clash of perspectives and the enriching contributions of diverse disciplines. Congeniality may also have reflected the likelihood that all had encountered the limitations of single model approaches in earlier phases of their training, fueling their desire to create a more promising intellectual milieu.

Akin to the crucial developmental move beyond split self-representations and object representations, we aspired toward a more unified representation of psychoanalysis. We wished to contribute to making the discipline other than the current sum of its parts, just as the integrated object of the depressive position is so very different from the separate, part objects characterizing the paranoid-schizoid situation. Such maturational advance, whether on an individual or disciplinary level, constitutes a quantum leap to new organizational status.

Grappling, like us, with problems of pluralism and paradigm shift, Fast (1998) noted that we are at an "exhilarating time of ferment in the construction of psychoanalytic perspectives. The long hegemony of ego psychology, with its firmly objectivist base, seems to be giving way to relational perspectives with a largely constructivist bent" (p. 170). In this unprecedented time of opportunity, our challenge is to "construct a relational framework for psychoanalysis that can accommodate the rich heritage of observation and conceptualization that derives from Freud's explorations, from ego psychology, and from other psychoanalytic perspectives." The comparative-integrative approach furnishes the framework Fast challenged the field to find.

Although agreeing with those who assert the moment is ripe for paradigm shift, the new framework cannot simply be something like self psychology instead of ego psychology, object relations instead of classical analysis, or any other *B* instead of *A*. A viable paradigm must, instead, promote serious study of all models, combining what proves substantial in each into a more comprehensive framework. Otherwise, one narrow set of ideas would simply be exchanged for a differently constricted belief system. That dismal possibility was sadly confirmed as a real probability in V. Hamilton's (1996) empirical study that found change in theoretical orientation was unlikely to widen the range of an analyst's belief.

Discussing the relationship between innovation and tradition in Part I, I utilized Kohut's (1984) ideas and clinical material to illustrate impediments to the evolution of psychoanalytic thought. My analysis accorded with V. Hamilton's sobering conclusion. Kohut's commitment to novel thinking had the adverse effect of preventing him from being able to draw on valuable classical insights, despite his effort to be open to both viewpoints. Hypercathecting self psychology, he could not avoid countercathecting/decathecting traditional analysis, thereby losing access to important ideas and ways of analyzing data (and patients).

WHEN TO BEGIN?

Not long ago, the *International Journal of Psycho-Analysis* invited papers on professional education, echoing Kernberg's (1986) earlier plea for much greater interchange of educational philosophies across institute boundaries. These calls reflected growing recognition that this "third and final component of our educational tripod has been given scant attention" (Gedo, 1984). The requests did not unleash a flood of fascinating ideas. Perhaps presenting our thoughts may encourage others to develop and share theirs.

To embody our commitment to comparative-integrative analysis, we created a radically new curriculum. Desirous that this perspective should become integral to our candidates' identity—a natural, automatic aspect of their thinking, theorizing, and practice—we introduce this philosophy in the first class. To add such considerations later would be too late.

Becoming proficient with analytic models is like learning languages. Educators specializing in bilingualism believe the earlier the immersion, the more likely one will acquire competence. Recent neuropsychological research supports that belief. Languages learned early are encoded in the same brain area. Those acquired later are located in separate neuronal networks, slightly removed from the original linguistic site. To absorb the comparative-integrative perspective, early immersion in a milieu containing multiple analytic tongues is ideal.

The plurality of analytic languages has been likened to a Tower of Babel (e.g., Aslan, 1989), a formidable obstacle to communication and cross-fertilization. Multiple monologues cannot bring us closer to heaven. We need multilingualism and, possibly, a lingua franca. It is not in our interest to scoff at dialects, criticizing those who speak imperfectly or who introduce "foreign" elements into their writing and teaching. Zealously rooting out alien concepts is more likely to impoverish than purify us.

Celebrating the scholarly role of making knowledge from one system comprehensible to others, Ogden (1986) pointed out that each language creates meaning that cannot be generated by the others. As "retriever of the alienated ... the interpreter safeguards the fullness of human discourse" (p. 1).

This positive, dialogic process was portrayed by three South American analysts (Junqueira, Menezes, & Meyer, 1988, as cited in Bernardi, 1992) who committed themselves to intensive, ongoing discussion of their different points of view, seeking areas of coincidence, contradiction, and complementarity. "What we had thought clear and evident was not really so," they discovered. This finding "forced us to carry out the disquieting work of rethinking the theoretical and technical presuppositions used in our practice. Our listening to each other simultaneously revealed how much threat is contained in a coexistence of this nature" (p. 516). They concluded that acceptance of the "reciprocal, disturbing action" of different paradigms should be considered an important advance.

Placing a comparative-integrative attitude at the center of an institute's philosophy is likely to create considerable reciprocal disturbing interaction. Introducing such discussions into training is not likely to create a reassuring, smooth course of studies. Nonetheless, like Junqueira et al. (1988), we believe such steps constitute necessary, significant advances for our field.

A "MODEL" CURRICULUM

> Anyone who hopes to penetrate the new dialectic of science must develop
> psychological empathy with the participants, and the best way to do this
> is to study the whole spectrum of complementary ideas.

> —Gaston Bachelard, *The New Scientific Spirit*

It is not helpful to discuss curricular matters too abstractly, but minutiae would
not interest many. Bearing these extremes in mind, a description of our curriculum may suffice to convey how it has been designed to foster the spirit we
espouse.

In labeling this a model curriculum, I do not mean to imply it is perfect. Placing it in the public domain, it can be played with, used, challenged, attacked, and
modified. It is not the last word, not even our final word. It is, rather, a model
responding to adaptive challenges in an ongoing evolutionary process that,
as Gedo, Holt, Wallerstein and Weinshel, and others have noted, had become
gummed up.

Our course begins with a seminar on our philosophy—reasons for it, goals,
and methods. Following that introduction, there are two seminars on a given
evening each week for 4 years. The first half of the night might not seem very dif
ferent from courses at some other institutes. During the first year, it follows the
evolution of the Freudian framework. In the second year, the first seminar each
evening concentrates on the evolution of Kleinian/Object Relational approaches.
In the third year, the first half of the night emphasizes evolving Self Psychological and Relational models together with analytically informed infancy research.
The fourth year allows for electives to fill lacunae perceived by candidates in the
course up to that point.

One's reaction to that first seminar over the first few years of the course might
depend on one's degree of experience with and preference for "straight-line"
(Rangell, 1988) theoretical evolution. From that vantage point, we might appear
to give excessive attention to Kleinian, object relational, self psychological, and
relational deviations.

Observers would note that our Institute adopted a historical approach in keeping with the continuing truth of Hartmann's (1948) assertion that "understanding
of analysis is hardly possible without a detailed knowledge of its history" (p. 69).
Here, he echoed Freud's (1923/1955c) belief that "The best way of understanding
psycho-analysis is still by tracing its origin and development" (p. 235).

The course departs radically from traditional curricula in the second seminar each night. In that class, a different faculty member discusses issues raised
in the first seminar from an alternative perspective. If the first class focused on

Freudian instinct theory, for example, the second might examine that topic from a self psychological point of view. In this way, the comparative-integrative challenge is presented *ab initio*. It quickly becomes clear to candidates that no school has a monopoly on truth. No perspective is awarded privileged status. That place is reserved for the comparative-integrative metaperspective.

This contrapuntal structure differs significantly from institutes that try to cope with multiplicity by establishing separate training streams. The British Institute, for example, offers Freudian, Kleinian, and Independent tracks. New York University's Postdoctoral Program in Psychoanalysis provides Freudian, Interpersonal, Relational, and Independent streams (Aron, 1996). Our curriculum differs even more radically from one-track institutes that simply acknowledge other perspectives by inserting brief modules on them late in training—a tack-on approach Glover (King & Steiner, 1991, p. 597) recommended.

Even David Rapaport might have found this novel course structure interesting. Rapaport's (in Gill & Klein, 1967) "historical approach had no mechanical respect for chronology. Not only was the contemporary scene to be surveyed against the background of history, but history was to be surveyed against the background of contemporary development" (p. 13). This methodology

> was not only a means of arriving at the most advanced understanding of a concept; it also made it possible to revive the usefulness of previously discarded concepts, which for one reason or another had not been digestible within the theory, by bringing them into relationship with later developments. (p. 13)

For Rapaport, "the historical approach was the guarantee *par excellence* against superficial theorizing."

Notwithstanding his stature as ego psychologist extraordinaire, and his dislike of certain other schools, our curriculum fosters many values Rapaport held dear. Studying a topic from a classical perspective in the first seminar during the first year and then from a more modern point of view during the second half of the evening enables candidates to survey contemporary developments against the background of history and vice versa. This approach facilitates understanding concepts and rekindles interest in heretofore ignored ideas by bringing them into relationship with subsequent developments, mitigating against "superficial theorizing," teaching, and practice. Building this philosophy into the core values of an institute and into its curriculum provides structural guarantees against provincialism and rigidity.

We encourage all faculty to teach from a comparative-integrative point of view. Even if they cannot or do not, the course structure ensures candidates will have the benefit of this perspective. They will be presented at least two sides of every issue.

NON IN USUM DELPHINI

When our program was proposed, some in our community who saw it as exciting, even inspired, believed it would be too difficult for candidates. Their reservations may have been based not only on empathy but also on projective identification, for a comparative-integrative perspective can be daunting for faculty as well.

Pondering why comparative analysis was so undeveloped, Schafer (1983) concluded it was because analyzing the structure of thought in just one school is formidable. Analysts within an orientation cannot agree on basic assumptions, relationships between propositions, what constitutes evidence, the relationship between evidence and practice, and so forth. These problems are compounded when comparing different schools. He therefore settled for the notion that although it is important to pay attention to what different schools propose to guard against one's fictions becoming myths, one needs "a firm base, a consistent orientation, a defined culture of one's own in which to work" (p. 285). From this point of view, comparative psychoanalysis, let alone comparative-integrative analysis, would not be a good place to begin training.

He shared his ideas favoring grounding in a particular perspective in his address to a graduating class. He also warned them that after one has become an analyst "of one persuasion or another" (p. 281), something peculiar happens:

> There are important things you begin to see in your work that your teachers told you were not there or were not important; or else they never led you to expect to see them and so, when you do see them, they startle and dismay you. ... You may for a time simply try to explain them away. At some point, however, you may face them directly and begin to raise some serious constructive questions about the tradition within which you work. (p. 286)

Schafer's approach was far more conservative than ours. Although attuned to certain problems of one-track education, a danger in his stance is that graduates may, and often do, forever overlook, or explain away, phenomena that do not fit their tradition. This likelihood concerned Kuhn (1970), who not only wrote about how paradigms change but also about their resistance to change. Working within a paradigm amounts to a "strenuous and devoted attempt to force nature into the conceptual boxes supplied by professional education" (p. 5). Phenomena "that will not fit the box are often not seen at all" (p. 24). This inability to perceive was my focus in Part I. Consequently, I feel candidates need something other than a "firm base, a consistent orientation, a defined culture" in which to work. They will benefit more from a firm, multicultural base embodying a consistent, comparative-integrative attitude.

The ability to form opinions on controversial matters was, Glover (King & Steiner, 1991) believed, too much to expect from most candidates. He viewed this problem as due to transferences that "handcuff him securely to his analytic mother or father" (p. 146). Similarly, Brierely believed Klein trainees often identi-fied their analysts with idealized objects, and then identified with them, becom-ing "follow-my-leader copyists. They would remain under the psychic necessity of swallowing their training whole and never using their teeth upon what they are taught" (p. 627). In such circumstances, there could be "no hope of steady prog-ress; only the chance of revolution. But while the trainee remained the echo of the trainer the result in both theory and practice could only be sterile repetition."

This unanalyzed idealization—a variant of Freud's (1912/1958a) "unobjection-able" (p. 105) positive transference—is especially common in training analyses, Hamilton (1996) warned. These "ideal analytic patients" set up mutually seduc-tive, transference-countertransference interplay that obscures defiance and rage. Glover (1942/1991) believed the major source of controversy in the British Insti-tute emanated from such "training transferences" (p. 614).

Identificatory processes in psychoanalytic education also concerned Rangell (1988). Such phenomena pertain to suggestion—something Freud strove to steer the analytic enterprise away from—rather than critical thinking.

> A major concern for the future is that a generation of candidates, parallel to the mechanism of children's becoming imprinted to their original figures and training conditions, become similarly imprinted to the milieu of the institute and orienta-tion in which they were trained. (pp. 327–328)

Amazingly, Rangell's concern seemed exclusively for current candidates who he felt were being initiated into inferior orientations. He appeared unconcerned about previous cohorts who had "imprinted" when his favored paradigm ruled more securely.

Schafer seemed to realize graduates might never transcend the boxes sup-plied by professional education, resulting in sterile repetition of what they were taught. This possibility at least seemed implicit in his citing Sartre's observation that experience usually consists of somebody's repeating the same errors long enough to feel entitled to claim absolute authority for doing things that way. Schafer added wryly, "Sometimes when one looks at one or another senior col-league, one cannot help thinking that there must be a lot of truth in what Sartre says" (p. 287). Such stasis illustrates "the tenacity with which the libido adheres to particular trends and objects" (Freud, 1916, p. 348)—a significant problem in analytic education.

Among those who become aware of their tradition's shortcomings, not all respond by raising constructive questions; fewer proceed to creative resolu-tions. Because of these dangers, we believe (as Schafer hinted) it is time for a paradigm shift but not to one that simply discards old models. That would be the revolutionary path Brierely (in King & Steiner, 1991) viewed as the sole hope for disgruntled graduates of programs that do not encourage critical evaluation. The new paradigm should not be any of the dashing new pretenders to the throne. Although these orientations are valuable, they are in certain respects like the old, single model emperor sporting new duds. In contrast, a comparative-integrative metamodel represents a radically different attitude toward all models including those not yet conceived.

Some analysts thought self psychology was the necessary revolutionary paradigm. Kohut seemed like a messiah, promising salvation from the "restrictive paradigm of the transference neuroses" (Gedo, 1991, p. 144). His kinder, gentler vision brought hope of hacksawing handcuffs, exorcising the infernal complexities, conundrums, and terminal "exhaustion of the ego-psychological paradigm" (Bacon & Gedo, 1993, p. 133). Hungry for something new, searching analysts embraced his doctrines enthusiastically. Sometimes their tight grip on the new squeezed out any positive regard for the old framework, to the dismay of their former fellow travelers.

How many converts to new orientations experienced earlier trainings that encouraged what Brierely described as swallowing what one was taught holus-bolus, never using one's teeth on it? From anecdotal evidence, it would seem quite a few. Under such circumstances, one may later use one's teeth with a vengeance.

The fate of the analytic object under these conditions can be intriguing. Some candidates feel they cannot just gulp down their training but feel a need to pretend they have. Others swallow but do not absorb much of what they have taken in. Their learning is encapsulated. It may pass through their system undigested. Others claim to have benefited greatly from training, yet their activities reflect destructive involvement with analytic programs. Under a cloak of idealization, their disavowed sentiments return to wreak subtle or not so subtle suffering on colleagues and programs. These outcomes can be seen as part of what Glover (in King & Steiner, p. 598) described as residual, concealed, negative training transferences.

Contra Schafer (1983), we believe the time to acquire the new, metaparadigm is, preferably, from the beginning. We do not want to graduate analysts of one or another of the extant "persuasions." We seek, rather, to develop scholars and practitioners committed to the idea that a more sophisticated epistemology is required to do justice to the multiplicity of models and complexity of clinical data. We wish to foster an open, creative attitude toward theories new, old, excommunicated, and as yet unborn.

Although our approach is challenging, it is consistent with Freud's (1916) thought-provoking and still relevant attitudes on analytic education:

In my prospectus, it is true, I announced a course of "Elementary Lectures to Serve as an Introduction to Psychoanalysis" but what I had in mind was nothing in the nature of a presentation *in usum delphini*, which would give you a smooth account with all the difficulties carefully concealed, with the gaps filled in and the doubts glossed over, so that you might believe with an easy mind that you had learned something new. No, for the very reason of your being beginners, I wanted to show you our science as it is, with its unevennesses and roughnesses, its demands and hesitations. For I know it is the same in all sciences and cannot possibly be otherwise, especially in their beginnings. I know also that ordinarily instruction is at pains to start out by concealing such difficulties and incompleteness from the learner. But that will not do for psychoanalysis. ... If any one finds the whole thing too laborious or insecure, or if any one is accustomed to higher certainties or more elegant deductions, he need go no further with us. I think, however, that he should leave psychological problems entirely alone, for it is to be feared that in this quarter he will find impassable the precise and secure path which he is prepared to follow. (p. 101)

Our curriculum, like Freud's, is no smooth account with difficulties concealed, gaps filled, doubts glossed over. It is, rather, an exposition of analysis as it is, uneven and rough, full of demands, hesitations, difficulties, and incompleteness. Beyond that, it provides a model of what psychoanalysis might become.

Regrettably, Freud's pedagogic principles were not always followed by subsequent generations of educators. As a consequence, they needed to be reiterated a half century later by Loewald (1966/1980b). Reviewing Arlow and Brenner's (1964) classic text, Loewald observed that

They do present their views clearly and concisely and leave no doubt as to where they stand. But the reader is left with the impression that in their view issues are settled, concepts well defined and precise, problems well understood and in no need of further inquiry, many of which are neither as clear-cut nor as simple and one-dimensional as they are represented to be by the authors. (p. 54)

Loewald raised the question:

Should the beginner in the study of psychoanalysis be expected simply to learn the facts and concepts as known and understood by the experts, in a similar fashion to the conventional learning of anatomy; or should he, too, be asked to learn by seeing problems, raising questions, considering issues as open and in need of further understanding, looking at the observable material with fresh eyes? (p. 54)

He concluded his review by warning that "In this book, I am afraid, more issues are closed than opened, more answers given than questions raised and discussed in the spirit of scientific inquiry" (p. 54).

Freud delivered his "Introductory Lectures on Psycho-Analysis" to a group of university students from diverse faculties. His perception of the need to present analysis in all its unfinished complexity would apply even more to educating today's candidates. Despite the often staggering shortcomings of current psychiatric and psychological education, these students generally have some knowledge not only of psychoanalysis but usually of more than one of its schools. Many candidates arrive having already formed preliminary allegiances to some part object orientation. To expect them to park that knowledge until there may be a module in that area is not optimal pedagogy. They are usually ready to come to grips with controversies if provided a facilitating structure. We therefore present difficulties, questions, and issues that might seem to have been settled for fresh examination, much as Loewald (1966/1980b) recommended. We avoid creating the impression that issues have been resolved, concepts precisely defined, problems well understood, and therefore continuing investigation is not needed.

We invite candidates to embark on an exciting, intellectual adventure, expanding their familiarity not only with orientations they know but with others with which they may only be dimly, if at all, familiar. We challenge them not to acquire information about other frameworks as exotic cultures or quaint deviations but rather to try to integrate them with what they know. We might urge them to consider, for example, how the Mahlerian concept of symbiosis may relate to Kohut's archaic merger fantasies; Winnicott's subjective object; or Freud's concepts of primary narcissism, primary identification, and the purified pleasure ego. Are these constructs identical, overlapping, incompatible, or complementary? What other theorists have addressed similar phenomena? How do these constructs relate to assertions about infantile experience and abilities emanating from contemporary research (e.g., Stern, 1985)? What new questions are raised when attempting to integrate hitherto separate models?

PROVISIONAL EVALUATION

Having experimented with this curriculum for several years, some impressions can be offered with respect to its effectiveness. I will discuss these reflections in relation to contemporary critiques of analytic education.

Our curriculum is indeed challenging, particularly at the outset. This quality, with a dollop of "culture shock," might characterize any cutting-edge course requiring candidates to use their teeth. The program may initially be less daunting and more appealing to students who already have considerable knowledge of psychoanalysis and are, furthermore, familiar to some extent with the history of ideas, the clash of paradigms, the necessity of viewing phenomena from multiple perspectives, and the desideratum of pulling together diverse bodies of thought.

"We are entering a period of curricular flux and challenge," Wallerstein and Weinshel (1989) noted. "The challenge will come from the significant influx into the institutes of the American of new categories of students, many of them non-medical and from university graduate backgrounds. ... They will be academically and perhaps theoretically more savvy" (p. 358). The comparative-integrative framework is sufficiently ambitious, sophisticated, and intellectually rigorous to meet the demands, challenge, and satisfy even the most well-prepared candidates.

Although this program sometimes can be confusing and difficult, candidates still find it attractive. Many are drawn to it because it accords with their view of reality. Welcoming vigorous, creative intercourse between perspectives, some go to considerable lengths to partake of this experience (e.g., commuting several hours). They might have simplified their lives by enrolling in more conventional programs. They do not, however, seem to want to wait years before coming to grips with the fact that what they were taught did not even approximate the whole truth, that different schools—minimized, devalued, or ignored—are not simply irrelevant or wrong but contain keys important for the overall picture and for working successfully with a wide range of patients. "The coming generation of psychoanalysts ... will demand a clinical theory that accounts for the observations of every analytic faction" (Gedo, 1991, p. 137). That generation has arrived.

"I emerged from my training in the usual split condition, having been significantly influenced by teachers with varied and seemingly incompatible points of view." This quotation was not garnered from one of our graduates, but from Roy Schafer (1999). Our curriculum increases the likelihood that a graduate will not emerge so split. He or she may still feel unintegrated but will likely be securely on the way toward cohesion.

Graduates from this course will not likely be in a state of intellectual dissociation either. They may, however, experience a vibrant condition of conflict. This latter state, as Phillips (2002) emphasized, constitutes the essence of the democratic mind. The most difficult and cherished manner of containing multiplicity yet envisioned, democracy provides a suitable educational ethos for our time.

Appreciative of the artistic gift to intuit tendencies in cultural evolution, Kohut would likely have understood Leonard Cohen's (1993) prophesizing that democracy would be coming to America first, "the cradle of the best and of the worst" (p. 368). Shortly before Kohut's death, the historic lawsuit against mainstream psychoanalysis (American Psychoanalytic Association, International Psychoanalytic Association, New York Psychoanalytic Institute, and Columbia University Psychoanalytic Institute) finally resulted in greater freedom for institutes to accept psychologists and others into full training and for their faculty to teach outside their mainly medical institutes. In this new, more democratic zeitgeist, previously ignored and denigrated orientations simultaneously, and surely not just coincidentally, began to be recognized as well.

Today, the North American psychoanalytic scene is much more democratic than it was in days not long past. Although antidemocratic forces resisted these changes vigorously and often bitterly, once the suit was settled, almost everyone seemed to agree it was a good thing. Without the invigorating input of analysts from diverse backgrounds, the new consensus seemed to be that American analysis might be in a sorry state.

We may not always succeed in inculcating a questioning, critical, comparative-integrative perspective in our candidates to the extent we would like. Nonetheless, it appears that all graduates are richer for having been immersed in this endeavor. If, for example, a student entered our program devoted almost exclusively to Klein, and continued so, we believe she or he will, nonetheless, be a better, less naïve, more knowledgeable, broad-minded, creative Kleinian for having engaged in this challenging discourse. We would prefer that such graduates would also consider themselves self psychological, ego-psychological, interpersonal, and so forth. For some, however, this broadening may only happen to a limited extent. Nonetheless, postgraduation, the seeds of dialogue with other perspectives may continue to germinate and bear increasingly large fruit. They will be much further ahead and better prepared for this growth than those of exclusively "one persuasion or another."

TO THINK, PERCHANCE TO DREAM

It is not a matter of teaching the analyst-to-be what he has to know, Green (in Wallerstein, 1993) remarked, "but rather of making him want to think" or, more precisely, to want to "think about what the field of psychoanalysis is" (p. 174). Although our Institute does lead candidates to explore certain basics we feel they "have to know," our philosophy and curriculum do accord with Green's prescription concerning the needs of students (and, I would add, faculty and graduates). By encouraging candidates to think intensively not only about what the field is but also what it could/should become, we go significantly beyond his prescription.

In the evolution of science, prior to consensus, "A new man entering the field was inevitably exposed to a variety of conflicting viewpoints; he was forced to examine the evidence for each, and there always was good evidence," Kuhn (1970, p. 231) stated. "This earlier mode of education was obviously more suited to produce a scientist without prejudice, alert to novel phenomena, and flexible in his approach to his field." Our curriculum does not convey any illusion of consensus. It should, therefore, help produce clinical investigators with the desirable (one might say essential) characteristics Kuhn described.

In contrast, reflecting Loewald's lament, psychoanalytic education has all too often been presented as if all issues were settled, and as if there were but one worthwhile paradigm. A third of a century after his remarks, Wallerstein and Weinshel (1989) still bemoaned the fact that

> Our curricula have mostly rigidly reflected the dominant theoretical position of the particular training center, and there has been little incentive to explore the literature of other perspectives. Until the rise of Kohut's self psychology, institutes in the United States have been almost monolithically within the dominant ego psychology paradigm. (p. 357)

The situation was not better in most other jurisdictions. "Until recent years, institutes in Latin America have been equally single-mindedly Kleinian and/or Bionian" (Wallerstein & Weinshel, 1989, p. 357). Aside from the shared beginnings in reading Freud, there have been almost no points of correspondence in what is read and integrated into one's psychoanalytic understanding and identity between those trained in the North American and in the South American contexts (p. 357).

Rather than encouraging students to think about what psychoanalysis is, let alone what it could become, noncomparative institutes constrict candidates' vision to a particular sector of the field. In contrast to Kuhn's description of the desirable outcome achieved prior to consensus in a science, such institutes, presenting an illusion of consensus, produce scientist-practitioners less open to ideas, phenomena, and patients. There is no future in such illusion.

Emphasizing that there is much to be gained from avoiding premature closure, Zen master Suzuki (1970) observed famously that in the mind of the "beginner there are many possibilities, but in the expert's there are few" (p. 21). We hope to facilitate candidate's cultivating and maintaining their delightful openness to multiple possibilities as they immerse themselves in clinical practice and the unfolding disciplinary discourse.

Despite his emphasis on dependence, Winnicott (Phillips, 1988) believed theoretical allegiance risked compliance, thereby preempting the personal and unexpected. This danger would not accompany a comparative-integrative perspective because it offers a very different sort of theory with which to affiliate. It is more a container for models and a methodology for theory creation. One can invest dependence in it without sacrificing freedom to experience novel phenomena and generate innovative theories. In fact, it facilitates such desiderata, beseeching all to partake in the dialectic, never settling for a thesis without awareness of potential or actual antitheses. This attitude may, therefore, help resolve traditional conflicts between dependence and counterdependence, compliance and defiance, swallowing and not swallowing. It has the capacity to foster an intellectual orientation embracing multiple sides of an issue, transmuting limited, dichotomous thinking into limitless, dialectical cognition.

RONALD WHO?

Candidates immersed in a comparative-integrative field find it increasingly strange to encounter senior colleagues who know little about key figures and concepts from other schools. They would find it jarring to hear Sutherland (1989) say "I have a strong impression that Kohut read Fairbairn. (I have been informed his work was talked about in the Institute of which Kohut was a member)" (p. 31). It would be hard for them to imagine that any analyst could be unfamiliar with a major theoretician, that innovative thinkers might not be studied and debated at centers of analytic excellence. Sutherland's musings might seem tantamount to raising the surely outrageous possibility that Kohut, his colleagues, and his Institute might have formed a center of narrow-mindedness and illiteracy despite their other exemplary qualities.

Our faculty would not be shocked by Sutherland's contemplations. Familiar with the constricted scope of much analytic education, they would not find his uncertainty unnerving. They might, nonetheless, still shake their heads in dismay on being reminded that such narrow educational standards once existed and still do in many places.

Students and faculty might react similarly to Wallerstein's (1992) description of his training during the 1950s. Sticking exclusively to ego psychology, it adhered strictly to the straight and narrow line from Freud to Anna Freud to Hartmann:

> This tradition constituted the totality of the literature that was prescribed in our clinical and theoretical course work. ... We knew, of course, that there was a large Kleinian literature in the pages of the ... *International Journal,* but it was not assigned and was not read. (p. 11)

Beyond simply not assigning orientation-alien literature, in many quarters it was actively shunned. "We were trained to be completely orthodox, completely compliant. If any student asked any question whatever, he was put down and told that he was resistant" (Ostow, in Bergmann, 2000). "It was really a religious orthodoxy complete with a scripture and with ideas of heresy. It would tolerate no other religion" (p. 233).

Many still regard such a "straight line of theoretical progression" (Rangell, 1988, p. 329) as optimal a half century after Wallerstein and others endured it. Wallerstein himself eventually peeked at the apostatic pages in the *International Journal,* much to his and our benefit. Some of his colleagues did not.

Our candidates would be dumbfounded by Bacal's (1987) speculation that classically trained American analysts may not have studied British object

relations theorists. They would wonder whether iron curtains separated conti-
nents and institutes despite international associations, congresses, and journals.
That unsavory, heavy metal, cold war image would be reinforced if they were to
read Marmor's (in Silver, 2000) description of "the repressive teaching climate"
(p. 22) he suffered during his training from 1937 to 1941. His portrayal echoed
Ostow's arresting reflections.

> No deviation from orthodox theory was tolerated and any questioning of it was
> invariably attributed to idiosyncratic neurotic "resistance." As candidates, we were
> forbidden to do any psychoanalytic reading other than assigned readings and we
> were not even allowed to come to the monthly scientific meetings of the society
> because we might hear something that was contradictory to prescribed precepts
> that would endanger our indoctrination. (p. 22)

Although we still have far to go, we may breathe a collective sigh of relief that
we have come a long way from the heyday of psychoanalytic McCarthyism. A few
too many of us, however, having gotten one or another psychoanalytic religion,
may still be perpetuating the old fundamentalism.

Lamenting the impact of American psychoanalytic totalitarianism on his
contemporaries, Anton Kris renounced the repressive ambience in which he
trained:

> The astonishing number of casualities in our field, among our own colleagues, at
> the hands of their teachers and their Institutes (or the Institutes that would not
> have them, or would have them only under demeaning conditions) has been a pow-
> erful influence on my development. (pp. 228–229)

Bacal's disquieting speculation about American classical analysts of that era
not having studied British object relations theorists was, unfortunately, confirmed by V. Hamilton's (1996) research. One of her subjects informed her that

> Most Americans of my generation who did analytic training never read anything
> by the British. Nothing of Melanie Klein, that is sure, or the whole Independent
> group. We never read a single paper by Ian Suttie, Fairbairn, Guntrip, Bowlby,
> Balint. Winnicott, yes, but only a few papers, the "Transitional Object" paper, the
> "Hate in the Countertransference" paper, probably no others. And of the Anna
> Freud group, we read only Anna Freud, not Willie Hoffer or anybody else. So
> basically you could be fully educated psychoanalytically in this country and have
> read only Anna Freud's "The Ego and the Mechanisms of Defense" and one or two
> papers by Winnicott. (p. 92)

Borrowing Rilke's evocative phrase, Hugh MacLennan entitled his novel portraying the relationship between French- and English-speaking Canadians *Two*

Solitudes. Relationships between analytic subcultures were, in the past, characterized by multiple solitudes. In many places, it is still much that way.

Fortunately, there is some evidence that the ferrous veil is lifting, at least
on one side of the Atlantic. From her investigation, V. Hamilton (1996) noted
that "American analysts appeared to be more widely read. … They tended to be
familiar with the British literature, whereas the majority of British analysts were
not conversant with the American psychoanalytic literature" (p. 14). Comparative illiteracy is evidently not merely a matter of geography; it is also affected by
orientation. Kleinian/Bionians and self psychologists were, for example, particularly unlikely to have acknowledged being influenced by sources outside their
groups. New orientations can be as closed minded as old ones.

Whereas Bacal and Sutherland only had impressionistic data, V. Hamilton
gathered empirical evidence. Some of V. Hamilton's findings were perturbing,
perhaps even shocking; others were more encouraging. For example, "Nearly
all the American 'classical' Freudians acknowledged 'some' influence by British object relations, Kohut, and Klein" (p. 39). At the same time, it remained
disheartening to learn that they still acknowledged "no influence by Bion or self
psychology after Kohut" (p. 39). Interestingly, analysts who included children in
their practice were more widely read and influenced. Working with those who
still have a "beginner's mind" may keep one more open and curious.

A FUNNY THING HAPPENED ON THE WAY TO THE FORUM

Given our characteristically constricted training models, it is not surprising that
Wallerstein (1992) described theoretical schools as metaphors "heuristically use
ful to us in terms of our varying training *indoctrinations* [italics added] (p. 283).
Although it can be useful to regard theories as metaphors (fictions, provisional
hypotheses), it is surely high time we shifted the pedagogic balance away from
"indoctrination" toward education, preferably critical education.

Over a half century ago, Glover (King & Steiner, 1991) described the British
Institute as "a propaganda system of training" (p. 146). More recently, Kernberg
(1986) echoed similar sentiments:

> Psychoanalytic education today is all too often conducted in an atmosphere of
> indoctrination rather than of open scientific exploration. Candidates as well as
> graduates and even faculty are prone to study and quote their teachers, often ignor-
> ing alternative psychoanalytic approaches. The disproportionate amount of time
> and energy given to Freud, in contrast to the brief and superficial review of other
> theorists, including contemporary psychoanalytic contributions (other than those
> of dominant local authorities), and the rigid presentation and uncritical discussion
> of Freud's work and theories in the light of contemporary knowledge give the educa-
> tional process a sense of flatness. (p. 799)

Kernberg's scathing criticism was echoed by Wallerstein and Weinshel (1989). They reported frequent complaints from students, especially so-called "research candidates," that teachers are "narrowly professional and overly dogmatic" (p. 356). (The term *research candidate* may send a shudder down the spines of those who recall the era in which that label was part of a system designed to prevent clinical psychologists and some others from practicing psychoanalysis. From the comparative-integrative perspective, one might now think more positively of all candidates being, in a different sense, research candidates.) Unfortunately,

> Rather than the classroom and seminar being experienced as a place for critical challenge of espoused viewpoints for purposes of comparison and contrast, the students complain that they become arenas for the mastery of material presented by teachers who brook no questions and make no effort to set their presentations within the context of the problems of the field and the limitations of theory. (p. 356)

Difficulties that plagued psychoanalytic pedagogy long ago evidently continue to stifle students and the educational process in many quarters to this day.

In contrast, the comparative-integrative philosophy and curriculum virtually guarantee the climate of free scientific exploration Kernberg, Wallerstein and Weinshel, and other activists have advocated. Giving equal time to classical, object relational, self psychological, relational, and other models neither ignores diversity nor dedicates disproportionate time to Freud. Furthermore, the contrapuntal seminar structure makes it impossible to present the findings of the founding father uncritically, isolated from contemporary knowledge.

Freud and ego psychology only occupy half of our initial year (first seminar each evening). That perspective does, however, continue to be discussed in the remaining years, particularly as a Stream Two counterpoint to Kleinian, self psychological, and object relational approaches. This structure meets Wallerstein and Weinshel's desideratum that

> There *is* virtue in understanding the origin of psychoanalytic concepts and why changes have occurred in them. But it is also true that our students need not repeat the whole evolution, step by step. ... The challenge would be to fashion a curriculum that fully reflects present-day knowledge while inculcating an appreciation of its historical derivation to illuminate how and why our knowledge base has developed the way it has. (p. 357)

Some of Kernberg's trenchant criticisms and suggestions had been articulated by his analytic forefathers over a half century ago. Strachey, for example, advocated introducing candidates to various tendencies, none privileged. Strachey's (as cited in Steiner, 1985) "open forum" (p. 43) was, unfortunately, never realized. We have established one. We also developed his prescient idea much further, challenging candidates to not only become familiar with diverse tendencies but also to compare and contrast them, struggling to see whether they might be integrated. In keeping with Strachey's wish, no school is privileged. Special status is given only to a methodology.

Strachey's ideas were controversial in his day (and still are in some quarters): "Though the idea of an open forum for psychoanalytic teaching may seem tempting at first glance, I personally doubt whether it could be carried out effectively and whether the result would not fall far short of the intentions," Anna Freud (in Steiner, 1985) cautioned persuasively. If Institutes developed in that direction, she warned, "This would probably lead to the gradual dissolving of psychoanalytic societies, which, after all, were founded for the propagation and development of a more or less unified and consistent theory and method" (pp. 45–46). One can understand why Glover believed the British Institute was a propaganda system of training.

Anna Freud's angst may seem to have been assuaged by history. The fears she communicated have, however, by no means been laid completely to rest. Proudly tracing his intellectual lineage back to the one Anna Freud prized, Rangell (1988) asserted that the ascension of object relational and self psychological heresies in the analytic marketplace profoundly endangered the survival of psychoanalysis. Their appeal threatened to undo "the major scientific advance of the past century" (p. 314).

Rangell did not stand alone in his dread. Based on her research, V. Hamilton (1996) concluded, "Confusing pluralism with relativism, psychoanalysts—especially those involved in the administration of psychoanalytic institutions—fear that psychoanalysis will degenerate into anarchy" (p. 22). V. Hamilton's finding that administrators are particularly prone to this panic is especially disturbing. One would prefer the illusion that the most open-minded, cutting-edge thinkers establish the educational ambience for the next generation of analysts.

Even someone favoring pluralistic education, such as de Saussure, nonetheless was careful to caution that such dialogue is risky. Such discourse must always be carefully contained within consensually accepted bounds, she (in Wallerstein, 1993) warned, because "There is always the danger that airing our differences will lead to splitting" (p. 166).

Similarly, calling for "a broadened, more 'tolerant' curriculum," Wallerstein and Weinshell (1989, p. 359) anticipated that speaking up for these democratic values would provoke attack from traditionalists. Attempting to preempt that critique, they stated, "Again, we wish to guard against misinterpretation. We do not intend this to be read as a call for an uncritical ecumenicism that equates each psychoanalytic perspective in all particulars with every other" (p. 360). They emphasized they were, rather, talking of a curriculum that would be

still integrated into an overall coherent theoretical perspective, or perhaps a creative amalgam of two or more. We will then be able to see more broadly and deeply
how the same clinical phenomena are conceptualized within other theoretical systems with their differing idioms. (p. 360)

Despite their careful attempt to reassure those inclined to panic and those
likely to take offense, their proposal was roundly attacked by conservatives. Nersessian (in Furer et al., 1998) saw no merit in their proposal:

> Would, in fact, an effort toward increased integration of the various psychoana-
> lytic theories—i.e., the various metaphors—really serve to advance the science, as
> Wallerstein suggests? Taking just one example of such an effort, that of Kernberg to
> integrate Freudian, Kleinian, and other derivative theories, one would be hard-put
> to say that the effort advanced the understanding of the mind. In fact, I feel that
> such a movement toward making our curriculum an amalgam would be regressive.
> (p. 64)

Evidently, it is considered acceptable to simply disparage and dismiss decades of
labor by investigators of Kernberg's caliber whose contributions, in other circles,
are profoundly respected. Such wanton devaluation challenges one's optimism
concerning the chances of receiving an open hearing, in some groups, for the
idea of an open forum, let alone for a comparative-integrative approach.

Like de Saussure and others, Wallerstein and Weinshel could only speak in
rather vague terms of a broader, more tolerant curriculum that would somehow
be integrated into an "overall coherent theoretical perspective, or perhaps a creative amalgam of two or more" (p. 360). They did not have the advantage of a
more developed, comparative-integrative point of view. Rather than being indef-
inite or unduly cautious, our philosophy furnishes the necessary clear, concrete
container that can help mitigate against fears that enlivened discourse will inevitably degenerate into anarchy, incoherence, blurring, and hostile splitting. Based
on over 15 years of experience, rather than fearing an "open forum" would be the
beginning of the end of analytic societies, we see such discourse as heralding the
end of the beginning phase in the evolution of psychoanalytic thought.

FIDGETING IN THE SEMINARY

"A final symptom of the sick psychoanalytic institutes is the diminished creative
thinking and scientific productivity on the part of faculty, students, and graduates," Kernberg (1986) lamented (no doubt earning himself even more animus
from the administrators).

> A narrow intellectual frame determined by the locally prevalent views within the
> broad spectrum of psychoanalysis, intellectual toadyism or kowtowing to venerable

fathers of the local group … and discouragement of original thinking are painful indicators that not all is well with psychoanalytic education. (p. 806)

Kernberg's diagnosis was echoed a decade later by Renik (1996): "Given that most of us receive psychoanalytic education under almost exclusively local circumstances, parochialism is endemic among psychoanalysts and constitutes an important constraint on psychoanalytic discourse" (p. 40).

In contrast, a comparative-integrative curriculum, by its very structure, cannot be confined to any parochial, national, or even internationally prevalent view. Furthermore, our candidates spend three weekends per year with Visiting Faculty representing the leading edge of analytic thought. Intensive immersion with outside teachers for approximately a quarter of their instruction time ensures the intellectual frame will not be limited to the views of a few local, venerable fathers (or mothers).

Designed like technical schools, with overtones of the religious seminary, institutes are generally unsuitable for conveying either the art or science of analysis, Kernberg (1993) concluded. Wallerstein and Weinshel (1989) similarly bemoaned "the general trade-school approach in what should be a graduate academic training program" (p. 356). A more appropriate milieu would combine features of university and art school, Kernberg suggested. Others (e.g., Holtzman, 1976) argued for environments akin to university graduate programs. The University of Michigan's Department of Psychology offered an outstanding program like that, and a few universities, such as New York University and Adelphi, have long established, vibrant postdoctoral programs of that nature. The ambiance in such settings differs dramatically from the usual "trade school atmosphere" (Gedo, 1984, p. 169).

A comparative-integrative curriculum encourages wide-ranging inquiry, lively debate, and critical, integrative thinking as in the finest graduate schools. Like Wallerstein and Weinshel (1989), we endorse and, beyond that, have actually produced a template for "a more self-conscious effort in curriculum making to include the best and most appropriate elements of professional school and of graduate academic education without being the intellectual captive of either" (p. 358). Our model may help others seeking to move beyond the seminary.

GENERATIVITY VERSUS STAGNATION

Troubled by the state of "stagnation" in psychoanalytic pedagogy, in Kernberg's (1986) ideal model, candidates

would have to be exposed to and educated with a critical sense regarding all theories and techniques … and would have to accept the uncertainty resulting from a critical examination of all knowledge, theories, and procedures in the light of all available evidence. (p. 827)

They "would have to absorb not only Freud's writings, but also those of psycho-analysts who reached theoretical and/or technical conclusions that differ from Freud's" (Kernberg, 1986, p. 811). A comparative-integrative curriculum meets these requirements. Students not only tolerate the uncertainty entailed but actually find the process challenging and satisfying.

Sharing Kernberg's concerns, Michels (1998) stated that

The dominant current institute structure is designed ideally to protect known truths, but not designed ideally to examine them, nor to modify and develop them. We may expect to see institute structures that are more attuned to these latter goals. (p. 5)

Enter the comparative-integrative structure. It fulfills all the new aims deemed essential by Michels. Through its dialectical method, it simultaneously preserves, negates, and transforms established "truths."

The comparative-integrative philosophy has a stimulating, beneficial impact not only on candidates but also on faculty. Teachers become familiar with per-spectives other than those they have habitually favored. This encounter may be unsettling, but there is usually a positive attitude toward such growing pains. Faculty begin to look inside conceptual doors they had never opened and oth-ers that had been closed prematurely. Instructors who dialogued mostly with "their own kind" become open to and interested in new conversations. Crossing boundaries, they discover new possibilities. As one senior teacher expressed it after a lively, challenging seminar, "I now know what I do not know." His com-ment reflected an educational ambience coconstructed with candidates, evoking useful, Socratic humility and commitment to continuing learning.

Instructors study articles assigned by faculty leading the seminar before or after them. They consider how their readings, clinical data, theoretical formula-tions, and interventions might be similar or different, how they might be inte-grated, obstacles to such synthesis, and so forth. The curriculum thus fosters fertilization as opposed to what Kernberg (1986) described as the more common "cross-sterilization." This latter quality is manifest in the

suspicious and envious way in which new ideas are received, faculty fearfulness of expressing new ideas that might challenge local dogma, and the general collusion in public applause of rehashed formulations, while privately many depreciate the monotonous repetition of concepts that, by the same token, also reassure the fac-ulty that nothing new is threatening their present convictions. (p. 806)

Kernberg's concern with stagnation was taken in different directions and amplified ominously by Meehl (1993): "Increasing heterogeneity and the unanswered challenges to technique and doctrine suggest that psychoanalysis may be a degenerating program" (p. 299), he warned. Several years later, a psychoanalytic researcher, Bornstein (2001), proclaimed even more bluntly that "Psychoanalysis is dying, and maybe it should" (p. 3).

From our perspective, it is only the lack of creative dialogue between viewpoints that is ominous, degenerative, and moribund. A comparative-integrative curriculum fears neither heterogeneity nor challenges to technique and doctrine. In fact, it welcomes both to ensure fructifying discourse and generative synthesis. If psychoanalysis is or was dying, the comparative-integrative perspective predicts a rousing resurrection.

Institutes must see their task as the creation of knowledge rather than simply transmission, Kernberg (1993) asserted. Seminars should stimulate new ideas. Candidates and faculty should be encouraged and rewarded for contributing to the development of psychoanalytic science, he said. A comparative-integrative curriculum fosters—even forces—such creative thinking. It stirs fertile ground in the minds of candidates and teachers in which new ideas are likely to take root and grow. We expect our model will stimulate increasing contributions from candidates, graduates, and faculty. There is some evidence it is already having this effect on students. For example, in Society scientific meetings during one recent year, half the presentations were by senior candidates.

The task posed by this curriculum is as challenging to faculty as it is to students. Rather than simply being delivered and received, knowledge is cogenerated by teachers and candidates. Struggling to master this perspective, faculty are perceived, and view themselves, not only as instructors but also as students and investigators. Faculty and candidates feel, like Modell (1985),

> We are now ready to begin the task that will be completed by future generations; that is, to step outside our respective traditions, to find areas of common agreement and understanding that have been masked by the idiosyncratic language and concepts of a particular "school." (pp. 99–100)

Reverberations and Amplifications

Among contemporary critiques of psychoanalytic pedagogy, we devoted particular attention to Kernberg's because it was clear, strong, and by no means idiosyncratic. His reveille resonated with plaints from leading educators around the world. Summarizing the Fifth IPA Conference of Training Analysts, "Between Chaos and Petrifaction: Problems in the Integration of Different Theoretico-Clinical Frameworks in the Formation of the Psychoanalyst," Wallerstein (1993) reported, "What is shared by these seven quite disparate presentations from so many ideologically and geographically diverse quarters is a widespread dissatis-faction with so many aspects of, and so many consequences of, the operation of our extant tripartite training structure" (p. 177).

Although participants at that symposium favored introducing greater diver-sity into curricula, they were not very specific as to how this could or should be done. Believing pluralism enriched education, de Saussure felt models needed to be taught by people believing in them. If an institute lacked such individuals, it should invite visiting speakers. Points of disagreement could be debated in scien-tific meetings. Like Strachey so long ago, Kligerman espoused equal teaching of all perspectives. Apart from such general support for change, there was a dearth of detail as to how diversification might actually be accomplished. In contrast, the comparative-integrative approach provides a clear model of how one might redress these fundamental problems in ways that far exceed interest in, tolerance of, or even considerable appreciation of multiplicity.

Outside a comparative-integrative perspective, pluralism may have woefully little to do with integration. "In much of Latin America psychoanalytic pedagogy is directed toward the candidates learning several methods of practicing psycho-analysis in anticipation that the candidates, in time, will select a method that best matches the candidates' emotional and intellectual needs" (Calder, 1998, p. 71). In like manner, Bernardi and Nieto (1989, as cited in Calder, 1998) advocated "a pluralistic atmosphere which will allow each candidate to adopt his preferred theory" (p. 72). According to Rangell (2000),

> Almost all institutes today … appeal to potential candidates with the promise to represent all theories equally in their training. In the spirit of democracy, the stu-dents then gravitate to the theoretical system with which they feel the most per-sonal kinship. (p. 452)

Although there may be diversity in such curricula—a major advance over repres-sive, monolithic structures—there is little emphasis on rigorous, critical thinking and especially, dialectical synthesis. In our program, we can live reasonably com-fortably with the idea that some of our graduates may come to or continue to pri-marily embrace one particular paradigm, but that is not our ideal outcome.

At the previously referred to Training Conference, Infante (in Wallerstein, 1993) articulated some of the crucial questions:

> How is it possible in the teaching of psychoanalysis to reconcile the need to main-tain a solid common foundation with the necessary openness to new ideas, which is an essential condition for scientific progress? … To achieve this goal, "It is neces-sary not only to reaffirm the spirit of pluralism and tolerance but to structure our institutions so as to ensure that this spirit prevails. (p. 172)

Infante did not specify how one might organize institutes to achieve these ends. I believe it necessary to spell out practical means for accomplishing these desiderata. Otherwise, they will remain lofty, but unrealized dreams. We must develop prototypes and then expose them to discussion, critique, evaluation, reality testing, refining, improving, and replacing as experience dictates. Otherwise, we may stay forever arrested at the point Anna Freud advocated over a half century ago, namely, that although an open forum might seem reasonable and tempting, it probably could not be carried out and might be dangerous to the existence of institutes. In contrast to A. Freud's conservative pessimism, we situate ourselves closer to Gedo's (1984) more optimistic, experimental outlook. "We are most likely to emerge from our time of troubles if a hundred flowers are indeed allowed to bloom and if the most viable alternatives are given an opportunity to prove themselves in action" (p. 170).

Moving far beyond generalities, I furnished a model balancing tradition and innovation. My concern with that very tension occupied the first half of this book. In the second half, I demonstrated one way institutes can not only affirm pluralism but actually enshrine it and something greater—that is, a challenging, comparative-integrative philosophy—at the core of their values, modus operandi, and being. I have also shown how one can create a curriculum to ensure that this vitalizing spirit prevails. Although there may be other ways of accomplishing these aims, they do not seem to have been detailed in the sparse literature devoted to this topic. This model may stimulate others to develop and share their seeds, their incipient ideas on these matters so that we may be privileged to witness the glorious spectacle of a hundred tall flowers sprouting up in the analytic garden.

THE LONG HAUL

The initial allure of this curriculum seems to hold. Graduates have generally reported that their education has been intellectually exciting and clinically valuable. They have been also, of course, generous with their criticism, enabling us to continuously reconsider and refine the program. Overall, they share our "strong dislike of simplifying things at the expense of truthfulness" (Freud, 1916, p. 282).

Faculty, too, continue to find it stimulating to teach in this program. The curriculum structure, in itself, poses challenging questions as do candidates and other faculty. Teachers from other institutes have sometimes remarked on the intellectual curiosity and lively, respectful discussions, both theoretical and clinical, in our classes. Their kindness, no doubt, is operative, but we may also attract a certain type of candidate (and faculty). We do believe our philosophy and curriculum help bring out certain characteristics in students and teachers, creating a milieu different from "the stifling rigidity, the suffocating indoctrination" (Lussier, in Wallerstein, p. 174), the "infantilisation, stultification and suffocation of autonomy and creativity" (Infante, in Wallerstein, p. 165) that are apparently still common in many institutes.

It will naturally take more time before we can say how successful our experiment has been and in what ways it could be improved. Optimally this trial should be replicated in other centers. That hope is one reason propelling writing this book. In the meantime, we are encouraged by our experience to date to feel we were correct in emulating Freud's (1916) example by refusing to present our candidates "a smooth account with all the difficulties carefully concealed, the gaps filled in and the doubts glossed over" (p. 108). Although our orientation could be criticized as cumbrous, we would nonetheless follow Freud in saying, "If anyone finds the whole thing too laborious or insecure, or if anyone is accustomed to higher certainties and more elegant deductions, he need go no further with us" (p. 101). We would also concur with the founder that such an individual should probably "leave psychological problems entirely alone" (p. 101).

ETERNAL EVOLUTION

No sooner had the inkjet sprayed its substance on the preceding page than our Curriculum Committee (which I chair) decided to act on some candidates' criticism. Particularly some relatively new to the field seemed to find the contrapuntal structure difficult. As one put it, "I don't have a grasp of any of the schools, so how can I appreciate how they challenge and oppose each other?" He did allow that during his second year, he began to get the hang of it. Nonetheless, representing his class on the Curriculum Committee, he relished the proposal of having the first year consist largely of modules outlining the major schools of analytic thought, following the sequence in which these various branches came into being. Only toward the end of the year would a case be studied from the comparative-integrative point of view in an attempt to pull together and integrate the diverse paradigms that had been studied during the year. Subsequent years would look at topics and cases from multiple perspectives in the comparative-integrative spirit.

In his study of curricula for the American Psychoanalytic Association, Kohut (1962) found that institutes either followed a chronological or a thematic structure. We have always combined these approaches. With our most recent revision, our first year follows the historical approach; subsequent years have a more thematic emphasis. Whatever the balance between these approaches, the superordinate need is to hold these dimensions and work with them within a comparative-integrative framework.

When we announced this curriculum change to our newest group of candidates, several were upset because they had been looking forward to the former structure they had heard or read about. Nonetheless, at our year-end meeting with them, there was a high level of satisfaction with this modified approach. There will, no doubt, be more changes in years ahead as we learn from experience and strive to meet the needs of new generations of students.

7

The Class Struggle

Hell is other people.

Jean-Paul Sartre, *No Exit*

On reading the first draft for this book, Dr. Lewis Aron suggested illustrating how a class might be conducted from a comparative-integrative point of view. Imagining such exposition might interest not just an eminent educator but others as well. I cast my mind's eye back in time, seeking a suitable exemplar. The last seminar I had taught with our first-year candidates sprang to mind. It had been interesting (as hopefully all are). The selection seemed reasonably random and, above all, freshest in my memory.

A few days later, I began a continuous case seminar with our third-year candidates. It struck me that it, too, would make an instructive chapter. The analyst presenting the material felt, however, that confidentiality mitigated against opening her consulting room to the public unless the material were disguised to the point that, I thought, it would lose too much authenticity. I therefore returned to the previous seminar.

Although the students and I believed at the time that we were in a class by ourselves, it seems appropriate now to open the doors to our larger professional community. Please come in and join us in our learning adventure.

Setting and Educational Goals

Eight candidates in our first-year class possessed a wide range of theoretical sophistication and clinical experience. Most were from medical and psychological backgrounds; a couple came from other academic/professional areas. For example, one was a professor of education at a university a couple hours' drive from Toronto where he also headed a major interdisciplinary program in social science. He had experience creating classroom milieus for troubled youth and used psychoanalytic ideas in his many publications. Another candidate had a strong background in religion, literature, and high school counseling. She had recently completed training at a self psychological institute and wanted to expand her clinical and theoretical knowledge base.

My goal in this 90-minute seminar was to expose the candidates to some inter-esting ideas, hoping they would find them stimulating and useful. I wanted to provide some context for these concepts, highlight some points, encourage them to consider these ideas in relation to their clinical work and theoretical knowledge, provide some clinical illustrations, and answer any queries they might have based on the assigned material they had read in preparation for the class. I thought these goals were largely achieved, but readers will be able to come to their own judgment in that regard.

Guntrip in Historical Context

Our first year commences with an overview of comparative-integrative philoso-phy. After this introduction, there is a module on the Freudian Framework fol-lowed by seminars on transitional figures who played important roles in shifting emphasis from drive/structure to a more relational/structure perspective (e.g., Abraham, Ferenczi). A module on the Kleinian Development is then followed by British Object Relations theory. The seminar in this chapter came after classes on Fairbairn.

Although some candidates like to dive right in to discuss the material they read for the seminar, most prefer having the instructor provide prefatory remarks to frame the topic before inviting questions and comments. Consequently, to position Guntrip in the history of psychoanalytic ideas, I mentioned that he was important, in part, because his inaugural book, *Personality Structure and Human Interaction* (1961), opened a window for many people. It afforded them a clear view of the seminal works of M. Klein, Fairbairn, Winnicott, and others. Published in New York, this volume was eye opening for those whose purview had been limited by the hegemony of the North American, ego psychological perspective.

With respect to our comparative-integrative sensibility, Guntrip's book on psychic structure and relationality bore a significant subtitle: *The Developing Synthesis of Psycho-Dynamic Theory* (my underlining). With those words, he announced and initiated an important project. Mitchell (1988) later continued that crucial undertaking in such works as his *Relational Concepts in Psycho-analysis: An Integration*. In the 27 years between those publications, there had been sufficient maturation in the field such that the "developing synthesis" could become "an integration." Our Institute strives to nurture the sensibility Guntrip and Mitchell fostered.

Eight years after his first book, Guntrip's (1969) *Schizoid Phenomena, Object Relations and the Self* established him as a compelling, innovative clinical writer in his own right. In this second book, he carefully combined rich, detailed obser-vations of behavior, symptoms, affects, and dreams of patients, supplemented by occasional excursions into philosophy and literature, to provide a vivid base for his theoretical formulations.

As with all British Object Relations theorists, Guntrip's writing helps one better understand early experience and its subsequent manifestations in adults. Venturing boldly into relatively uncharted waters, these pioneers have provided valuable maps of strange new worlds. As those relational realms became increasingly familiar and sensible to us, we could better comprehend and help patients.

Guntrip's second book appeared shortly before Kohut's volumes focused the psychoanalytic community's attention increasingly on the self, the concept Guntrip had positioned so prominently in his title. Given his early grasp of the centrality of this construct, one can readily understand why self psychologists Bacal and Newman (1990) acknowledged him in their book, *Theories of Object Relations: Bridges to Self Psychology,* as one of the major architects of that link to their favorite destination.

The key distinction Kohut (1977) articulated between Guilty (oedipal) and Tragic (preoedipal) Man was clearly prefigured by Guntrip. Guntrip distinguished the moral standpoint of the oedipal level, concerned with guilt and the control of impulses, from the fear and futility characterizing the schizoid situation. In that premoral position, there is no well-developed, integrated self-possessing sufficient ego strength to enable the individual to accept moral responsibility and social education.

Within the British Independent Group around the same time, Balint (1968) also discussed these two different levels. He referred to them as the oedipal or triangular level versus the area of basic *fault.* This latter term suggests a fundamental personality flaw analogous to a geological fault line or structural weakness in a crystal. This vivid, evocative phrase, pointing to a potentially tragic ego weakness resonates with Fairbairn's use of the word *schizoid* to highlight early splits in core personality formation.

Like these British Middle Group authors, Kohut wanted to give the earliest level its own name (Tragic Man) rather than defining it in relation to a later, privileged phase as was commonly done in Freudian circles. Feeling he needed to devote his energy to spelling out his own thoughts, Kohut was not inclined to cite contributions of like-minded authors. He left those comparative-integrative reflections to others who would come after him.

Regarding the link between British object relations theory and self psychology, Mitchell held a different view than Bacal and Newman. From Mitchell's more encompassing perspective, the work of Guntrip and other British nonaligned theorists, rather than being steps toward self psychology, is better viewed, together with self psychology, as contributing to a more overarching, relational psychoanalysis. From this perspective, the Kohutian self's relationships with its self-objects are a form of object relations, albeit less differentiated than some other types. Self-objects have something in common with other objects that are not perceived as having fully developed distinctiveness and subjectivity (e.g., Freudian narcissistic objects and objects of primary identification, Kleinian part objects, and ego psychology's need-satisfying objects and auxiliary egos).

Guntrip's integrative, relational outlook was strikingly similar to the one Mitchell later promulgated. Abundantly clear in the British writer's first two books, this constructive perspective was further elaborated in his final volume, *Psychoanalytic Theory, Therapy and the Self.* He emphasized the significant roles Sullivan and Erikson played in North America, paralleling those of Klein and the object relations theorists in the United Kingdom. In his opinion, Klein and Erikson were transitional figures who made great leaps forward but never completely escaped what he, like Mitchell, regarded as constraining, outdated, biological, drive theory. In contrast, he believed Sullivan and the British Middle Group succeeded fully in advancing the discourse to a truly person-centered, psychological level.

This final book was based on lectures he had been invited to deliver to the William Alanson White Institute in New York City. Those talks and their subsequent publication constituted further, significant steps exposing North Americans to the seminal contributions of Klein, Fairbairn, Winnicott, and others. His integrative approach would have helped his audience understand how their interpersonal approach fit with object relational theories in an ever-widening synthesis.

Given that Guntrip delivered those lectures in the home of interpersonal analysis, they probably sparked interest in his audience in further integrating object relational and interpersonal thinking. One might imagine young analysts such as Greenberg, and especially Mitchell, important members of the White community, being inspired by that historical event to pursue even more diligently their interest in studying and synthesizing these perspectives.

Guntrip's Clinical Theory

The Lost Heart of the Self
Having recently studied Fairbairn, you will have grasped from tonight's readings that Guntrip extended the work of his first analyst (Fairbairn) on ego and object splitting. In the first, Fairbairnian fracture, the originally unitary ego withdraws from objects in the external world because they are felt to be intolerable. Because they are also desperately needed, the ego does not sever connections from them entirely. Instead, it retreats to an imaginary realm where it can preserve these vital attachments and attempt to master the problem. The ego strives to not have its cake and eat it too.

In the complex, internalized struggle Fairbairn portrayed, the psyche strategically split itself into libidinal, antilibidinal, and central egos, each with a corresponding object. Guntrip believed that this arrangement did not bring final resolution to the thorny problems with which the now divided self continued to struggle. Difficulties that originated in the external world proceeded internally in an equally problematic manner. Consequently, he envisioned, a further split occurred. The libidinal ego, itself, divided. One portion of it remained entrenched in bad internal object relations, much as Fairbairn described. The other, new, detached segment retreated even further from reality, seeking to escape even from internalized object relations. This regressed part of the self yearned to return to something safely encompassing, like the prenatal state, far removed from the maddening world of relationships

Resisting

Guntrip's regressed ego resembles what his second analyst, Winnicott (1963), referred to as the incommunicado, true self, forever isolated, not wanting to be found. Winnicott's nonrelating self was rather mysterious. Guntrip made it much easier to understand this enigmatic entity. With vivid images and stories, he fleshed out how, where, and why this "lost heart of the self" heads and hides. You may recall, for example, his patient's dream in which he refused to be born. Doctors and others tried everything to pull him out, even enlisting teams of horses with ropes. All efforts proved futile. The regressed ego wants nothing to do with the human world.

The greatest treatment resistance, Fairbairn believed, was based on attachment to bad objects. This problem embodied the force Freud (1916–1917) described as adhesiveness of the libido. In contrast to his mentor (Fairbairn), Guntrip envisioned the supreme source of resistance as the desire to retreat from all relationships including bad, internal ones. His forlorn ego objected to all objects.

Immersing oneself in the early, disturbed realm of object relations that leads to such resistance, one might recall Freud's "narcissistic neuroses." He believed such patients were beyond the reach of analysis because they could not form a transference relationship. From a Guntripian perspective, the problem would not so much be that they cannot form a transference (deficit) but rather that they will not (conflict).

Retreat from object relations is not only desirable; it is also horrifying. This dangerous pull is resisted. It is felt as ego weakness, provoking terror of dissolution. In the context of such bivalence, continuing attachment to bad objects was viewed by Guntrip as a defense against the more profound, regressive wish. He usefully detailed many manifestations of the fight against these threatening, passive yearnings such as compulsive activity and insomnia.

At times there is a more positive note in Guntrip's ideas about the ultimate aim of the regressed ego. Sometimes, he believed, this lost heart of the self embodies the hope that the sought-after state of vegetative passivity—similar to the one that fostered primordial, intrauterine growth—might facilitate contemporary recuperation. With respect to this locus for restoration of the self, he mirrored Winnicott's (1963/1972) "true self" placed into cold storage, hoping some day it may be able to emerge, thaw, and resume development in a more facilitating milieu.

De-Attachment Research

Those of you familiar with the work of the Robertsons and Bowlby (1979) on separation and loss may recognize that they have dealt with phenomena pertinent to those that captured Fairbairn and Guntrip's attention. They described young children struggling with relational frustration pursuing turbulent paths from protest through despair to detachment. The first two phases in that sequence (protest, despair) involve something similar to the sadomasochistic attachment to objects that Fairbairn described.

In protest, angry interaction with the external object world continues. Noisy claims on others represent continuing engagement. One can understand why Winnicott (1967) viewed phenomena such as delinquency as a sign of hope.

Despair, on the other hand, signals giving up on the environment. As the self loses heart, bad object relations are abandoned. The individual now has diminished interest and energy for external objects. These primal attachments do, however, persist in a deeper, less visible preoccupation in the internal world.

If this deteriorating slide from protest to despair is not remedied by a suitable object becoming available, the third phase in this downhill sequence will be reached. The journey to this final, dangerous detachment parallels Guntrip's portrait of the trajectory of the regressed ego.

Attachment researchers, like the two Marys, Ainsworth and Main, built on Bowlby's (1979) foundational labor. They have shown how children develop idiosyncratic attachment styles to cope with relational frustration. Their longitudinal studies have demonstrated how these distorted, defensive patterns can be passed on intergenerationally and can be terribly enduring. Bearing Fairbairn and Guntrip's contributions in mind, these attachment patterns might well be called *detachment* styles.

These researchers might describe the semidetached children who have begun consolidating solutions to their dilemmas in the third phase of the previously mentioned sequence as having insecure attachment, avoidant type. Guntrip might have regarded these descriptors as understatement. He would also likely have underscored the chronic approach–avoidance conflict enshrined in such structures. Apparent characterological stability would be based, in his view, on an underlying balance of conflicting forces, a struggle between attachment and detachment drives.

Going far beyond the primarily behavioral level of description usefully furnished by the Robertsons, Bowlby, and the attachment researchers, Guntrip's refined observations and theorizing help us understand why, how, and where the detaching ego goes, how it separates not only from external object relations but also from internal ones, and so forth. Whereas Bowlby's group spoke somewhat vaguely of "internal working models" paralleling or underlying behavior, Guntrip fleshed out important aspects of these schemas and described modifications they undergo. As a result of his efforts, these working (and not working) models have become much more clear, comprehensible, and useful in the therapeutic situation.

Class Discussion: Question A

Dr. A (a pseudonym for one of the candidates) asked if Guntrip's regressed ego could be related to Freud's death instinct. I responded that there were similarities and differences. The death drive was a highly speculative, biological hypothesis. Freud (1920/1955b) imagined that when the original life form evolved out of inanimate matter, it found itself in a terribly challenging position. It might, consequently, have "longed" to return to the simpler, unalive state. This primal conflict between pro-life and pro-death forces was, Freud hypothesized, built into the cellular foundations of all subsequent beings.

In contrast to Freud's metapsychological hypothesis based on a unicellular entity emerging from some primordial soup, Guntrip's regressed ego derived from his endeavor to comprehend actual human reactions to difficult experiences with early caretakers. His concern was the transition from the relative calmness of uterine life to postnatal turbulence. Drawing inferences from dreams and other clinical material, he talked from an experience-near level. Freud's musings about the death instinct came from a very different, experience-distant place.

In the struggle Freud depicted between Eros and Thanatos, desire for death would always, ultimately, be victorious. In famously disturbing words, he (1920) proclaimed, "The aim of all life is death" (p. 38). Guntrip was similarly shocking in declaring that the fundamental human desire was to flee all relationships. In their tragic views of the human condition, these theorists assigned similar weight to profoundly regressive tendencies.

Freud's death instinct attracted more criticism than any of his other ideas. Guntrip's dark theory deserves equal challenge. My criticism would not be that his contribution was wrong, but rather that he overgeneralized. The phenomenon he described may be very important with some patients. The problem is that he increasingly tended to see this issue as the fundamental problem of all patients and, for that matter, all human beings.

Overextension of a construct is a danger to which many analytic theorists have succumbed. This process can lead not only to overshadowing but even to excluding other valid ideas. This problematic relationship between innovation and tradition (explored in Part I) is one reason a comparative-integrative approach is essential. Without it, one is in danger of losing the necessary dialectical tension between one's view and others. One risks becoming ensorcelled in one's construct.

Portraying a fundamental struggle between progressive and regressive thrusts, Freud and Guntrip have highlighted a key dimension of human experience. In a past life, I regularly utilized the Anna Freud (Hampstead) Metapsychological (Developmental) Profile. The item in that thorough assessment instrument concerning the balance between progressive and regressive forces struck me as most important. At that time, I was working primarily with profoundly disturbed children. For them, this conflict is a most vital matter, diagnostically and prognostically.

Guntrip's and Freud's belief in the supraordinate position of their regressive drives, in conflict with life forces, can be related to Matte-Blanco's (1988) interesting ideas about the nature of mind. Viewing Freud's death drive as a bi-logical conception rather than an instinct, Matte-Blanco believed important light could be cast on the nature of life. (I am indebted to Skelton's [2000] recent contribution on this subject.)

The radically different postnatal milieu precipitates intense desires and impulses that are "asymmetrical" (Matte-Blanco, 1988). The newborn's new world is one of differences and separation. In contrast, "symmetry," sameness, and unity prevail prenatally. Infants seek to avoid conflict between these radically divergent experiences by giving each its due. A division is created in the psyche. At the conscious level, asymmetry, rational logic, and either/or thinking is embraced. At a deeper (unconscious) level, symmetry, stillness, unity, and both/and thinking prevail.

Although Matte-Blanco's terminology is unique, his conceptualization parallels Freud's. Conscious life becomes increasingly divided in terms of stable categories such as space and time, Freud emphasized, whereas the unconscious remains fluid, subject to condensation, displacement, and timeless. In the unconscious, "Contraries are not kept apart but treated as though they were identical" (p. 169). With such ideas, Freud described how sameness and unity (symmetry) prevail unconsciously, whereas opposite conditions (asymmetry) obtain in consciousness.

The simultaneous functioning of symmetrical and asymmetrical modes in different parts of the mind produces paradoxes. From the conscious, spatiotemporal point of view, life and death are opposites; in the unconscious, they may be identical. An individual courting death may feel on the way to life everlasting.

From Freud's Darwinian perspective, life strives to preserve itself; from the point of view of the death instinct, life aims at self-destruction.

Freud's death drive strives for a previous state that, for Matte-Blanco, was the still, indivisible, symmetrical mode. There must almost inevitably be confusion between this mode and death, Matte-Blanco wrote, for people are used to identifying lack of movement with mortality. I am reminded in this regard of the French words for still life painting, *nature morte*. A literal translation of the Gallic expression would be dead nature. The French seem to have drawn on the natural confusion between inanimacy and death that Matte-Blanco referred to to create this term.

In view of the preceding, it is not surprising that yearning for symmetry and stillness in a turbulent, asymmetrical world might be experienced as a dangerous, implosive force threatening to pull the individual backwards and inwards to an undifferentiated state (Grotstein, 1996). This fusional anxiety can transform the image of an idealized womb offering safety into an ominous black hole guaranteeing destruction.

Concern with contrasting forms of logic and distinctions between conscious and unconscious modes of experience aligns Matte-Blanco with Freud. Emphasis on differences between prenatal and postnatal existence coupled with yearnings to stay in or return to the earlier experiential mode aligns him with Guntrip. Belief in how the continuing pull of symmetry can be experienced as both profoundly attractive and dangerous puts him at one with both Freud and Guntrip's views on the powerfully ambivalent nature of regressive urges.

Question B

Each system, Dr. B noted, seemed to posit a primal bad object. Freud's (and Klein's) was the death instinct, an internal force threatening annihilation. Dr. B wondered about the nature of Guntrip's bad object.

I pointed out that in contrast to the death drive, Fairbairn's bad object was initially an aspect of the external parent. The intolerable features of this caretaker were transposed to the internal theatre. This solution eventually became, for Guntrip, the next problem. Beleaguered by endless struggles with internal objects, part of the ego longed to escape. This desire to flee into objectless oblivion, in turn, became a major problem. The siren call of the schizoid solution transmogrified into Guntrip's uber bad object. It acquired all the ambivalence initially experienced with respect to the external bad object. Part of the ego therefore clung to the sadomasochistic relationships of the internal world to avoid being consumed by the desire for regressive retreat into the ebony hole of the womb.

Like Freud's death instinct, Guntrip's bad object was also an internal force or situation. Guntrip's was, however, derived from unmanageable experience in object relationships (initially external, subsequently internal). Freud's supremely bad object, the death drive, was, in contrast, derivative of a more abstract, speculative, inherited, biological base. The external situation reflected was one that came into being long before humans even existed.

Quite apart from Freud's controversial death instinct theory, Freud believed the first human object is, in a sense, inherently bad. It is, in fact, the experience of badness that makes it an object. Like Matte-Blanco, Freud believed infants are unaware of separate objects until they experience painful frustration. At that moment, they become aware of something distinct from themselves. The very first "reality" separate from themselves is thus, simultaneously, the first object, and it is not good. Resonating with this primal relationship between reality and bad objects, T. S. Eliot reminded us (in "Burnt Norton") that "Human kind cannot bear very much reality." In sync with such ideas, Fairbairn, Guntrip, and others have emphasized the ego's desperate flight from reality to inner world.

This first, frustrating, frightening, painful encounter with the world of separate entities becomes the basis for the infant's conception of the object world. In this view, bad objects (Klein's paranoid-schizoid position) precede good ones. Reality sucks. Alternatively, it bites. Sometimes the best one can do, in provocative defiance, is to challenge the bad object to "bite me." These common expressions capture oral components of our inaugural experience of externality. Whether reality sucks, bites, or rocks, it is surely spiced up by powerful projections of infantile, oral-aggressive drive derivatives.

In Erikson's (1950) psychosocial elaboration of Freudian theory, this fundamental, harsh aspect of object relations provided the basis for profound suspicion. This sentiment was destined to be an essential ingredient in the infant's first dialectical challenge: trust versus mistrust. This core opposition has much to do with the crucial balance between progressive and regressive tendencies.

Among contemporary relational thinkers, Hoffman (1998) penned thoughts most relevant to this discussion concerning the uber bad object. For Hoffman, this role belonged to none other than death itself. Like Erikson's inaugural and continuing conflict between trust and mistrust, Hoffman described a similarly crucial dialectic between living and dying. Hoffman's insightful perspective on mortality skillfully blends existentialism with object relations theory.

Maintaining a watchful eye over all humans, even before we are born, death stalks us throughout the life cycle. It waits for opportune moments, confident its day will come. As time goes by, like the casino, it always gains the upper hand. In this universal drama, the roles of time and death merge easily. Contemplating the conclusion of each calendar year, we conjure up images of elderly Father Time with his scythe. At the end of the day, time triumphs, harvesting us like hay. We are destined to return to the symmetrical, inanimate, timeless realm. Unlike the

Grim Reaper's companion, the celebrated first babe of the new year, it is not clear whether we are slated for rebirth.

Question C

"Hasn't Freud's death instinct been thoroughly discredited" Dr. C asked? Lacking scientific validity, she thought it had been abandoned by all except diehard Kleinians who had isolated themselves and failed to keep abreast with developments in psychoanalysis and the broader scientific discourse. I replied that her strong view was shared by many. From her perspective, I suspected, Guntrip's (or Matte-Blanco's) idea of dangerous regressive forces and our discussion of bad objects might seem more scientifically acceptable and clinically useful. Dr. C agreed.

Nonetheless, I suggested, for all its problems, Freud's provocative proposal continued to have some heuristic value. It still intrigues some bright analysts trying to get a handle on fundamental matters. I thought Dr. C might be interested in two recent contributions from a symposium our institute cohosted at Trinity College Dublin with the Irish Psychoanalytic Forum and the psychoanalytic societies of the William Alanson White Institute and New York University and Adelphi University's Postdoctoral Programs in Psychoanalysis (Willock, Bohm, & Curtis, 2007). One of these chapters (referred to earlier) is by Skelton (2007). The other, by Lombardi (2007) discusses Freud and Klein's different views on the death instinct in relation to contemporary theorizing on the negative (e.g., Kristeva, 1979; Green 1986, 1999a).

Far from being completely dead, in some circles, the death instinct still seems very much alive. French analyst André Green penned two books related to the topic: *The Work of the Negative* (1999b) and *Life Narcissism, Death Narcissism* (2001). For him, the death drive was the motor of self-destruction. The life drive's purpose, in contrast, is to ensure an "objectalising function" (1999b, p. 85), that is, creation and investment in objects. The death drive aims instead for "deobjectalization" or decathexis. This latter function can be related to what Bion (1959) called "Attacks on Linking." Deobjectalization goes hand in hand with self-abasement and "an aspiration to nothingness" (2002, p.6). "Blank psychosis" is a radical solution to catastrophic object loss (Green, 1986). This pathology arises consequent to the loss of meaning infants experience when a mother becomes emotionally "dead." With nowhere to turn to metabolize affects, a child may resort to massive decathexis of emotion, resulting in a blank state of mind. This breakdown is in a specific area—"a hole in the texture of object relations with the mother" (Green, 1986, p. 151).

Translating the death drive into a disobjectalizing function reactive to traumatic relational experience exemplifies the theoretical tactic Greenberg and Mitchell (1983) referred to as accommodation. Greenberg and Mitchell concentrated on how Freud responded to challenges to libidinal drive theory, modifying his model, making it less vulnerable to attack. In Green's work, one detects a similar strategy for preserving the dual-drive model. Accommodating relational critique, Eros and Thanatos become objectalizing and disobjectalizing functions. (A somewhat similar strategy was reflected in ego psychology's attempt to encompass object relations theory by positing object relations as one of many ego functions.)

Via Green's accommodation, the theory of life and death drives becomes a relational perspective focusing our attention on attachment and detachment. Although he does not refer to Guntrip, Green's dual-drive framework resembles Guntrip's core ideas concerning commitment to versus flight from object relations.

Is it time to bury the death instinct? Perhaps. Alternatively, one might keep it on life support at least awhile longer because of its continuing heuristic value. Flawed though it may be, the concept still has power to point to important phenomena that need attention. Not the least of these matters concerns the ongoing importance of death, if not the death instinct, in our lives.

Question D

Dr. D wondered whether these theorists were talking of a fantasy of returning to the womb or an actual drive to become dead. I replied that Guntrip described the agenda of the regressed ego as complete retreat from object relations, even internal ones. Because attachments are necessary for life, at least for a dependent child (as Spitz [1945, 1946] has demonstrated), achievement of this goal would be tantamount to death. In this spirit, Green aligned the death drive with the disobjectalizing function. Nonetheless, in Guntrip's examples, this morbid outcome was not necessarily the goal. Some of his patients sought a return to the safety, comforts, and provisions of the womb or its equivalent. Other, more suicidal patients longed for the eternal quiescence of the tomb. These destinations easily become confused.

With respect to the latter, seemingly terminal aspiration, recall Matte-Blanco's (1988) point that in the symmetrical world of the unconscious, life and death may not be differentiated and incompatible. In Green's language, such patients long for "nothingness." That nirvana state might be the absolute stillness Matte-Blanco described. In its most extreme, desperate form, it would be death.

In trying to comprehend more precisely what these patients might be striving for, these theorists have not had or have not utilized the important, neo-Kleinian contributions of Ogden. His work provides a potentially significant piece of the puzzle underlying Dr. D's question.

The Primal Position

From the 1930s until the early 1970s, discussion in British object relations theory revolved around the work of such luminaries as Klein, Fairbairn, Winnicott, and Bion. In the late 1960s, the conversation shifted to innovative work with autistic children conducted by clinicians such as Bick , Meltzer, and Tustin. Pulling together findings from this latter dialogue, Ogden (1989) posited an autistic-contiguous position with a period of primacy prior to Klein's two psychological organizations (PS and D). All three positions coexist dialectically from the beginning. Ogden's contribution is profound and underappreciated.

In the autistic-contiguous mode, sensory impressions are organized to constitute bounded surfaces. On these, the experience of self has its origins. Here Ogden followed Freud (1923) who wrote not only that "The ego [the "I"] is first and foremost a bodily ego" (p. 26) but also that "The ego is ultimately derived from bodily sensations, chiefly from those springing from the surface of the body" (p. 26, footnote).

The autistic-contiguous mode usually recedes from phase primacy as development proceeds. It continues, nonetheless, to contribute the barely perceptible but essential background of sensory boundedness that accompanies subjective experience throughout life. During this seminar you may, for example, be subliminally aware of sensations from holding your pen, the pressure of your leg on your knee, your back touching the "back" of the chair, and so forth. Without these sensations, something would be disturbingly absent from our relationship with the world, possibly leading to feelings of depersonalization and derealization.

The rudimentary feeling of I-ness that arises from relationships of sensory contiguity over time generates the sense of a cohesive, bounded surface where one's experience occurs. This containedness provides the foundation for the experience of a place where one feels, thinks, and lives. This entity has shape, hardness, coldness, warmth, texture, and other essential qualities of who one is.

Each of the three coexisting psychological organizations has a characteristic form of anxiety. Depressive anxiety relates to the fear that one has harmed or driven away a love object. Paranoid-schizoid anxiety entails a sense of impending annihilation via fragmenting attacks on self and object. Autistic-contiguous anxiety involves fear of one's sensory surface, or what Tustin (1986) called the containing "rhythm of safety," disintegrating. Such dissolution results in feelings of leaking into endless, shapeless space. One may fear plummeting through the sensory floor, the stage on which the otherwise foundational dramas of PS and D take place.

Winnicott (1974) knew about these discrete levels of anxiety. "Primitive agonies" (1974, p. 104), such as fear of falling forever, make other horrors, such as being boiled alive and eaten by cannibals, seem like mere bagatelles, he asserted. This enigmatic declaration becomes more comprehensible with Ogden's help.

Translated into this neo-Kleinian conceptual framework, Winnicott seemed to be trying to convey, in his vivid, challenging, mysterious way, that autistic-contiguous anxieties (falling forever) are more terrifying than even extreme, paranoid-schizoid fears. The earliest terrors, experienced when the self and its boundaries are still in process of formation and consolidation, may be worse than any that can arise later when self and object are more evolved and differentiated.

Guntrip and Ogden

As he did with Kohut and Mitchell, Guntrip also prefigured Ogden's work in some important ways. He appreciated how Klein borrowed from Fairbairn's work on schizoid processes, merging Fairbairn's ideas about splitting with her own conceptualizations about paranoid, projective operations. Fairbairn's influence was memorialized by her wedding the name of her position to his to form the renowned paranoid-schizoid couple. Despite the near sacred status of that marriage, Guntrip believed it was ultimately incorrect and undesirable to have lost the distinction between the paranoid and what he called the schizoid position. In his opinion, analogous to Ogden, each of these modes has unique object relations, anxieties, defenses, and psychopathological potential. The paranoid position, for example, is highly aggressive (fighting objects). The schizoid position, in contrast, entails a very different *flight* from relationships. Based on a feeling of ego weakness, it reflects inability and unwillingness to do battle with frustrating objects.

Like Ogden, Guntrip believed there were three basic positions. Although their emendations to customary Kleinian views have quite a bit in common, they are not identical. Ogden did not emphasize prenatal experience—something I consider highly germane to the schizoid and autistic-contiguous positions. His illustrations of contiguity generating boundedness were typically selected from the oral stage. For example, he mentioned the infant feeling its cheek on mother's breast, continuity and predictability of shape derived from rhythmicity and regularity of sucking, rhythm of cooing dialogue with mother, and feelings of edgedness generated by the infant's gums pressing tightly on mother's nipple or finger. Vital though these experiences are, I believe we need to look to antenatal sensation to locate the origins of autistic-contiguous experience. From a comparative-integrative perspective, I am arguing for the advantages of integrating something that was at least implicit in Guntrip's British object relational views with Ogden's neo-Kleinian perspective.

In the womb, one might imagine, the foetus would generally feel safely held. Such words may, however, suggest greater self–other differentiation than is actually present. Inside the undifferentiated "environment mother," as opposed to the more delineated "object mother" (Winnicott, 1963), the gestating infant begins generating sensory experience, forming the basis for a rudimentary sense of "me." A sensation self not clearly delineated from an "autosensuous object"

(Tustin, 1984, p. 282) provides a comforting sense of contact and boundedness for one's being.

Birth threatens the sensory contiguity that defines this preliminary, sensation self. Leaving the primordial, aquatic milieu for terrestrial life is a momentous event. Seeming to intuitively understand something of the autistic-contiguous experience, adult caretakers do what they can to reduce the potential trauma of this radical disruption. They envelope the vulnerable baby in soft fabrics, cradling the newborn in their arms, close to their warm chests. They ward off unfamiliar, disturbing stimulation, such as loud sound and bright light, that might impinge and disturb their baby. In these ways, they protect their offspring's fragile self, optimizing the infant's chances of sustaining that bedrock sense Winnicott (1956) referred to as "going on being" (p. 303).

To Matte-Blanco's (1988) description of the symmetry, stillness, and sameness of the womb, I would add a fourth essential S-word. *Sensation* enables us to know we are alive. It permits us to avoid confusing stillness with death. An appropriate degree of sensation is vital prenatally and throughout life.

Each evening, we retreat into nocturnal wombs. Embedded in warm, dark retreats, supported and surrounded by firm mattresses, soft pillows, and cozy blankets, we try to obliterate obnoxious external stimulation and detach ourselves from troubling internal thoughts. In this drift toward oblivion, we may fear excessive discontinuity could unglue us from essential, life-sustaining moorings. This terror could contribute to the feeling many people occasionally have as they are "falling" asleep that they are about to drop off the bed or off some cliff. That feeling of abrupt discontiguity jerks them awake with a somatic rush. The fright needs to be processed. Reassuring themselves that they are safely ensconced in a benevolent bed, they can let themselves continue the process of detachment from waking life and thought.

Considering prenatal origins of the autistic-contiguous position brings Guntrip and Ogden together in mutually enriching ways. Guntrip's emotionally aloof, schizoid patients with their intense, approach–avoidance conflicts concerning human relationships seem similar to the deeply troubled individuals Ogden described. Guntrip believed these patients longed to retreat from all object relations. Ogden's framework enables us to characterize their yearning more accurately. These individuals do not necessarily want to abandon all relations. Rather, they may be withdrawing from higher level, depressive, and paranoid relationships to more primitive, autistic-contiguous ones.

That these patients frequently seek boundaried, containing sensations in fantasies of returning to the womb suggests prenatal origins of autistic-contiguous experience. In these reveries of the right to return through "the unknown, remembered gate" (Eliot, "Four Quartets") to the tranquil, "unthought known" (Bollas, 1987), they do not seek complete objectlessness. Rather, they crave a realm of simple, soothing sensation, safely ensconced inside a suitably containing, auto-sensuous object.

Grasping the importance of the prenatal, Freud (1926a) wrote insightfully that "There is much more continuity between intra-uterine life and earliest infancy than the impressive caesura of the act of birth would have us believe" (p. 138). He went on to explain:

> What happens is that the child's biological situation as a foetus is replaced for it by a psychical object-relation to its mother. But we must not forget that during its intra-uterine life the mother was not an object for the foetus, and that at that time there were no objects at all. (p. 138)

The work of Ogden and other object relational investigators enables one to understand and describe perinatal continuity, transition, and change more clearly than Freud could have done.

In recent years, Freud has been roundly criticized in some quarters for having talked of an original, objectless condition (autoeroticism, primary narcissism). Out of that state, Freud hypothesized, object relations slowly and tentatively evolve. Ogden's framework enables us to appreciate that Freud might not have been completely off base. The autistic-contiguous position represents such a primitive, preverbal, undifferentiated mode of relating that one might be forgiven for thinking it indicates a completely objectless state rather than a realm of autosensuous objects and "shapes" (Tustin, 1984).

Ogden believed this autistic-contiguous state has primacy in earliest life but that higher levels of relatedness (PS, D) coexist with it *ab initio*. His formulation is useful from a comparative-integrative perspective. It allows something akin to Freud's objectless state to be rescued from the rubbish heap where some infancy researchers tossed it. Cleaned up a little, this autosensuous realm can be integrated with the simultaneously operative, more differentiated relational abilities (PS, D) emphasized by infancy researchers. Freud may have grasped an essential component of early (prenatal) and continuing object relations that many contemporary analysts and infancy researchers do not yet have in their conceptual armamentarium.

Schizoid dreams of being in a coffin or tomb can be viewed as womb variations. We are incapable of really imagining ourselves dead, Freud (1915) stressed. We may not even be able to completely imagine others being dead. In a humorous manner, when French people say someone is eating daisies by the roots, they manage to convey that someone is dead and that death is not total. Anglophones communicate the same things when they say someone would roll over in their grave if they heard something shocking. When we imagine our own death, we remain vaguely present and alive, observing our inanimate bodies. In the stillness of the imagined casket, autistic-contiguous contact, sensation, and boundedness persist. Continuing to enjoy containment and stimulation, we are simultaneously protected from noxious impingement (bad objects).

Returning to Dr. D's query as to whether these patients seek womb or tomb, we might now answer that it could be either or even both—a "wombtomb." They crave a quiet, still place with no "woom" for toxic others.

Long ago, in the village of Germelshausen, legend has it, a stern pope punished the people of the parish. Condemned by this bad (parental) object, they sank beneath the surface of the earth. Neither dead nor alive, every hundred years they were allowed to resurface and enjoy life on earth for a day (Gerstacker, 1902). Applying Guntrip's theory to this grim tale, one might detect not only horror but also a schizoid wish to retreat almost completely from object relations. It is surely more than coincidental that Eliot (2000) alluded to this legend in *Four Quartets*, the poetic series in which he commented on humankind's limited capacity to endure reality (Vianu, 1997).

Comorbidity

In Green's (1999b) discussion of the death drive as a deobjectalizing function leading to "sensations of a gap, of bottomless holes, of an abyss" (p. 84), one recognizes the "primitive agonies" Winnicott (1958a) described (such as endlessly falling). Ogden's work enables one to understand these fears as autistic-contiguous anxieties concerning unboundedness and disintegration.

With this insight, rather than simply being what Green (2002) referred to as deobjectalizing with "an aspiration to nothingness" (p. 6), one can consider other possible aims of his death drive. Its real goal might be to dismantle object relations of the depressive and paranoid positions, leaving the autistic-contiguous mode intact. These peculiar processes may, therefore, aspire to something, even as they seem dedicated to annulling other things. The sensation something they seek is sufficiently subtle and primitive that one can be forgiven for mistaking it for nothingness (much as Matte-Blanco [1988] described the natural tendency to confuse stillness and death).

Dismantling large portions of the more differentiated object relations that constitute two of the three basic modes of engaging the world leaves one increasingly with just one line of reality contact. One is brought to the edge of the abyss. Death, disintegration, dissolution, and other depressing, horrifying possibilities stare back from the bottom(less).

In Meltzer, Bremner, Hoxter, Weddell, and Wittenberg's (1975) work with autistic children, dismantling emerged as a central concept. This construct may be relevant for comprehending aspects of the object relations of some adult patients, especially those with prominent schizoid features.

In Green's (1999b) "fears of annihilation or … of bottomless holes"(p. 84), one senses a mixture of anxieties from paranoid (annihilation) and autistic-contiguous (bottomless) positions. Coexistence of terrors from diverse modes of psychic organization fits with Ogden's insistence that all three modes are always present, to some degree, in dialectic interaction. For Guntrip, coexistence of multiple levels of anxiety reflected clinging to higher level object relations (e.g., paranoid) as a defense against precipitous regression from all relationships (schizoid).

Referring to blank psychosis resulting from dysphoric experience with a depressed, "dead" mother (again that natural confusion between stillness and death), Green (1986) noted that this breakdown was only in a specific area. That is to say, it coexisted with other levels of object relationship, anxiety, and defense. The partial nature of the breakdown parallels Guntrip's underscoring that when the libidinal ego splits to create the schizoid, part ego, the nonregressive component of the libidinal ego continues to engage in more differentiated (sadomasochistic) object relations.

Blank psychosis reflects "a hole in the texture of object relations with the mother" (1986, p. 151). Green's (1986) word choice, *texture*, evokes the sensuous, tactile quality of autistic-contiguous relations. His idea of a breach in that fabric, elucidated by Ogden's ideas, alludes to the corresponding, autistic-contiguous anxieties of self-substance draining, leaking, and falling through that hole.

Attachment to blankness may also suggest another subtle contribution from the autistic-contiguous mode of generating (and degenerating) experience. In this aspiration and attachment to "nothingness," a primitive level of an autosensuous relationship continues. This bond with the blank screen does, however, at least partially preclude the more lively play of dramas characterizing more differentiated levels of relatedness.

FIRST CLINICAL ILLUSTRATION

Yew, an attractive 21-year-old single mother, emigrated from Malaysia under stressful circumstances. Through family connections, she secured reasonably satisfying employment in the retail electronics industry in a small city near Ann Arbor, Michigan. Referred to me by a colleague in the Department of Psychiatry at the University of Michigan Medical Center, she was depressed, anxious, and had numerous relationship concerns.

After we had been working productively for several months, Yew was feeling considerably better about herself and her life in the new world. When I announced that I would be taking a vacation, she became distressed. She dreamt that a Big Ben style clock, like the one on the corner bookshelf in my consulting room, was dissolving. Her Dali-esque image graphically illustrated autistic-contiguous anxiety precipitated by the prospect of separation.

On the subjective level (Jung, 1916/1969a), the melting clock likely represented Yew's disintegrating self. Contemplating loss of her analyst, she felt she was losing her core shape. Her sense of boundedness that was shored up by the regularity of our contact (Tustin's [1986] rhythm of safety) was threatened. A discontiguity crisis erupted. As the connection with her analyst became less certain, Yew felt in danger of dissolving. She could go over the edge, succumbing to the same fate as the timepieces in the surrealist's masterpiece.

At the objective level (Jung, 1916/1969a), the dissolving clock would represent Yew's analyst. From this point of view, the vision was not only a self-state dream (Kohut, 1977) as I described previously but also what one might call an other-state dream. The dissolving timepiece portrayed the precarious state of her source of support. The rock on which she had steadied herself was disintegrating.

As time ticked away, the dreaded end of the hour of the prevacation period approached. The usually manageable, small separation between sessions would soon become huge. The abyss of eternal absence loomed menacingly on the rapidly approaching horizon. Before her very eyes, the reliable reality she had come to know, trust, and count on was collapsing.

Between views of the clock as either self-representation or object representation, one could also regard it as an amalgam of the two, that is, as projective identification. This potential would be based on an underlying conception of the object as originally, in large measure, a self-object (autosensuous object). Intolerable terrors of bad things happening to her that she could not contain as she contemplated separation could be projected into the timepiece associated with and representing her analyst. Perhaps he could hold her toxic fear, confusion, and rage. If not, better he should dissolve than she. Better still, "it" should disintegrate (displacement) rather than he.

Ego psychologists might traditionally have thought of Yew displacing anxiety onto her representation of the clock rather than lodging part of herself in it via projective identification as Kleinians would have it. Kernberg helped make projective identification more familiar and acceptable to ego psychologists. Although this notion may still sometimes strike their ears as a bit foreign, or overused in Kleinian linguistic circles, it is no longer reflexively derided or avoided. It would now usually be felt worthy of consideration, its merits weighed in relation to other concepts.

With the help of Matte-Blanco (1988) and Guntrip, one can consider the possibility that self-dissolution (the clock) may not only be feared, but also desired. This counterintuitive idea brings one closer to Freud's core principle concerning dreams as wish fulfillments. When life in the asymmetrical, conscious mode with its focus on separation and difference becomes intolerable (as it had for Yew), one may want to dissolve those painful distinctions. Time, symbolized by the clock, and space, represented by its distinct, three-dimensional form, had become key coordinates of an increasingly persecutory, asymmetrical world. Time was "running out." Doomsday was at hand. Space was transforming from what Balint (1955) called a "friendly expanse" into a "horrid empty space" (p. 225). In a desperate drive to escape disaster, space and time—the fundamental pillars of reality—needed to be attacked and annihilated. This is a paranoid-schizoid situation.

The more encompassing aim, of which attacks on time and space are a part, would be to dismantle the entire, increasingly paranoid-schizoid object relational world to achieve a symmetrical, fluid, timeless, contiguous state. In Winnicottian terms, the underlying strategy would be to de-differentiate the object mother (and the objective self) to merge with the environment mother, thereby returning to a world prior to separation. Desperate times demand desperate measures.

In Balint's (1968) terminology, the wish would be to reactivate "primary object relations" to realize a "harmonious interpenetrating mix-up"(p. 68). At this fundamental level, self and other become more like primary substances (e.g., water, sand, air) rather than discrete entities. Texture, feel, and flow predominate rather than the stability of objects with distinct, hard, stable boundaries. These qualities resemble those Tustin (1984) called autosensuous.

For Yew, the impingement of an unwanted vacation sufficed to sound the alarm. The object mother had proved his unreliability. It was time to retreat to the more secure realm of the environment mother. This regression required vacating her usually more sophisticated level of representation and relatedness. She needed to flow to a lower level the way liquids inevitably do. It was time to abandon the mother ship, even her own shape. Time to flow in search of a more suitable container now that the hitherto trustworthy one had sprung a leak.

Question E

Given Yew's intense anxiety, Dr. E wondered whether it is appropriate to give such patients telephone numbers so they can reach their analysts at their vacation spots should the need arise. Dr. E's proposed intervention seemed humane and might allay some anxiety. One needs, however, to consider not only the analysand but how the analyst, too, feels about vacation contact.

It is also beneficial to contemplate such moves in relation to alternatives. One should, for example, ponder whether provision of such concrete support is optimal responsiveness (Bacal, 1985) or whether one should place more emphasis on interpreting the patient's fundamental fear and associated defenses.

Interpreting the deepest anxiety is a hallmark of classical Kleinian technique. Ego psychologists favor a more cautious style. They are inclined to interpret successive layers of defense before addressing the basic anxiety and, finally, the underlying impulse. Some ego psychologists would wonder whether interpretation is appropriate for patients with basic ego weakness such as that hinted at by the disintegrating object representation (clock). They might favor a less intense, more supportive treatment approach.

From a comparative-integrative perspective, interpretive, supportive, Freudian, Kleinian, and other approaches would not necessarily be ruled incompatible. They can complement one another. In the case under discussion, it would be useful to explore the patient's ability to engage and benefit from an interpretive approach before deciding whether more supportive measures might also be required.

Some extra-analytic interventions (such as vacation phone contact) would be seen by some as "dissolving" the therapeutic frame—a move that may or may not be necessary, beneficial, and advisable. Classical analysts, be they Freudian or Kleinian, would be more inclined to maintain the frame, perhaps at all cost (cf. Langs, 1973). Relational analysts are usually more open to considering alternatives. Not wanting at the end of the day to be in the position of saying the frame survived but the patient did not, one might opt for a framework possessing a certain amount of elasticity.

Combining the virtues of supportive and interpretive approaches, one might say to such a patient that her anxiety and its representation in the dream appear to have been stimulated by the upcoming separation. She seems to fear all her gains, which have made her feel so much more solid, are in danger of dissolving like the clock. This interpretation might lead to discussing whether her current degree of separation agitation is warranted, what other supports she has to sustain her sense of security, and so forth.

This mode of intervention might be understood from an ego-psychological perspective as interpreting upward (cf. Langs, 1973). It addresses what are probably conscious or near conscious fears pertaining to the current adaptive challenge. It does not go back too quickly in time to possible infantile origins of the transference anxiety. The analyst gauges from the patient's response whether to explore the historical bases of these fears or, instead, focus mostly on the present context and on more ego supportive measures.

In contrast, if one were to interpret downward to the deepest level of anxiety, one might say the patient felt the floor had been precipitously pulled out from under her by an uncaring analyst, perhaps even a hostile one who loathed her dependence, causing her to fear she would fall forever and completely disintegrate into oblivion. In face of such terror, she longed to return to the security of the breast, even imagining herself as the flowing milk rather than being the abandoned baby. She would even like to slip back into the womb, seeking a safe, uterine harbor to shelter her from the current affective storm, surrendering realistic adult functioning, merging with the amniotic fluid, biding her time until her good analyst returns to rescue her from her necessary retreat from the bad analyst, just as she must have felt when her mother, … and so forth.

Supportive interventions have often been viewed by ego psychologists as primarily intended to shore up failing defenses. The concept of defense, although still a central pillar of the ego-psychological model, used to loom even larger in their considerations. Other frameworks would not see such interventions so much in terms of defense. They would focus more on the relational dimension. Bion, for example, discussed projective identification not only as a defense but also as a mode of communication. Bion emphasized the necessity for the analyst to serve as a receptive, transforming container for the patient's anxieties. From this point of view, Big Ben, the analyst, would need to demonstrate that he could take in his patient's distress without fragmenting, dissolving, or going defensively rigid. He would have to respond flexibly, showing he comprehended what made his patient tick and what made her sick. He would have to reflect back that he understood she feared she would not be able to keep on ticking and talking in his absence and that she would, instead, become completely unwound, and so forth.

SECOND CLINICAL ILLUSTRATION

Our discipline can be divided into several domains: traditional treatment several times weekly on the couch, applied psychoanalysis, child analysis, and so forth. Despite psychoanalysis' emphasis on the early years of the life cycle, training programs are often weak with respect to material from actual child treatments. Sometimes the only such case to which candidates are exposed is Freud's 100-year-old write-up of his mostly indirect work with Little Hans. That historically important treatment embodied the founder's intense interest in both child observation and child analysis, activities to which his daughter, Anna, devoted herself.

The final illustration I shared with the class came from a challenging child treatment. It was selected not only to exemplify issues we were discussing in the seminar but also to complement, update, and hopefully stimulate their understanding of children and their treatment needs. The way youngsters present material (e.g., play) differs in some important ways from adult analysands. There are also some different technical issues. Otherwise, the two domains have a great deal in common and much to say to each other. Ferenczi (1931) was not the only eminent analyst to believe that the more adult treatment resembled child therapy, the better it was.

A Cool Womb

Rory was referred to me shortly before his eighth birthday. A school psychologist had found him to be very bright, with a possible learning disability. It was Rory's personality that most concerned, even alarmed him. This youngster was the most resistant child he had ever encountered. His teacher described Rory's attitude as that of a high school dropout. The present was problematic, the future unpromising.

When I first encountered Rory, he was seated on his mother's lap in the waiting room near my office at the University of Michigan Medical Center. He looked unhappy about being at the hospital. With zero zest, he accompanied me to my office. Gradually, he warmed up and was able to talk about various subjects.

Rory spoke most enthusiastically about a snow fort he had constructed on the weekend when his parents were hosting a sleepover (for another couple). His building differed from the average child's winter creation. Inside there was a refrigerator, toilet, a cache of weapons, and his dog. Outside, his father attacked with a double-barreled shotgun.

Although much of the content of Rory's story was hard to believe, the segment concerning his father's gun particularly challenged credulity. Rory, however, had no trouble lending credulity to his narrative. He insisted it was so. This discrepancy in our beliefs raised questions about his ability to distinguish fantasy from reality—an important diagnostic consideration. How difficult might it be more generally for him to differentiate unconscious fantasy productions from conscious perceptions? How much delusion might he be capable of generating?

In his important work on the internal dreaming couple (analogous to Bion's [1962a] thinking couple and perhaps Fonagy, Gergely, Jurist, & Target's [2002] reflective function), Grotstein (1981) noted that the dreamer who dreams the dream must find a narrative solution acceptable to the dreamer who understands the dream. The two must work together toward that end. "The failure of their harmony is psychosis, in which case harmony is produced by the alternative of altering the integral structure and coherence of the mind" (Grotstein, 1981, p. 365). In this latter, autoplastic solution, a form of "harmonious interpenetrating mix-up" (Balint, 1968) is established by dissolving the firm categories of the mind, resulting in the characteristic of psychosis.

Children's play can be likened to dreaming. As in the nocturnal state, there is a dreamer (or daydreamer, or player) who creates the play and one (another part of the child) who witnesses, understands, and benefits from it. A difference might be that play generally takes place in what Winnicott (1952/1971b) called the transitional realm, whereas one might say that dreaming occurs in the hallucinatory zone of the subjective object.

To achieve harmony within himself, Rory seems to have collapsed the distinction between these domains. Listeners to his tale experience a jarring disjunction between what should be pretend versus real. Rory did not seem particularly troubled by that con-fusion.

The snow fort tale is relevant to issues we have been discussing in today's seminar. In his fantasy, Rory retreated to an enclosed, self-sufficient, womb-like setting much as Guntrip described. There, he had nutritional supplies (refrigerator) and a means of eliminating bodily waste (toilet) just as he enjoyed inside his mother. There was no incentive or pressing need for him to leave his shelter. It was far too hostile out there. His fortification and weapons afforded him some protection from a seemingly deranged parent determined to maim or kill him.

Rory's insistence on the truth of his tale indicated just how real this object relational situation was for him, at least on the level of psychic reality, a domain he seemed unable to distinguish to the extent one might wish from consensual, objective reality. In keeping with Guntrip's description, Rory's retreat from bad objects was by no means total (e.g., he still had the family dog with him inside his fort). Nonetheless, in addition to the disturbing content of his narrative, slippage in his reality testing raised concerns about how far his regression could go.

Despite these difficulties, this teller of tales had managed to leave the womb of his mother's lap to accompany me to my office. (As treatment "progressed," he vehemently resisted such transitions.) Although suspicious, he did allow himself to "come in from the cold." Gradually he warmed up sufficiently to share his poignant plight via metaphorical messaging.

Both Rory's manner and story conveyed that he had by no means totally abandoned object relations. In paranoid fashion, he maintained intense commitment to bad objects. Barricading himself against them in his self-sufficient retreat with his stash of weaponry, he was ready to battle needed foes. Schizoid flight was balanced by preparedness for paranoid fight.

Guntrip would likely see that latter, aggressive stance as a defense against the more frightened, demoralized part of the self that longed for more total regression. One should, however, be open to the possibility that patients like Rory do not totally want to retreat to the womb. They may also be genuinely committed to higher level object relations, including paranoid and healthy, progressive ones. In keeping with this alternative hypothesis, in addition to keeping one foot firmly engaged in the schizoid position and another in the paranoid position, the inclusion of the family dog in Rory's cool womb hinted at the continuing presence of more advanced object relations. Because Rory did not say anything else about this pet, one cannot know much more about her significance. (She may partly have been a source of heat and contact comfort, furnishing soft, warm, reassuring sensations—something like a primary transitional object—different from those he could derive from his weaponry and the icy walls of his fort.)

Duality, Freud (1900/1953a) claimed, symbolizes breasts. From this viewpoint, the double-barreled shotgun outside Rory's womb might represent a dangerous set of mammaries. This possibility accords with the early developmental conflicts that provoke schizoidal regression. Such breasts, transmogrified into potent, discharging barrels, parallel the deadly weaponry Rory possessed inside. These external organs had presumably been pumped up with projected aggression.

Supplementing Guntripian and Kleinian analysis with classical Freudian considerations would lead one to contemplate the heavily armed father as an oedipal presence. From this vantage point, Rory's symbolic possession of the maternal womb, coupled with his continuing commitment to struggle with his dangerously phallic father, suggests a lesser degree of regression. Father's double-barreled shotgun, as a phallic symbol, might allude to the insult inflicted to Rory's narcissism and to his relationship with his parents when his father's potent buckshot successfully penetrated his mother, causing his son to suffer the births of a brother and sister. Rory's mentioning his parents' sleepover suggests he may have wanted to reference an analogous, exciting event from which he was partly excluded, adding further insult to his oedipal injury.

Considering the complete Oedipus complex, one would have to entertain the possibility that Rory also wished to replace all rivals, particularly his mother, and become the main object of his father's desire. In his story, his hyperaroused father certainly appeared to have hot feelings for his son. The provocative, elusive youngster seemed capable of stimulating overwhelming interest, passion, and pursuit. Papa seemed truly, madly, deeply determined to penetrate his feisty offspring's defenses, to get his hands on him, perhaps penetrating his butt with bullets or whatever it might take to compel him to surrender.

Rory's multiple desires would simultaneously have been highly conflicted, fraught with anxiety, subject to punitive superego disapproval, and deeply defended. His story was a clever compromise formation, synthesizing these numerous, contradictory aims. One can understand that he would have experienced considerable satisfaction with himself for having woven this multidetermined narrative, successfully disguising, balancing, and gratifying so many conflicting goals.

Although classical hypotheses shed considerable light on Rory's fantasies, one is still struck by the nature and extent of his regression. His retreat to a chilly but seemingly self-sufficient womb has elements more severe (psychosexually, structurally, and relationally) than Freud's description of the lesser regression to anality characteristically manifested in obsessive–compulsive neurosis and in phobias like Little Hans's.

Guntrip would likely view Rory's continuing phallic-oedipal conflict as a defense against a more complete retreat from object relations. One can also think about this matter in both/and terms—an attitude favored by comparative-integrative analysis. From this more inclusive perspective, one might hypothesize that Rory found an appropriate compromise between his wish to retreat and his equally authentic desire to continue struggling to succeed with more developmentally advanced relational dilemmas. The equilibrium he achieved pertains to what Anna Freud's Developmental Profile described as the crucial balance between progressive and regressive forces.

Without the benefit of at least a three-pronged model—schizoid (autistic-contiguous), paranoid (paranoid-schizoid), and phallic-oedipal (depressive)—one would be unable to generate, and at a loss to comprehend, the multiple meanings encapsulated in Rory's snow fort story. Because his narrative, if well understood, is replete with diagnostic significance and treatment implications, it is essential to comprehend it as fully as possible. To get an adequate handle on such material, one needs the complex, balanced perspective a comparative-integrative outlook affords. To explore this story solely in terms of schizoid retreat would be as one-sidedly insufficient as to view it strictly as indicative of oedipal conflict. One needs, instead, to consider both what self psychologist Marion Tolpin (2002) referred to as the trailing edge as well as the forward edge of the developmental process. In Rory's case, the trailing edge would be schizoid retreat, whereas the forward edge might be oedipal conflict. Besides these two edges, one also needs to be attuned to intermediate zones such as the paranoid position.

It has been said that the initial dream an analysand shares, often in the first session, frequently tells the story of the analysis that will unfold. One cannot always decipher the full meaning and implications of such inaugural dreams, but their significance may become clearer as treatment proceeds. This likelihood is increased substantially if one has a comparative-integrative outlook.

One might attribute similar significance to initial fantasies presented in words, deeds, or play by children. In Rory's case, one could even wonder whether his story might have been not just a memory suffused with fantastic distortions but also a dream. If so, he may not have been aware of having dreamt these events. To illustrate this possibility, I refer to another bright child I saw around the same time in Michigan. Slightly older than Rory, Chris told me that when he was younger, he used to have scary, repetitive dreams. In them, his father came to his bed at night, led him downstairs, and then turned him over to a witch. I asked Chris if he ever told his parents about this nightmare. He replied he never had done that because he had not known they were dreams. How terrifying must that be, remembering such horrifying events in subsequent days, believing they actually happened? How would one feel about and relate to one's parents in the daytime when one thought they had perpetrated such ghastly things on previous nights and, presumably, would continue to do so on subsequent evenings? (These processes could be relevant for understanding other phenomena such as so-called false memory syndrome.)

Rory and Chris both seem to have had difficulty effecting full Fairbairnian transformations in object relations. If they could have been more successful in that regard, there would have been clearer distinctions between their inner and outer worlds. They would have been able to sheer off excessively exciting and rejecting parts of parental images, shifting these to the internal theatre. Removed from external reality, these bad objects could be subjected to repression, displacement, condensation, disguise, and other operations, rendering them less disturbing. Despite whatever bad dreams or nightmares they might have then had, they would not be so liable to mistake their parents for monsters in waking life, perhaps not even in their dreams.

Psychotics might be considered dreamers who are trying to dream a dream (Grotstein, 2000, p. 13). Unable to successfully handle stress, fears, and traumas that way, they are prone to experiencing frightening delusions, hallucinations, and other symptoms instead. Chris and Rory seemed to have had some similar difficulty dreaming. As a result, some delusional and hallucinatory features haunted their waking lives.

It would, of course, exceed the scope of this chapter to explore the entirety of Rory's analysis to see whether his troubling tale might parallel the significance of an adult analysand's inaugural dream. We can, nonetheless, examine at least one additional source of data to consider how it might support (or disconfirm) our interpretation of his snow fort story (particularly with respect to Guntrip's ideas that have been the major focus of this seminar).

Born on the Rorschach

The lack of attention paid to projective tests in graduate psychology programs in the currently troubled state of our culture is sufficient to make a sensitive soul weep. Times have changed so much from when luminaries like Rapaport, Gill, and Schafer (1968) and Blatt (e.g., Allison, Blatt, & Zimet, 1968) presented their important work with these techniques. Psychologists, not to mention other mental health professionals and their patients, are increasingly deprived of the benefits of these investigative methods.

Knowing that I taught projective techniques at the University of Michigan and that psychoanalytic approaches to these instruments were of considerable interest to me, the psychologist referring Rory shared some of his Rorschach responses with me. I wanted to discuss one with the class so they might increase their familiarity with these methods. Anyone not conversant with this test can simply regard the following example as they might a dream image for purposes of this exposition. Readers interested in learning more about this approach to projective assessment might consult "Projection, Transitional Phenomena, and the Rorschach" (Willock, 1992).

On the first card, Rory perceived scary aliens. "One pinches and eats with his little mouth," he noted. "There's another inside the first one that gets smaller and smaller and eventually dies because he cannot get much food."

Like Rory's igloo story, his initial response suggests his object world can feel alien, ungratifying, and dangerous. (Subsequent responses portrayed remains of aliens; missiles; something eaten by Spiderwoman; devils; mechanical, robotic beings; and damaged things.) In such a terrifying milieu one sees, once again, his desire to retreat to the womb. This defense does not, however, seem completely satisfactory as a long-term solution. The sheltering womb is destined to become a tomb. This frightening fate reflects Rory's dilemma: emerge into the dangerous, postnatal world and be annihilated or stay inside and die of alimentary insufficiency. The latter outcome may indicate a wish to retreat even further than the womb, that is to die, declaring a final no to the torments life offers (as in the legend of Germelshausen but here not even coming above ground one day each 100 years).

Dr. D's earlier question about whether schizoid individuals seek the security of the womb or death is germane to understanding the fantasies embodied in Rory's Rorschach response. From his percept, it seems a solution (retreat to the womb) becomes a problem (insufficient nurturance), leading to a more drastic "solution" (death). This "progression," whereby answers become problems, parallels the sequence discussed earlier wherein external frustration propels a retreat to an inner world (Fairbairn), then that solution becomes sufficiently problematic so that a further ego split is undertaken (Guntrip), provoking regression to an "objectless" state, and so on.

In terms of developmental history, when Rory was little, he did not like to be cuddled. Might that be an early indication of schizoid traits emerging? His mother felt he had been more oriented toward things than people. He did not play with toys as they are supposed to be used. One would want to know more about that latter observation. On the surface, it is reminiscent of a point Tustin emphasized in her work with autistic children. They use toys in idiosyncratic ways to provide sensations rather than either exploring their physical and functional properties or using them to enact fantasies in transitional space. These thoughts are not meant to suggest Rory was autistic, but some concepts concerning the autistic-contiguous or schizoid position could be relevant to understanding aspects of his psychopathology.

Nearly out of time (in the seminar), I could only share a few vignettes from later in the treatment indicating the utility of classical Kleinian and other views for elucidating Rory's material and the analytic process. The candidates seemed intrigued by how theoretical constructs from different frameworks could complement each other and illuminate clinical data. They raised questions about technical aspects of working with deeply disturbed, difficult patients.

SUMMARY

In this chapter, I have attempted to provide some idea of how classes might function in a comparative-integrative program. There are, of course, many ways to teach from this point of view. In all cases, candidates and instructors are encouraged to consider concepts and clinical phenomena from multiple perspectives. Contributions by authors from widely disparate times and traditions are brought together to explore how their ideas may be similar and different and how they might challenge, contradict, and complement each other. Our overall aim is to provide students a number of tools for understanding clinical phenomena, enabling them to raise more and better hypotheses than would be possible from any single vertex, ultimately affording them a richer array of options for analytic intervention.

8

The Comparative-Integrative Spirit

A science in the early stage of disunity does not have the full power of science, and it is not considered to be a full science. That power and recognition await the beginning of the science's advancement to unification.

—Arthur Staats, "The Disunity–Unity Dimension"

We have barely begun exploring the scientific and professional implications of pluralism, Wallerstein (1992) declared. Wallerstein's (1992) simple statement of what is seemed, simultaneously, a proclamation of what should be, that is, a call to action. To the growing chorus of scholars and clinicians committed to investigating those implications, one more voice has now been added. This contribution, based not only on certain values, but also on experience, may stimulate and prove useful to others seeking to comprehend and creatively engage the sometimes overwhelming richness of the contemporary psychoanalytic scene.

Confronting the current state of disciplinary fragmentation, one might derive some solace from the fact that not only psychoanalysis but also the entire field of psychology is in considerable disarray. That overarching discipline, of which psychoanalysis is but one part, constitutes "a modern disunified science, with a plethora of diverse and unrelated scientific products but with little investment in unifying those products" (Staats, 2004, p. 273). Lest psychologists and psychoanalysts become excessively discouraged by this state of affairs, they might take heart from Staats's observation that "All sciences begin in disunity and only advance toward unification by dint of hard and lengthy scientific achievement. … Those who help begin that journey will be centrally important to the development of the science" (p. 273).

In our quest to achieve a suitable method and form of unification, we can learn from psychology's struggles to become more than a "would-be science" (Toulmin, 1972). In turn, psychology may learn something from our efforts to formulate a methodology appropriate for our area of specialization. As discussed earlier with respect to clinical formulation, there should be a mutually facilitating interaction between part and whole.

Progress in science "can come about only in two ways: by gathering new perceptual experiences, or by better organizing those which are available already" (Frank, as cited in Popper, 1959, p. 279). The latter thrust has been the prime focus of our labor. At the same time, as one arranges currently available findings and formulations from diverse schools of analysis through a comparative-integrative process, lively dialogue inevitably ensues, giving rise to new perceptual experiences, problems, and questions.

HALLELUJAH CHORUS

> Now I've heard there was a secret chord / That David played, and it pleased the Lord / But you don't really care for music, do you? / It goes like this / The fourth, the fifth / The minor fall, the major lift / The baffled king / composing Hallelujah.

> —Leonard Cohen, "Hallelujah"

To capture the complexity of individuation, Kohut (as cited in Cocks, 1994) enlisted the help of an artistic analogy: "Great music is not just a perfect chord" (p. 25), he wrote. Beyond that, it "is always a deviation into dissonance and a complex way of coming back again to the consonance." He believed "This is what drives music through the tunes and harmonies until it finally rests or alludes again at the rest of balance. And so, he concluded, "we are spurred on by the necessary shortcomings" (in Cocks, 1994, p. 25).

As with great art and the human condition, so it is with psychoanalysis. The best music in our discipline has never struck an absolutely perfect chord, at least not for long. Discord has always been close at hand. Imperfections in theory and technique regularly spur us on to create alternative models. This "deviation into dissonance" constitutes a crucial aspect of dialectical development. It also describes a longstanding state of our discipline, too long divided into cacophonous schools of thought.

Like composers in any medium, we are destined to find our own "complex way of coming back again to the consonance." At this stage in the evolution of our discipline, the comparative-integrative path we are paving may be especially helpful in the quest for return to equilibrium. On this royal road, harmony will emerge through dialogue culminating in innovative synthesis, permitting us to sojourn, at least briefly, at "the rest of balance." This blissful state will surely have shortcomings, spurring us on to struggle to create something even better.

Comparative-integrative psychoanalysis provides a perspective and methodology to encompass and make sense of all phases in this endless, evolutionary process. It suggests the need to shift from a solo instrument (any single analytic model) to something more like a sextet, or small symphony orchestra, an ensemble containing different voices that together can make a more interesting, complex, cooperative, creative statement than might be possible for any individual player.

Consistent with the idea of the inevitability, perhaps even the desirability of deviations into dissonance, together with the need to discover a way back to consonance, Bergmann (1997) noted that "The history of psychoanalysis ... shows that nearly every deviation contained a kernel of truth to which psychoanalysis returned at a later date" (p. 84). The wartime "British Psychoanalytic Society's Controversial Discussions" in London were significant for being "the first time that psychoanalysis was able to hold such a deviation within the movement," Freud (Steiner, 1985, p. 57) remarked appreciatively. Emerging from a seething cauldron of angst, acrimony, passion, and purpose, that historic moment permitted thesis and antithesis to come together in vigorous dialogue.

It took our field a half century to mature to that point in its dialectical evolution. Now, another half century later, we may be able not just to hold but actually to transcend splits between theses and antitheses. If so, we will be privileged witnesses to another grand, historical moment—the completion of the first, full cycle in our discipline's dialectical development—as we discover our own "complex way of coming back again to the consonance."

One of the most far-reaching, creative thinkers in our field, James Grotstein (1981), stated that "The goal of analysis is to gather the splits and allow a coherence of at-one-ment" (p. 212). Although his Kleinian-based theoretical frame and mode of intervention differ significantly from self psychology's, his formulation nonetheless resembles Kohut's emphasis on the necessity of overcoming fragmentation to achieve a cohesive sense of self. In similar vein, a prominent classical analyst, Rangell (1990), observed that "Integration (Hartmann, 1950/1964), or synthesis (Nunberg, 1931/1948), is as close as we have been able to come to a definition of 'normal,' or of 'mental health'" (p. 854).

All these analysts, from such widely divergent schools, are essentially being true to Freud's (1919) overall vision concerning the conflicted mind and its treatment needs: "The neurotic patient presents us with a torn mind, divided by resistances," he wrote.

> As we analyze it and remove resistances, it grows together; the great unity which we call the ego fits into itself all the instinctual impulses which before had been split off and held apart from it. The psychosynthesis is thus achieved. ... We have created the conditions for it by breaking up the symptoms into their elements and by removing the resistances. (p. 161)

The comparative-integrative approach advocates a strikingly similar method for achieving the equally necessary psychosynthesis with respect to the fragmented character of our discipline. It provides a means whereby the great disunity that we call psychoanalysis can fit into itself all the trends and traditions that hitherto have stood apart.

With perspicacity, Freud (1919/1955d) remarked that "In mental life we have to deal with trends that are under a compulsion toward unification" (p. 161). Clinicians have harnessed that vital force for their patients' advantage. Now we must utilize that primal power to confront and resolve our discipline's difficulties.

A DISSONANT VOICE

Compared to the delightfully harmonious sound of the preceding, multicultural choir, a seemingly discordant note was struck by one influential, relational analyst. "Health is not integration," Bromberg (1998) averred. Rather, it "is the ability to stand in the spaces between realities without losing any of them" (p. 186).

Despite his opening beat, Bromberg's (1998) stance may not be so different from the preceding authors. His declaration might be viewed as another way of gathering the splits. His image of health (the ability to grasp multiple realities simultaneously) might be viewed as the precondition for a comparative or even a comparative-integrative venture.

Enabling his patients to access many self-narratives at the same time helps them move from mental structures organized dissociatively to new ones organized conflictually. In this manner, an "experience of 'wholeness' is achieved" (p. 566). This progression, from dissociation to conflict to increasing integration, parallels the path advocated by comparative-integrative psychoanalysis for our discipline.

Bromberg's patient is encouraged to allow the various selves that define separate realities to have voices by forming relationships with the analyst. In this process, each self can also build bridges to the others rather than operating as a dissociated island of truth in a rigid, unadaptive view of reality. The dissociative structure and the patient's blind dependence on it must change. Analogously, psychoanalysts' blind dependence on isolated islands of truth needs transformation via a new, comparative-integrative vision.

Mental health is "the ability of the individual to access a broad range of self-states that participate in the ultimate resolution of conflicting meanings" (Bromberg, p. 556). Instead of self-states, if we were to substitute the psychoanalysts' capacity to access a broad array of theoretical frameworks, enabling them to participate in the resolution of conflicting meanings, we would have a good description of a mentally healthy discipline.

Back to the Consonance

For the interpersonal psychoanalyst Donnel Stern (2003), dissociation is a restriction on freedom of thought and experience. The treatment goal and method is to destabilize and diminish dissociation. Comparative-integrative psychoanalysis strives similarly to disequilibrate the status quo, reducing dissociative barriers between schools of thought to facilitate freedom of thinking, experience, and action.

Currently, the principal need of our field is exactly what these exemplary analysts from such diverse traditions—Freud, Grotstein, Kohut, Rangell, Bromberg, Stern, and others—have declared the essential requirement of analysands to be—dialogue to diminish dissociation and promote integration. This striking isomorphism between individual and disciplinary needs is surely more than coincidental. Rather, it would seem that the fundamentals of psychoanalysis are sufficiently potent to be applicable not only to the complexities of individual personality, pathology, and treatment but also to elucidating a far wider range of crucial endeavors, including the analysis and treatment of our complex discipline.

Healing the problems of our field will simultaneously enable us to better address the difficulties with which our patients struggle. In these regards, the comparative-integrative point of view may prove useful to others, as it already has to us, permitting us to "gather the splits," to achieve balance and coherence, enabling us to access and mobilize our considerable resources to progress more optimally as a vigorous, invigorating science and discipline.

9

Last Words

The ultimate cause of progress ... has to be sought in the force fields that new associations of ideas set up in our minds, fields whose strength measures the good fortune of scientists lucky enough to bring those ideas together.

—G. Juvet, *La Structure*

When Juvet (1933) suggestively alluded to "force fields" created in the mind by bringing together different concepts, Bachelard (1934) wrote, he encouraged us to "interpret the traditional association of ideas in a more dynamic light and to give to Fouillée's notion of an idea force an almost physical interpretation" (p. 175). In a similar spirit, the comparative-integrative philosophy and curriculum has been designed to bring together concepts that, by their very association, will stimulate students (and teachers) to forge new connections, fostering innovative thoughts. Our "good fortune" has been the opportunity to have played a part in this play of ideas, in this evolutionary process.

The comparative-integrative attitude is all about free association. Valorized by psychoanalysis in certain contexts, this ideal has been underpursued in others. Tightly bound associations have often thwarted cathectic mobility, fragmenting thought processes and the discipline of psychoanalysis. Comparative-integration advocates more fluid associations, bringing together thinkers and theories from diverse realms, confident that commingling perspectives will energize rather than corrupt cognition, propelling us beyond hitherto self-imposed limits, advancing our discipline and practice.

AFTER EATING, ALL ANIMALS ARE SLEEPY

Having nearly finished this book, you may be in the mood to muse on what you have encountered. You are what you eat, a 1960s maxim famously proclaimed. That insightful adage was partly right. A fuller version might be: You are what you do with what you consume. Having welcomed at least some of the preceding treatise into your psychic digestive system, object usage (Winnicott, 1969) can now commence.

Some ideas in this book may be easily embraced, merging readily with pre-existing thoughts, setting up force fields that will enliven and enrich thinking, practice, teaching, and research. Others may be swallowed less easily, needing to be chewed longer. Hopefully a considerable portion of the perspective I have presented in these pages will stand up to the most spirited digestive attack, from the teeth on down, permitting something substantial in the idea of a compara-tive-integrative attitude to endure or be replaced in time by something even more useful.

Among thinkers on the forward edge of our field, pluralism and compara-tive analysis are increasingly valued. This contribution endeavors to propel those attitudes forward, adding a complementary ideal, integration, to this already ambitious agenda. Important steps in this direction have already been taken by visionaries like Guntrip (1961), Gedo and Goldberg (1973), Mitchell (1988), Pine (1990), and Slavin and Kriegman (1992). The infusion of energy, direction, and sensibility that the comparative-integrative attitude affords our discipline will make the venture ahead more challenging, exciting, worthwhile, and productive. Mobilization of this "idea force" is not only of theoretical but also of immense practical import.

BACK TO BACHELARD

Throughout this work, I alluded to ideas of Gaston Bachelard (1934/1985, 1960/1969) who, like Freud, transcended the usual gulfs between science, human-ities, and the arts. It seems appropriate, therefore, to give the penultimate word to him and to thinkers he respected. Referring to Lalande's *pensées*, Bachelard noted that science does not aim solely at "reconciling things with other things but even more at reconciling minds with other minds" (p. 11). If this volume helps reconnect and reconcile some heretofore isolated and dissociated ideas and minds, I would be delighted indeed. If it were to achieve anything more, that would be icing on the cake.

References

Abraham, K. (1973a). The influence of oral eroticism on character-formation. In E. Jones (Ed.), *Selected papers of Karl Abraham* (pp. 393–406). London: Hogarth Press. (Original work published 1924.)

Abraham, K. (1973b). A short study of the development of the libido viewed in the light of mental disorders: Part I. Manic-depressive states and the pregenital levels of the libido. In E. Jones (Ed.), *Selected papers of Karl Abraham* (pp. 418–501). London: Hogarth Press. (Original work published 1924.)

Adorno, T. W. (1973). *Negative dialectics* (E. B. Aston, Trans.). New York: Seabury Press. (Original work published 1966.)

Allison, J., Blatt, S. J., & Zimet, C. N. (1968). *The interpretation of psychological tests*. New York: Harper & Row.

Alvarez, A. (1992). *Live company: Psychoanalytic psychotherapy with autistic, borderline, deprived and abused children*. London: Tavistock/Routledge.

Arlow, J. (1985). The structural hypothesis. In A. Rothstein (Ed.), *Models of the mind: Their relationship to clinical work* (pp. 21–34). New York: International Universities Press.

Arlow, J., & Brenner, C. (1964). *Structural concepts and the structural theory*. New York: International Universities Press.

Aron, L. (1995). The internalized primal scene. *Psychoanalytic Dialogues, 5*, 195–238.

Aron, L. (1996). *A meeting of minds: Mutuality in psychoanalysis*. Hillsdale, NJ: Analytic Press.

Aslan, C. M. (1989). Common ground in psychoanalysis: Aims and clinical process. *International Journal of Psycho-Analysis, 70*, 12–15.

Astor, J. (1998). Some Jungian and Freudian perspectives on the Oedipus myth and beyond. *International Journal of Psycho-Analysis, 79*, 697–712.

Bacal, H. A. (1985). Optimal responsiveness and the therapeutic process. *Progress in Self Psychology, 1*, 202–227.

Bacal, H. A. (1987). British object-relations theorists and self-psychology: Some critical reflections. *International Journal of Psycho-Analysis, 68*, 81–98.

Bacal, H. A., & Newman, K. M. (1990). *Theories of object relations: Bridges to self psychology*. New York: Columbia University Press.

Bach, S. (1994). *The language of perversion and the language of love*. Northvale, NJ: Jason Aronson.

Bachelard, G. (1969). *The poetics of reverie* (D. Russell, Trans.). New York: Orion Press. (Original work publshed 1960.)

Bachelard, G. (1985). *The new scientific spirit* (A. Goldhammer, Trans.). Boston: Beacon Press. (Original work published 1934.)

Bacon, K., & Gedo, J. (1993). Ferenczi's contributions to psychoanalysis: Essays in dialogue. In L. Aron & A. Harris (Eds.), *The legacy of Sandor Ferenczi* (pp. 121–140). Hillsdale, NJ: The Analytic Press.

Balint, M. (1955). Friendly expanses—Horrid empty spaces. *International Journal of Psycho-Analysis, 36,* 225–241.

Balint, M. (1968). *The basic fault: Therapeutic aspects of regression.* London: Tavistock.

Barratt, B. B. (1994). Critical notes on the psychoanalyst's theorizing activity. *Journal of the American Psychoanalytic Association, 42,* 697–726.

Barrett, W. (1958). *Irrational man.* Garden City, NY: Doubleday.

Becker, E. (1973). *The denial of death.* New York: Free Press.

Benjamin, J. (1988). *The bonds of love.* New York: Pantheon.

Benjamin, J. (1995). *Like subjects, love objects: Essays on recognition and sexual difference.* New Haven, CT: Yale University Press.

Benjamin, J. (1998). *The shadow of the other.* New York: Routledge.

Bergmann, M. (1997). The historical roots of psychoanalytic orthodoxy. *International Journal of Psycho-Analysis, 78,* 69–86.

Bergmann, M. (Ed.). (2000). *The Hartmann era.* New York: Other Press.

Bernardi, R. (1992). On pluralism in psychoanalysis. *Psychoanalytic Inquiry, 12,* 506–525.

Bernardi, R., & Nieto, M. (1989, July). *What makes the training analysis "good enough?"* Paper presented at the 4th IPA Conference of Training Analysts, Rome.

Bettelheim, B. (1950). *Love is not enough—The treatment of emotionally disturbed children.* Glencoe, IL: Free Press.

Bick, E. (1968). The experience of the skin in early object relations. *International Journal of Psycho-Analysis, 49,* 484–486.

Bion, W. R. (1959). Attacks on linking. *International Journal of Psycho-Analysis, 40,* 308–315.

Bion, W. R. (1961). *Experiences in groups and other papers.* London: Tavistock.

Bion, W. R. (1962a). *Learning from experience.* London: Heineman.

Bion, W. R. (1962b). A theory of thinking. *International Journal of Psycho-Analysis, 43,* 306–310.

Bion, W. R. (1970). *Attention and interpretation.* London: Tavistock.

Blatt, S. J., & Shichman, S. (1983). Two primary configurations of psychopathology. *Psychoanalysis and Contemporary Thought, 6,* 187–254.

Bolgar, H. (1965). The case study method. In B.B. Wolman (Ed.), *Handbook of clinical psychology* (pp. 28–29). New York: McGraw-Hill.

Bollas, C. (1986). Who does self psychology cure? *Psychoanalytic Inquiry, 6,* 429–436.

Bollas, C. (1987). *The shadow of the object: Psychoanalysis of the unthought known.* New York: Columbia University Press.

Bollas, C. (1989). *Forces of destiny: Psychoanalysis and the human idiom.* London: Free Association Books.

Bollas, C. (1992). *Being a character: Psychoanalysis and self-experience.* New York: Hill and Wang.

Bornstein, R. (2001). The impending death of psychoanalysis. *Psychoanalytic & Psychology, 18,* 3–20.

Bowlby, J. (1979). *The making and breaking of affectional bonds.* London: Tavistock.

Brenneis, C. B. (1975). Theoretical notes on the manifest dream. *International Journal of Psycho-Analysis, 56,* 197–206.

Brenner, C. (1955). *An elementary textbook of psychoanalysis*. New York: International Universities Press.

Breuer, J., & Freud, S. (1955). Studies on hysteria. In J. Strachey (Ed. & Trans.), *The standard edition of the complete psychological works of Sigmund Freud* (Vol. 2). London: Hogarth Press. (Original work published 1895.)

Bromberg, P. (1998). *Standing in the spaces: Essays on clinical process, trauma, and dissociation*. Hillsdale, NJ: Analytic Press.

Calder, K. T. (1998). The "common ground" of psychoanalysis. In M. Furer, E. Nersessian, & C. Perri (Eds.), *Controversies in contemporary psychoanalysis* (pp. 71–74). Madison, CT: International Universities Press.

Campbell, D., & Stanley, J. (1963). *Experimental and quasi-experimental designs for research*. Chicago: Rand McNally.

Carpenter, S. (2001, April). Sights unseen. *Monitor on Psychology, 32*, 54–57.

Carveth, D. (1984). The analyst's metaphors: A deconstructionist perspective. *Psychoanalysis and Contemporary Thought, 7*, 491–560.

Carveth, D. (1994). Selfobject and intersubjectivity theory: A dialectical critique: Part I. Monism, dualism, dialectic. *Canadian Journal of Psychoanalysis/Revue Canadienne de Psychoanalyse, 2*, 151–168.

Casey, E. S. (1990). The subdominance of the pleasure principle. In R. A. Glick & S. Bone (Eds.), *Pleasure beyond the pleasure principle* (pp. 239–258). New Haven, CT: Yale University Press.

Chasseguet-Smirgel, J. (1984). *Creativity and perversion*. New York: Norton.

Chasseguet-Smirgel, J. (1991). Review of R. Britton, M. Feldman, E. O'Shaughnessy, "The Oedipus Complex Today." *International Journal of Psycho-Analysis, 72*, 727–730.

Chomsky, N. (1972). *Language and mind*. San Diego, CA: Harcourt Brace Jovanovich.

Cocks, G. (1994). *The curve of life: Correspondence of Heinz Kohut, 1923–1981*. Chicago: University of Chicago Press.

Cohen, L. (1993). *Stranger music: Selected poems and songs*. New York: Pantheon, 367–369.

Cooper, A. (1985). A historical review of psychoanalytic paradigms. In A. Rothstein (Ed.), *Models of the mind: Their relationships to clinical work* (pp. 5–20). New York: International Universities Press.

Edelson, M. (1984). *Hypothesis and evidence in psychoanalysis*. Chicago: University of Chicago Press.

Edelson, M. (1985). The hermeneutic turn and the single case study in psychoanalysis. *Psychoanalysis and Contemporary Thought, 8*, 567–614.

Edelson, M. (1988). *Psychoanalysis: A theory in crisis*. Chicago: University of Chicago Press.

Eigen, M. (1993). *The electrified tightrope*. Northvale, NJ: Jason Aronson.

Einstein, A. (1998). Viewpoints. *The Bulletin of the Appalachian Psychoanalytic Society, 8*(2), 23.

Eisold, K. (1994). The intolerance of diversity in psychoanalytic institutes. *International Journal of Psycho-Analysis, 75*, 785–800.

Eissler, K. R. (1965). *Medical orthodoxy and the future of psychoanalysis*. New York: International Universities Press.

Eliot, T. S. (1951). Tradition and individual talent. In *Selected essays* (pp. 13–22). London: Faber & Faber. (Original work published 1919.)

Eliot, T. S. (1939). Last words. *The Criterion: A Literary Review, 71*, 269–275.

Eliot, T. S. (2000). *Four quartets*. London: Faber and Faber.

Elkins, J. (1996). *The object stares back: On the nature of seeing*. New York: Simon & Schuster.

Erikson, E. H. (1950). *Childhood and society*. New York: Norton.

Erikson, E. H. (1954). The dream specimen of psychoanalysis. *Journal of the American Psychoanalytic Association, 2,* 5 56.

Erikson, E. H. (1959). *Identity and the life cycle*. New York: International Universities Press.

Erikson, E. H. (1975). *Life history and the historical moment*. New York: Norton.

Erikson, E. H. (1998). The nature of clinical evidence. In R. Wallerstein & L. Goldberger (Eds.), *Ideas and identities: The life and work of Erik Erikson* (pp. 245–276). Madison, CT: International Universities Press. (Original work published 1958)

Fast, I. (1978). Developments in gender identity: The original matrix. *International Review of Psycho-Analysis, 5,* 265–273.

Fast, I. (1998). *Selving: A relational theory of self organization*. Hillsdale, NJ: Analytic Press.

Fenichel, O. (1945). *The psychoanalytic theory of neurosis*. New York: Norton.

Ferenczi, S. (1925). Psycho-analysis of sexual habits. *International Journal of Psycho-Analysis, 6,* 372–404.

Ferenczi, S. (1931). Child-analysis in the analysis of adults. *International Journal of Psycho-Analysis, 12,* 468–482.

Ferenczi, S. (1949). Confusion of tongues between adult and child. *International Journal of Psycho-Analysis, 30,* 225–230.

Fine, B., Moore, B., & Waldhorn, H. (1969). The manifest content of the dream. *Kris Study Group Monograph III*. New York: International Universities Press.

Fonagy, P., Gergely, G., Jurist, E. L., & Target, M. (2002). *Affect regulation, mentalization, and the development of the self*. New York: Other Press.

Fosshage, J. L. (1983). The psychological function of dreams: A revised psychoanalytic perspective. In M. R. Lansky (Ed.), *Essential papers on dreams* (pp. 249–271). New York: New York University Press.

Freud, S. (1953a). The interpretation of dreams. In J. Strachey (Ed. & Trans.), *Standard edition of the complete psychological works of Sigmund Freud* (Vols. 4 & 5, pp. 1–625). London: Hogarth Press. (Original work published 1900.)

Freud, S. (1953b)). Three essays on the theory of sexuality. In J. Strachey (Ed. & Trans.), *Standard edition of the complete psychological works of Sigmund Freud* (Vol. 7, pp. 125–248). London: Hogarth Press. (Original work published 1905.)

Freud, S. (1954). *The origins of psycho-analysis: Letters to Wilhelm Fliess, drafts and notes, 1887–1902* (M. Bonaparte, A. Freud, & E. Kris, Eds.). New York: Basic Books.

Freud, S. (1955a). Analysis of a phobia in a five-year-old boy. In J. Strachey (Ed. & Trans.), *Standard edition of the complete psychological works of Sigmund Freud* (Vol. 10, pp. 5–149). London: Hogarth Press. (Original work published 1909.)

Freud, S. (1955b). Beyond the pleasure principle. In J. Strachey (Ed. & Trans.), *Standard edition of the complete psychological works of Sigmund Freud* (Vol. 18, pp. 1–66). London: Hogarth Press. (Original work published 1920.)

Freud, S. (1955c). Encyclopaedia article: "Psychoanalysis." In J. Strachey (Ed. & Trans.), *Standard edition of the complete psychological works of Sigmund Freud* (Vol. 18, pp. 235–259). London: Hogarth Press. (Original work published 1923.)

Freud, S. (1955d). The *Moses* of Michelangelo. In J. Strachey (Ed. & Trans.), *Standard edition of the complete psychological works of Sigmund Freud* (Vol. 13, pp. 211–238). London: Hogarth. (Original work published 1914.)

Freud, S. (1955e). Lines of advance in psychoanalytic psychotherapy. In J. Strachey (Ed. & Trans.), *Standard edition of the complete psychological works of Sigmund Freud* (Vol. 17, pp. 159–168). London: Hogarth Press. (Original work published 1919.)

Freud, S. (1957a). Instincts and their vicissitudes. In J. Strachey (Ed. & Trans.), *Standard edition of the complete psychological works of Sigmund Freud* (Vol. 14, pp. 109–140). London: Hogarth Press. (Original work published 1915.)

Freud, S. (1957b). On the history of the psycho-analytic movement. In J. Strachey (Ed. & Trans.), *Standard edition of the complete psychological works of Sigmund Freud* (Vol. 14, pp. 7–66). London: Hogarth Press. (Original work published 1914.)

Freud, S. (1957c). The taboo on virginity. In J. Strachey (Ed. & Trans.), *Standard edition of the complete psychological works of Sigmund Freud* (Vol. 11, pp. 191–208). London: Hogarth Press. (Original work published 1918.)

Freud, S. (1957d). Thoughts for the times on war and death. In J. Strachey (Ed. & Trans.), *Standard edition of the complete psychological works of Sigmund Freud* (Vol. 14, pp. 273–300). London: Hogarth Press. (Original work published 1915.)

Freud, S. (1957e). "Wild" psycho-analysis. In J. Strachey (Ed. & Trans.), *Standard edition of the complete psychological works of Sigmund Freud* (Vol. 11, pp. 219–230). London: Hogarth Press. (Original work published 1910.)

Freud, S. (1958a). The dynamics of transference. In J. Strachey (Ed. & Trans.), *Standard edition of the complete psychological works of Sigmund Freud* (Vol. 12, pp. 97–108). London: Hogarth Press. (Original work published 1912.)

Freud, S. (1958b). Formulations on the two principles of mental functioning. In J. Strachey (Ed. & Trans.), *Standard edition of the complete psychological works of Sigmund Freud* (Vol. 12, pp. 218–226). London: Hogarth Press. (Original work published 1911.)

Freud, S. (1958c). A note on the unconscious in psycho-analysis. In J. Strachey (Ed. & Trans.), *Standard edition of the complete psychological works of Sigmund Freud* (Vol. 12, pp. 255–266). London: Hogarth Press. (Original work published 1912.)

Freud, S. (1958d). Recommendations to physicians practicing psycho-analysis. In J. Strachey (Ed. & Trans.), *Standard edition of the complete psychological works of Sigmund Freud* (Vol. 12, pp. 111–120). London: Hogarth Press. (Original work published 1912.)

Freud, S. (1959a). Inhibitions, symptoms and anxiety. In J. Strachey (Ed. & Trans.), *Standard edition of the complete psychological works of Sigmund Freud* (Vol. 20, pp. 87–172). London: Hogarth Press. (Original work published 1926.)

Freud, S. (1959b). The question of lay analysis. In J. Strachey (Ed. & Trans.), *Standard edition of the complete psychological works of Sigmund Freud* (Vol. 20, pp. 179–258). London: Hogarth Press. (Original work published 1926.)

Freud, S. (1960). The psychopathology of everyday life. In J. Strachey (Ed. & Trans.), *Standard edition of the complete psychological works of Sigmund Freud* (Vol. 6, pp. 1–290). London: Hogarth Press. (Original work published 1901.)

Freud, S. (1961). Civilization and its discontents. In J. Strachey (Ed. & Trans.), *Standard edition of the complete psychological works of Sigmund Freud* (Vol. 21, pp. 57–157). London: Hogarth Press. (Original work published 1930.)

Freud, S. (1962). Charcot. In J. Strachey (Ed. & Trans.), *Standard edition of the complete psychological works of Sigmund Freud* (Vol. 3, pp. 9–24). London: Hogarth Press. (Original work published 1893.)

Freud, S. (1963). Introductory lectures on psycho-analysis. In J. Strachey (Ed. & Trans.), *Standard edition of the complete psychological works of Sigmund Freud* (Vols. 15–16). London: Hogarth Press. (Original work published 1916–1917.)

Freud, S. (1964a). An outline of psycho-analysis. In J. Strachey (Ed. & Trans.), *Standard edition of the complete psychological works of Sigmund Freud* (Vol. 23, pp. 139–207). London: Hogarth Press. (Original work published 1940.)

Freud, S. (1964b). Analysis terminable and interminable. In J. Strachey (Ed. & Trans.), *Standard edition of the complete psychological works of Sigmund Freud* (Vol. 23, pp. 216–253). London: Hogarth Press. (Original work published 1937.)

Freud, S. (1964c). New introductory lectures on psycho-analysis. In J. Strachey (Ed. & Trans.), *Standard edition of the complete psychological works of Sigmund Freud* (Vol. 22, pp. 1–184). London: Hogarth Press. (Original work published 1933.)

Freud, S. (1964d). Why war? In J. Strachey (Ed. & Trans.), *Standard edition of the complete psychological works of Sigmund Freud* (Vol. 22, pp. 203–215). London: Hogarth Press. (Original work published 1933.)

Freud, S. (1972). Letter dated 25.5.16. In E. Pfeiffer (Ed.), & W. Robson-Scott & E. Robson-Scott (Trans.), *Sigmund Freud and Lou Andreas-Salomé: Letters* (p. 45). New York: Harcourt Brace Jovanovich. (Original work published 1916.)

Freud, S. (1987). Overview of the transference neuroses. In I. Grubrich-Simitis (Ed.), *A phylogenetic fantasy*. Cambridge, MA: Harvard University Press. (Original work published 1915.)

Fromm, E. (1941). *Escape from freedom*. New York: Farrar & Rinehart.

Fromm, E. (1947). *Man for himself: An inquiry into the psychology of ethics*. New York: Holt, Rinehart & Winston.

Fromm, E. (1955). *The sane society*. New York: Holt, Rinehart & Winston.

Furer, M., Nersessian, E., & Perri, C. (1998). *Controversies in contemporary psychoanalysis*. Madison, CT: International Universities Press.

Gaddini, E. (1982). Early defensive fantasies and the psychoanalytical process. *International Journal of Psycho-Analysis, 63*, 379–388.

Gedo, J. (1979). A psychoanalyst reports at mid-career. *American Journal of Psychiatry, 136*, 646–649.

Gedo, J. (1980). Reflections on some current controversies in psychoanalysis. *Journal of the American Psychoanalytic Association, 28*, 363–383.

Gedo, J. (1981). *Advances in clinical psychoanalysis*. New York: International Universities Press.

Gedo, J. (1984). *Psychoanalysis and its discontents*. New York: Guilford.

Gedo, J. (1986). *Conceptual issues in psychoanalysis*. Hillsdale, NJ: Analytic Press.

Gedo, J. (1991). *The biology of clinical encounters*. Hillsdale, NJ: Analytic Press.

Gedo, J. (1992). Review of drive, ego, object, and self, by Fred Pine. *Psychoanalytic Quarterly, 61*, 286–291.

Gedo, J. (1994). Academicism, romanticism, and science in the psychoanalytic enterprise. *Psychoanalytic Inquiry, 14*, 295–312.

Gedo, J. (1999). *The evolution of psychoanalysis*. New York: Other Press.

Gedo, J., & Goldberg, A. (1973). *Models of the mind: A psychoanalytic theory*. Chicago: University of Chicago Press.

Gedo, J., & Pollock, G. (Eds.). (1976). Freud: The fusion of science and humanism—The intellectual history of psychoanalysis. *Psychological Issues, Monograph 34.* New York: International Universities Press.

Gerstäcker, F. (1902). *Germelshausen.* Boston: D.C. Health and Co.

Gill, M. M. (1979). The analysis of transference. *Journal of the American Psychoanalytic Association, 27,* 267–288.

Gill, M. M. (1994). *Psychoanalysis in transition: A personal view.* Hillsdale, NJ: Analytic Press.

Gill, M. M., & Klein, G. S. (1967). The structuring of drive and reality: David Rapaport's contributions to psychoanalysis and psychology. In M. M. Gill (Ed.), *The collected papers of David Rapaport* (pp. 8–36). New York: Basic Books.

Glover, E. (1991). Edward Glover's response to memorandum by James Strachey. In P. King & R. Steiner (Eds.), *The Freud–Klein Controversies 1941–1945* (pp. 611–616). London: Routledge/Tavistock. (Original work published 1942.)

Goldberg, A. (1978). *The psychology of the self: A casebook.* New York: International Universities Press.

Goldberg, A. (1984a). Introduction. In H. Kohut, *How does analysis cure?* Chicago: University of Chicago Press.

Goldberg, A. (1984b). One theory or many? In J. Gedo & G. Pollock (Eds.), *Psychoanalysis: The vital issues: Vol. I. Psychoanalysis as an intellectual discipline* (pp. 377–394). New York: International Universities Press.

Goldberg, A. (1987). A self psychological perspective. *Psychoanalytic Inquiry, 7,* 181–188.

Goldberg, A. (1990). *The prisonhouse of psychoanalysis.* Hillsdale, NJ: Analytic Press.

Goldner, V. (1991). Toward a critical relational theory of gender. *Psychoanalytic Dialogues, 1,* 249–272.

Green, A. (1986). The dead mother. In *On private madness* (pp. 142–173). New York: International Universities Press.

Green, A. (1999a). The intuition of the negative in *Playing and reality.* In G. Kohon (Ed.), *The dead mother: The work of André Green* (pp. 205–221). London: Brunner-Routledge.

Green, A. (1999b). *The work of the negative* (A. Weller, Trans.). London: Free Association Books.

Green, A. (2000). The central phobic position: A new formulation of the free association method. *International Journal of Psycho-Analysis, 81,* 419–451.

Green, A. (2001). *Life narcissism, death narcissism* (A. Weller, Trans.). London: Free Association Books.

Green, A. (2002, February). *A dual conception of narcissism: Positive and negative organizations.* Paper presented at Journal of the American Psychoanalytic Association Conference: Narcissism revisited: Clinical and conceptual challenges. Mount Sinai Hospital, New York City.

Greenberg, J. (1991). *Oedipus and beyond: A clinical theory.* Cambridge, MA: Harvard University Press.

Greenberg, J., & Mitchell, S. (1983). *Object relations in psychoanalytic theory.* Cambridge, MA: Harvard University Press.

Grotstein, J. S. (1981). *Splitting and projective identification.* New York: Aronson.

Grotstein, J. S. (1983). *Dare I disturb the universe? A memorial to Wilfrid R. Bion.* London Karnac.

Grotstein, J. S. (1996) Review of *Thinking, Feeling and Being:* Clinical reflections on the fundamental antinomy of human beings & world. *International Journal of Psycho-Analysis, 77,* 1053–1058.

Grotstein, J. S. (2000). *Who is the dreamer who dreams the dream? A study of psychic presences.* Hillsdale, NJ: Analytic Press.

Guntrip, H. (1961). *Personality structure and human interaction.* New York: International Universities Press.

Guntrip, H. (1969). *Schizoid phenomena, object relations and the self.* New York: International Universities Press.

Guntrip, H. (1971). *Psychoanalytic theory, therapy and the self.* New York: Basic Books.

Hamilton, V. (1996). *The analyst's preconscious.* Hillsdale, NJ: Analytic Press.

Hamilton, W. D. (1964). The genetical evolution of social behavior. *Journal of Theoretical Biology, 7,* 1–52.

Hanly, C. (1990). The concept of truth in psychoanalysis. *International Journal of Psycho-Analysis, 71,* 375–383.

Hanly, C., & Hanly, M. (1999, January). *A dialogue on subjectivity and objectivity: Towards a definition of terms.* Paper presented at the Toronto Psychoanalytic Society, Toronto, Ontario, Canada.

Hartmann, H. (1948). Comments on the psychoanalytic theory of instinctual drives. *Psychoanalytic Quarterly, 17,* 368–388.

Hartmann, H. (1958). Ego psychology and the problem of adaptation (D. Rapaport, Trans.). New York: International Universities Press. (Original work published 1939.)

Hartmann, H. (1964). Comments on the psychoanalytic theory of the ego. In *Essays on ego psychology: Selected problems in psychoanalytic theory* (pp. 113–141). New York: International Universities Press. (Original work published 1950.)

Hartmann, H., Kris, E., & Loewenstein, R. (1953). The function of theory in psychoanalysis. *Psychological Issues, 14,* 117–143.

Hatcher, R. L., & Krohn, A. (1980). Level of object representation and capacity for intensive psychotherapy in neurotics and borderlines. In J. S. Kwawer, H. D. Lerner, & A. Sugarman (Eds.), *Borderline phenomena and the Rorschach Test* (pp. 299–320). New York: International Universities Press.

Hayman, A. (1994). Some remarks about the "Controversial Discussions." *International Journal of Psycho-Analysis, 75,* 343–358.

Hebb, D. O. (1958). *A textbook of psychology.* Philadelphia: W. B. Saunders.

Hegel, G. W. T. (1910). *The phenomenology of mind* (Vols. 1–2, J. Baillie, Trans.). New York: Macmillan. (Original work published 1807.)

Henry, J. (1963). *Culture against man.* New York: Random House.

Hoffman, I. (1998). *Ritual and spontaneity in the psychoanalytic process. A Dialectical-constructivist view.* Hillsdale, NJ: Analytic Press.

Holt, R. (1976). Drive or wish? A reconsideration of the psychoanalytic theory of motivation. In M. Gill & P. Holzman (Eds.), Psychology versus metapsychology: Psychoanalytic essays in honor of George S. Klein. *Psychological Issues, Monograph 36.* New York: International Universities Press.

Holt, R. (1992). The contemporary crises of psychoanalysis. *Psychoanalysis and Contemporary Thought, 15,* 375–403.

Holzman, P. S. (1976). The future of psychoanalysis and its institutes. *Psychoanalytic Quarterly, 45,* 250–273.

Ikonen, P., & Rechardt, E. (1984). Universal nature of primal scene fantasies. *International Journal of Psycho-Analysis, 65*, 63–72.

Isaacs, S. (1952). The nature and function of phantasy. In M. Klein, P. Heimann, S. Isaacs, & J. Riviere (Eds.), *Developments in psycho-analysis* (pp. 67–121). London: Hogarth Press. (Original work published 1948.)

Jacobson, L. (2003). Mitchell's return to Freud: A review essay of two books by Stephen A. Mitchell. *Contemporary Psychoanalysis, 39*, 509–530.

Jessee, S. S. (1995). Classics revisited: Heinz Kohut's *The analysis of the self. Journal of the American Psychoanalytic Association, 43*, 187–195.

Jones, E. (1957). *The life and work of Sigmund Freud* (Vol. 3). New York: Basic Books.

Jung, C. (1969a). General aspects of dream psychology. In *Collected Works* (Vol. 8, pp. 237–280). Princeton, NJ: Princeton University Press. (Original work published 1916.)

Jung, C. (1969b). The transcendent function. In *Collected Works* (Vol. 8, pp. 67–91). Princeton, NJ: Princeton University Press. (Original work published 1912.)

Junqueira, L. C., Menezes, L. C., & Meyer, L. (1988). Recentes avances na teoria e no tecnica psicanalitica [Recent advances in psychoanalytic theory and technique]. *Rev. Bras. de Psicoanál., 27*, 91–117.

Juvet, G. (1933). *La Structure* [The structure]. Paris: F. Alcan.

Kahr, B . (1996). *D. W. Winnicott: A biographical portrait.* Madison, CT: International Universities Press.

Kernberg, O. F. (1975). *Borderline conditions and pathological narcissism.* New York: Aronson.

Kernberg, O. F. (1986). Institutional problems of psychoanalytic education. *Journal of the American Psychoanalytic Association, 34*, 799–834.

Kernberg, O. F. (1993). The current status of psychoanalysis. *Journal of the American Psychoanalytic Association, 41*, 45-62.

King, P., & Steiner R. (1991), *The Freud-Klein controversies 1941–45.* London: Routledge.

Kipling, R. (2004). *The long trail: Selected poems/Rudyard Kipling* (II. Ricketts, Ed.). Manchester, England: Carcanet.

Kirsner, D. (1982). Self psychology and the psychoanalytic movement: An interview with Heinz Kohut. *Psychoanalysis and Contemporary Thought, 5*, 483–495.

Klein, G. (1976). *Psychoanalytic theory: An exploration of essentials.* New York: International Universities Press.

Klumpner, G. H., & Frank, A. (1991). On methods of reporting clinical material. *Journal of the American Psychoanalytic Association, 39*, 537–551.

Kohlberg, L. (1981). *The philosophy of moral development.* San Francisco: Harper & Row.

Kohut, E. (1984). Preface. In H. Kohut, *How does analysis cure?* (A. Goldberg, Ed., p. ix, p. xi). Chicago: University of Chicago Press.

Kohut, H. (1962). The psychoanalytic curriculum. *Journal of the American Psychoanalytic Association, 10*, 153–163.

Kohut, H. (1977). *The restoration of the self.* New York: International Universities Press.

Kohut, H. (1979). The two analyses of Mr Z. *International Journal of Psycho-Analysis, 60*, 3–27.

Kohut, H. (1984). *How does analysis cure?* (A. Goldberg, Ed.). Chicago: University of Chicago Press.

Kris, E. (1952). *Psychoanalytic explorations in art.* New York: International Universities Press.

Kristeva, J. (1986). The true-real. In T. Moi (Ed.), *The Kristeva reader* (pp. 214–237). New York: Columbia University Press. (Original work published 1979.)

Krohn, A., & Mayman, M. (1974). Level of object representation in dreams and projective tests. *Bulletin of the Menninger Clinic, 38*, 445–466.

Kuhn, T. S. (1959). The essential tension: Tradition and innovation in scientific research. In C. W. Taylor (Ed.), *The Third (1959) University of Utah Research Conference on the Identification of Creative Scientific Talent* (pp. 162–177). Salt Lake City: University of Utah Press.

Kuhn, T. S. (1970). *The structure of scientific revolutions* (2nd ed.). Chicago: University of Chicago Press.

Kuhn, T. S. (1977). *The essential tension: Selected studies in scientific tradition and change.* Chicago: University of Chicago Press.

Kuspit, D. (1994). Review of *A most dangerous method: The story of Jung, Freud, and Sabina Spielrein*, by John Kerr. *Journal of the American Psychoanalytic Association, 42*, 883–892.

Laing, R. D. (1960). *The divided self.* London: Tavistock.

Langs, R. (1966). Manifest dreams from three clinical groups. *Archives of General Psychiatry, 14*, 634–643.

Langs, R. (1973). *The technique of psychoanalytic psychotherapy* (Vols. 1 & 2). New York: Jason Aronson.

Lansky, M. R. (1992). The legacy of *The Interpretation of Dreams*. In M. R. Lansky (Ed.), *Essential papers on dreams* (pp. 3–31). New York: New York University Press.

Laplanche, J. (1989). New foundations for psychoanalysis (D. Macey, Trans.). Oxford: Basil Blackwell. (Original work published 1987.)

Laplanche, J., & Pontalis, J. (1973). *The language of psychoanalysis.* New York: Norton.

Lasch, C. (1978). *The culture of narcissism: American life in an age of diminishing expectations.* New York: Norton.

Laudan, L. (1977). *Progress and its problems: Towards a theory of scientific growth.* Berkeley: University of California Press.

Layton, L. (1998). *Who's that girl? Who's that boy? Clinical practice meets postmodern gender theory.* Northvale, NJ: Aronson.

Levenson, E. (1992). *Harry Stack Sullivan: From interpersonal psychiatry to interpersonal psychoanalysis.* New York: Contemporary Psychoanalytic Books.

Lewontin, R. (1997). Billions and billions of demons. *New York Review of Books, 44*, 28–32.

Lewy, E. (1941). The return of the repression. *Bulletin of the Menninger Clinic, 5*, 47–55.

Lichtenberg, J. (1995, September). Modes of therapeutic action and techniques that accord with them. Paper presented to the Toronto Society for Contemporary Psychoanalysis, Toronto, Ontario, Canada.

Loewald, H. (1978). *Psychoanalysis and the history of the individual.* New Haven, CT: Yale University Press.

Loewald, H. (1979). The waning of the Oedipus complex. *Journal of the American Psychoanalytic Association, 27*, 751–776.

Loewald, H. (1980a). Book review: Heinz Kohut, *The analysis of the self*. In *Papers on psychoanalysis* (pp. 342–352). New Haven, CT: Yale University Press. (Original work published 1973.)

Loewald, H. (1980b). Book review: Jacob A. Arlow and Charles Brenner, *Psychoanalytic concepts and the structural theory*. In *Papers on psychoanalysis* (pp. 53–58). New Haven, CT: Yale University Press. (Original work published 1966.)

Loewald, H. (1980c). Some instinctual manifestations of superego formation. In *Papers on psychoanalysis* (pp. 326–346). New Haven, CT: Yale University Press. (Original work published 1973.)

Loewald, H. (1988). *Sublimation*. New Haven, CT: Yale University Press.

Lombardi, K. (2007). Notes on negativity. In B. Willock, L. Bohm, & R. C. Curtis (Eds.), *On deaths and endings: Psychoanalysts' reflections on finality, transformations and new beginnings*. London: Routledge.

Luria, A. (1968). *The mind of a mnemonist*. New York: Basic Books.

Lussier, A. (1991). The search for common ground: A critique. *International Journal of Psycho-Analysis, 72*, 57–62.

Mack, A., & Rock, I. (1998). *Inattentional blindness*. Cambridge, MA: MIT Press.

MacLennan, H. (1945). *Two solitudes*. New York: Duell, Sloan and Pearce.

Mahler, M. S. (1972). On the first three subphases of the separation-individuation process. *International Journal of Psycho-Analysis, 53*, 333–338.

Mahony, P. (1982). *Freud as a writer*. New York: International Universities Press.

Matte-Blanco, I. (1988). *Thinking, feeling and being*. Routledge: London.

McDougall, J. (1995). *The many faces of Eros: A psychoanalytic exploration of human sexuality*. London: Free Association Books.

McLuhan, M., & Powers, B. R. (1989). *The global village: Transformations in world life and media in the 21st century*. New York: Oxford University Press.

Meehl, P. (1993). If Freud could define psychoanalysis, why can't ABPP? *Psychoanalysis and Contemporary Thought, 16*, 299–326.

Meisel, P., & Kendrick, W. (1985). *Bloomsbury/Freud: The letters of James and Alix Strachey, 1924–1925*. New York: Basic Books.

Meloche, M. (1998). Notes and comments about a videotape done for the 90th anniversary of W. C. M. Scott (1993). In M. Grignon (Ed.), *Psychoanalysis and the zest for living: Reflections and psychoanalytic writings in memory of W. C. M. Scott*. Binghamton, NY: Esf Publishers.

Meltzer, J., Bremner, J., Hoxter, S., Weddell, D., & Wittenberg, I. (1975). *Explorations in autism*. Scotland: Clunie Press.

Michels, R. (1998). Current conflicts and the future of psychoanalysis. In M. Furer, E. Nersessian, & C. Perri (Eds.), *Controversies in contemporary psychoanalysis* (pp. 3–10). Madison, CT: International Universities Press.

Mitchell, S. A. (1988). *Relational concepts in psychoanalysis: An integration*. Cambridge, MA: Harvard University Press.

Mitchell, S. A. (1993). Aggression and the endangered self. *Psychoanalysis Quarterly, 62*, 351–382.

Mitchell, S. A. (1997). *Influence and autonomy in psychoanalysis*. Hillsdale, NJ: The Analytic Press.

Mitchell, S. A. (2000). *Relationality: From attachment to Intersubjectivity*. Hillsdale, NJ: The Analytic Press.

Mitchell, S. A., & Black, M. (1995). *Freud and beyond: A history of modern psychoanalytic thought*. New York: Basic Books.

Modell, A. H. (1984). *Psychoanalysis in a new context*. Madison, CT: International Universities Press.

Modell, A. H. (1985). Object relations theory. In A. Rothstein (Ed.), *Models of the mind* (pp. 85–100). New York: International Universities Press.

Modell, A. H. (1987). How theory shapes technique: An object relations perspective. *Psychoanalytic Inquiry, 7,* 233–240.

Morrison, A. P. (1994). The breadth and boundaries of a self-psychological immersion in shame: A one-and-a-half person perspective. *Psychoanalytic Dialogues, 4,* 19–36.

Munroe, R. (1955). *Schools of psychoanalytic thought: An exposition, critique, and attempted integration.* New York: Dryden Press.

Nunberg, H. (1948). The synthetic function of the ego. In *Practice and theory of psychoanalysis* (Vol. 1, pp. 120–136). New York: International Universities Press. (Original work published 1931.)

Nunberg, H. (1948). Ego strength and ego weakness. In *Practice and theory of psychoanalysis* (Vol. 1). New York: International Universities Press.

Ogden, T. H. (1986). *The matrix of the mind: Object relations and the psychoanalytic dialogue.* Northvale, NJ: Aronson.

Ogden, T. H. (1989). On the concept of an autistic-contiguous position. *International Journal of Psycho-Analysis, 70,* 127–140.

Ogden, T. H. (1992). The dialectically constituted/decentered subject of psychoanalysis: II. The contributions of Klein and Winnicott. *International Journal of Psycho-Analysis, 73,* 613–626.

O'Shaughnessy, E. (1989). The invisible Oedipus complex. In R. Britton, M. Feldman, & E. O'Shaughnessy, *The Oedipus Complex today: Clinical implications* (pp. 129–150). London: Karnac.

Palombo, S. R. (1984). Deconstructing the manifest dream. *Journal of the American Psychoanalytic Association, 32,* 405–420.

Paniagua, C. (1995). Common ground, uncommon methods. *International Journal of Psycho-Analysis, 76,* 357–372.

Paton, A. (1953). *Too late the phalarope.* New York: Scribner's.

Phillips, A. (1988). *Winnicott.* London: Fontana Press.

Phillips, A. (1994). *On flirtation.* Cambridge, MA: Harvard University Press.

Phillips, A. (1995). *Terrors and experts.* London: Faber & Faber.

Phillips, A. (2002). *Equals.* London: Faber & Faber.

Piaget, J. (1955). *The language and thought of the child* (M. Gabain, Trans.). New York: Meridian Books.

Pine, F. (1990). *Drive, ego, object, and self: A synthesis for clinical work.* New York: Basic Books.

Pine, F. (1994). Multiple models, clinical practice, and psychoanalytic theory: Response to discussants. *Psychoanalytic Inquiry, 14,* 212–234.

Pine, F. (1998). *Diversity and direction in psychoanalytic technique.* New Haven, CT: Yale University Press.

Pizer, S. (1998). *Building bridges: The negotiation of paradox in psychoanalysis.* Hillsdale, NJ: The Analytic Press.

Polanyi, M. (1964). *Personal knowledge: Towards a post-critical philosophy.* New York: Harper & Row. (Original work published 1958.)

Popper, K. (1968). *The logic of scientific discovery, revised.* New York: Harper & Row. (Original work published 1959.)

Popper, K. (1963). *Conjectures and refutations.* New York: Harper & Row.

Prince, R. M. (1999). *The death of psychoanalysis: Murder? Suicide? Or rumor greatly exaggerated?* Northvale, NJ: Aronson.

Pulver, S. (1987). How theory shapes technique: Perspectives on a clinical study. *Psychoanalytic Inquiry, 7,* 141–299.

Pulver, S. (1993). The eclectic analyst. *Journal of the American Psychoanalytic Association, 41,* 339–358.

Rachman, A. W. (1999). Death by silence (*Todschweigen*): The traditional method of silencing the dissident in psychoanalysis. In R. M. Prince (Ed.), *The Death of psychoanalysis: Murder? Suicide? Or rumor greatly exaggerated?* (pp. 153–164). Northvale, NJ: Aronson.

Rangell, L. (1988). The future of psychoanalysis: The scientific crossroads, *Psychoanalytic Quarterly, 57,* 313–340.

Rangell, L. (1990). *The human core* (Vols. 1–2). Madison, CT: International Universities Press.

Rangell, L. (2000). Psychoanalysis at the millenium: A unitary theory. *Psychoanalytic Psychology, 17,* 451–466.

Rapaport, D. (1967b). Paul Schilder's contributions to the theory of thought processes. In M. M. Gill & G. S. Klein (Eds.), *The collected papers of David Rapaport* (pp. 368–384). New York: Basic Books. (Original work published 1951.)

Rapaport, D. (1967a). A historical survey of psychoanalytic ego psychology. In M. M. Gill & G. S. Klein (Eds.), *The collected papers of David Rapaport* (pp. 745–757). New York: Basic Books. (Original work published 1959.)

Rapaport, D., Gill, M. M., & Schafer, R. (1968). Diagnostic psychological testing (Rev. ed, R. R. Holt, Ed.). New York: International Universities Press.

Renik, O. (1996). Reflections on the 40th IPA Congress theme. *International Journal of Psycho-Analysis, 5,* 38–40.

Reisner, S. (1992). Eros reclaimed: Recovering Freud's relational theory. In N. J. Skolnick & S. C. Warshaw (Eds.), *Relational perspectives in psychoanalysis* (pp. 281–312). Hillsdale, NJ: The Analytic Press.

Richards, A. D. (1992). Commentary on Trop and Stolorow's "Defense analysis in self psychology." *Psychoanalytic Dialogues, 2,* 455–465.

Rickman, J. (1957a). The factor of number in individual and group dynamics. In W. C. M. Scott (Ed.), *Selected contributions to psycho-analysis* (pp. 165-169). London: The Hogarth Press. (Original work published 1950.)

Rickman, J. (1957b). Number and the human sciences. In W. C. M. Scott (Ed.), *Selected contributions to psycho-analysis* (pp. 218–223). London: The Hogarth Press. (Original work published 1951.)

Ricoeur, P. (1977). The question of proof in Freud's psychoanalytic writings. *Journal of the American Psychoanalytic Association, 25,* 835–871.

Rivera, M. (1989). Linking the psychological and the social: Feminism, poststructuralism, and multiple personality. *Dissociation, 2,* 24–31.

Roazen, P. (2002). *The trauma of Freud: Controversies in psychoanalysis.* New Brunswick, NJ: Transactions Publishers.

Rodman, F. (Ed.). (1987). *The spontaneous gesture: Selected letters of D. W. Winnicott.* Cambridge, MA: Harvard University Press.

Rosenbaum, M. (1965). Dreams in which the analyst appears undisguised: A clinical and statistical study. *International Journal of Psycho-Analysis, 46,* 429–437.

Rothenberg, A. (1987). To err is human. In J. L. Sacksteder, D. P. Schwartz, & Y. Akabane (Eds.), *Attachment and the therapeutic process* (pp. 155–181). Madison, CT: International Universities Press.

Rothstein, A. (1980). Psychoanalytic paradigms and their narcissistic investment. *Journal of the American Psychoanalytic Association, 28,* 385–395.

Rubin, J. B. (1998). *A psychoanalysis for our time.* New York: New York University Press.

Sandler, J. (1983). Reflections on some relations between psychoanalytic concepts and psychoanalytic practice. *International Journal of Psycho-Analysis, 64,* 35–45.

Sandler, P. C. (1997). The apprehension of psychic reality: Extensions of Bion's theory of alpha-function. *International Journal of Psycho-Analysis, 78,* 43–52.

Saul, L. J., Snyder, T. R., & Sheppard, E. (1956). On reading manifest dreams and other unconscious material. In L. Rangell (reporter), The dream in the practice of psychoanalysis. *Journal of the American Psychoanalytic Association, 4,* 125–127.

Schafer, R. (1976). *A new language for psychoanalysis.* New Haven, CT: Yale University Press.

Schafer, R. (1981). *Narrative actions in psychoanalysis.* Worcester, MA: Clark University Press.

Schafer, R. (1983). *The analytic attitude.* London: Hogarth Press.

Schafer, R. (1985). Wild analysis. *Journal of the American Psychoanalytic Association, 33,* 275–299.

Schafer, R. (1990). The search for common ground. *International Journal of Psycho-Analysis, 71,* 49–52.

Schafer, R. (1994a). Commentary: Traditional Freudian and Kleinian Freudian analysis. *Psychoanalytic Inquiry, 14,* 462–475.

Schafer, R. (1994b). The contemporary Kleinians of London. *Psychoanalytic Quarterly, 63,* 409–432.

Schafer, R. (1997a). *The contemporary Kleinians of London.* Madison, CT: International Universities Press.

Schafer, R. (1997b). *Tradition and change in psychoanalysis.* Madison, CT: International Universities Press.

Schafer, R. (1999). Recentering psychoanalysis: From Heinz Hartmann to British Kleinians. *Psychoanalytic Psychology, 16,* 339–354.

Schwaber, E. A. (1987). Models of the mind and data-gathering in clinical work. *Psychoanalytic Inquiry, 7,* 261–275.

Schwaber, E. A. (1990). The psychoanalyst's methodological stance: Some comments based on a response to Max Hernandez. *International Journal of Psycho-Analysis, 71,* 31–36.

Segal, H. (1964). *Introduction to the work of Melanie Klein.* New York: Basic Books.

Shane, E. (1987). Varieties of psychoanalytic experience. *Psychoanalytic Inquiry, 7,* 277–288.

Shengold, L. (1989). *Soul murder: The effects of childhood abuse and deprivation.* New Haven, CT: Yale University Press.

Silver, A. S. (2000). American Academy: Long history of success. *The American Psychoanalyst, 34,* 22–29.

Silverman, M. A. (1987). The analyst's response. *Psychoanalytic Inquiry, 7,* 277–288.

Simon, B. (1991). Is the Oedipus complex still the cornerstone of psychoanalysis? Three obstacles to answering the question. *Journal of the American Psychoanalytic Association, 39,* 641–668.

Skelton, R. M. (2007). Matte-Blanco, the death drive and timelessness. In B. Willock, L. Bohm, & R. C. Curtis (Eds.), *On deaths and endings: Psychoanalysts' reflections on finality, transformations and new beginnings*. London: Routledge.

Slavin, M., & Kriegman, J. (1992). *The adaptive design of the human psyche: Psychoanalysis, evolutionary biology, and the therapeutic process*. New York: Guilford.

Snibbe, A. C. (2004, November). Taking the "vs." out of nature vs. nurture. *Monitor on Psychology, 35*, 22–25.

Spanjaard, J. (1969). The manifest dream content and its significance to the interpretation of dreams. *International Journal of Psycho-Analysis, 50*, 221–35.

Spence, D. (1994). *The rhetorical voice of psychoanalysis: Displacement of evidence by theory.* Cambridge, MA: Harvard University Press.

Spezzano, C. (1993). *Affect in psychoanalysis*. Hillsdale, NJ: Analytic Press.

Spitz, R. (1945). Hospitalism. *The Psychoanalytic Study of the Child, 1*, 53–74.

Spitz, R. (1946). Hospitalism: A follow-up report. *The Psychoanalytic Study of the Child, 2*, 113–117.

Staats, A. W. (2004). The disunity-unity dimension. *American Psychologist, 59*, 273.

Steele, R. S. (1979). Psychoanalysis and hermeneutics. *International Review of Psycho-Analysis, 6*, 389–412.

Stein, S. (1991). The influence of theory on psychoanalyst's countertransference. *International Journal of Psycho-Analysis, 72*, 325–334.

Steiner, J. (1985). Some thoughts about tradition and change arising from an examination of the British Psychoanalytical Society's Controversial Discussions (1943–1944). *International Review of Psycho-Analysis, 12*, 27–71.

Stepansky, P. E. (1983). Perspectives on dissent: Adler, Kohut and the idea of a psychoanalytic research tradition. *Annual of Psychoanalysis, 11*, 51–76.

Stern, D. N. (1985). *The interpersonal world of the infant*. New York: Basic Books.

Stern, D. (1997). *Unformulated experience: From dissociation to imagination in psychoanalysis*. Hillsdale, NJ: Analytic Press.

Stern, D. (2003, September 13). Dissociation and enactment. Presentation to workshop sponsored by the Toronto Institute for Contemporary Psychoanalysis.

Stewart, W. (1967). Comments on the manifest content of certain types of unusual dreams. *Psychoanalytic Quarterly, 36*, 329–341.

Stolorow, R. D., & Trop, J. L. (1992). Reply to Richards and Mitchell. *Psychoanalytic Dialogues, 2*, 467–473.

Sutherland, J. D. (1989). *Fairbairn's journey into the interior*. London: Free Association Books.

Suzuki, S. (1970). *Zen mind, beginner's mind*. New York: Weatherhill.

Tolpin, M. (2002). Doing psychoanalysis of normal development: Forward edge transferences. *Progress in Self Psychology, 18*, 167–190.

Toulmin, S. E. (1972). *Human understanding* (Vol. 1). Princeton, NJ: Princeton University Press.

Tustin, F. (1984). Autistic shapes. *International Review of Psycho-Analysis, 11*, 279–290.

Tustin, F. (1986). *Autistic barriers in neurotic patients*. New Haven, CT: Yale University Press.

Vianu, L. (1997). *T. S. Eliot—An author for all seasons*. Bucharest: Paideia.

Waelder, R. (1930). The principle of multiple function. In S. A. Guttman (Ed.), *Psychoanalysis: Observation, theory, application* (pp. 68–83). New York: International Universities Press.

Wallerstein, R. S. (1988). One psychoanalysis or many? *International Journal of Psycho-Analysis, 69,* 5–1.

Wallerstein, R. S. (1990). Psychoanalysis: The common ground. *International Journal of Psycho-Analysis, 7,* 3–20.

Wallerstein, R. S. (Ed.). (1992). *The common ground of psychoanalysis.* Northvale, NJ: Aronson.

Wallerstein, R. S. (1993). Between chaos and petrifaction: A summary of the fifth IPA conference of training analysts. *International Journal of Psycho-Analysis, 74,* 165–178.

Wallerstein, R. S., & Weinshel, E. M. (1989). The future of psychoanalysis. *The Psychoanalytic Quarterly, 58,* 341–373.

Weiss, J., Sampson, H., & the Mount Zion Psychotherapy Research Group. (1986). *The psychoanalytic process: Theory, observations, and empirical research.* New York: Guilford.

Willock, B. (1992). Projection, transitional phenomena, and the Rorschach. *Journal of Personality Assessment, 59,* 99–116.

Willock, B., Bohm, L., & Curtis, R. (2007). *On deaths and endings: Psychoanalysts' reflections on finality, transformations and new beginnings.* London: Routledge.

Willock, B., Bohm, L., & Curtis, R. (in press). *Taboo or not taboo? Forbidden thoughts, forbidden acts in psychoanalysis.* Madison, CT: International Universities Press.

Winerman, L. (2006, February). The culture-cognition connection. *Monitor on Psychology, 64–65.*

Winnicott, D. W. (1949). Hate in the counter-transference. *International Journal of Psycho-Analysis, 30,* 69–74.

Winnicott, D. W. (1958a). The capacity to be alone. *International Journal of Psycho-Analysis, 39,* 416–420.

Winnicott, D. W. (1958b). Primary maternal preoccupation. In *Collected papers: Through paediatrics to psycho-analysis* (pp. 300–305). London: Tavistock. (Original work published 1956.)

Winnicott, D. W. (1965a). The development of the capacity for concern. In *The maturational processes and the facilitating environment: Studies in the theory of emotional development* (pp. 73–82). New York: International Universities Press. (Original work published 1963.)

Winnicott, D. W. (1965b). Ego distortion in terms of true and false self. In *The maturational process and the facilitating environment* (pp. 140–152). New York: International Universities Press. (Original work published 1960.)

Winnicott, D. W. (1969). The use of an object. *International Journal of Psycho-Analysis, 50,* 711–716.

Winnicott, D. W. (1971a). *Playing and reality.* London: Tavistock.

Winnicott, D. W. (1971b). Transitional objects and transitional phenomena. In *Playing and reality* (pp. 38–57). New York: Basic Books. (Original work published 1952.)

Winnicott, D. W. (1972). Communicating and not communicating leading to a study of certain opposites. In *The maturational process and the facilitating environment* (pp. 179–192). London: Hogarth Press. (Original work published 1963.)

Winnicott, D. W. (1973). Delinquency as a sign of hope. In S. C. Feinstein & P. L. Giovacchini (Eds.), *Adolescent psychiatry* (Vol. 2, pp. 363–371). New York: Basic Books. (Original work published 1967.)

Winnicott, D. W. (1974). Fear of breakdown. *International Review of Psycho-Analysis, 1,* 103–107.

Winnicott, D. W. (1988). *Human nature.* London: Free Association Books.

Index

A

Abraham, K., 39, 123
Adaptive advantage, 77
Advertising, 56–57
Alienation, 78–79
Alpha function, 105
Anal/hydraulic model, 56
Anality, 25
Analytic attitude, 96–98
Analytic objects, 155
Analytic theories
    assimilation of new, 55–56
    incompatibility between, 65–67
    integration of, 68–69
    personality factors affecting, 39–41
    splitting within, 102–107
    synthesis of, 71
Anti-alpha function, 105
Anxiety, 187–192
Aron, L., 14–15, 29–30, 101, 175
Attachment research, 180–181
Attachment styles, 39–40
Authoritarianism, 110
Autistic-contiguous anxiety, 187–190

B

Bacal, H. A., 161–162
Bach, S., 108
Bachelard, Gaston, 1, 3, 35, 53, 107, 123, 142, 151, 211, 212
Balint, M., 120, 132, 142, 177
Barratt, B., 94, 95
Barrett, William, 45, 54
Becker, Ernest, 54
Benjamin, J., 96, 118, 123, 126
Bergmann, M., 99, 121, 122, 207
Bion, W. R., 136
Birth, 189
Bisexuality, 24–25

Blatt, S. J., 78–80
Blind spots, 140
Blindness, 49, 50–51
Bollas, C., 109–110, 136, 138
Bornstein, R., 98
Breuer, J., 108, 113
British Independent Group, 177
Bromberg, P., 122, 208

C

Camera, 23, 24–25
Carveth, D., 112, 126
Castration anxiety, 27, 29
Categorical thought, 110–111
Censored self, 76–77
Charcotian principle, 46
Chasseguet-Smirgel, J., 110, 138
China, 69–70
Classical analysis
    criticisms of, 13
    dream interpretation in, 21
    inability of Kohut to draw from, 35–36, 38–41
    protection of, 120–121
    resistance-defense in, 29
Clinical illustrations, 192–202
Clinical theory, vs. general theory, 131–134
Clinical work, relevance of comparative-integrative approach for, 131–146
Cognition, 50
Cohen, L., 158
Collective countertransference, 137–139
Colonialism, 108
Commitment, 57
Comorbidity, 191–192
Comparative analysis, 92–93, 153, 212
Comparative-integrative analysis, 75–78

approach, 96–98
class example, 175–203
clinical relevance of, 131–146
mature genitality and, 123–128
need for, 92–96
progress toward, 113–128
psychoanalytic history and, 98–102
as road to equilibrium, 206–208
significance of, for psychoanalytic
  education, 147–173
Complementarity, 47, 61, 62, 66
Conflict resolution, 116–117
Constant objects, 48
Consumerism, 56–57
Contemporary Freudian, 117–118
Control-mastery theory, 26
Convergent thinking, 60–61
Cooper, A., 132
Correspondence theory of truth, 101
Counterdepressive strategies, 23
Countertransference, 137–139
Cultural context, 55–61
Culture
  affect of, on perception, 74–75
  of narcissism, 57
Curriculum, model, 151–157

D

Data collection methods, 46–47
Death, imaging own, 190–191
Death instinct, 181–186, 202
De-attachment research, 180–181
De-differentiation, 126
Defense, 29
Defragmentation, 48–49
Demythification, 115
Depressive position, 102, 104
*Developing Synthesis of Psycho-Dynamic
  Theory* (Guntrip), 176
Dialectical resolution, 59, 63–64
Dialectical thinking, 74–75
Dichotomous thinking, 74–75
Dissociation, 113, 209
Divergent thinking, 60–61
Dominance, 107

Dream formation, 12
Dream interpretation
  Freud and, 8–9
  by Kohut, 8–33, 35–38
  manifest content and, 8–10
Drive/structure model
  Eros and, 85–87
  Freud's shift to, 67–68
  Greenberg on, 72–73
  incompatibility between relational/
    structure model and, 65–67
  integration of, 68–69, 75–78
  Mitchell on, 73
  persistence of, 70–71
Dual-drive theory, 72–73, 78
Dual-track model, 78–80
Dyadic perspectives, 13–14

E

East–West dichotomy, 69–70, 74–75
Eclecticism, 137
Edelson, M., 43
Edenic controversy, 106–107
Educational implications, 51–55
Ego, 126
Ego instincts, 85, 103
Ego psychology, 101, 111
Ego strength, 129
Eissler, K. R., 137
Eliminative inductivism, 16
Eliot, T. S., 51, 52–53
Elkins, James, 48, 49, 50–51
Empathy, 17
Erikson, Eric, 9, 10, 78–79, 122, 184
Eros, 85–87, 133, 186
Errors, usefulness of, 31–32, 37–38
Escher, M. C., 84–85
Evidence, scientific evaluation of, 16
Evolutionary biology, 76
Evolutionary theory, 76–78
Exhibitionism, 11–12, 19, 22, 29
Experiments, 133
Extension, 121–122
External verification process, 43

F

False self, 77
Fast, I., 116, 149
Father, identification with, 27–28
Fear, 112–113
Fenichel, O., 29, 124–125
Ferenczi, S., 109
Fetish, 112–113
Fixation, 111–112
Fragmentation, 48–49
Free association, 211
Freud, Anna, 108, 117, 165, 171
Freud, Sigmund, 128
    on analytic education, 155–156, 157
    critique of, 96
    death instinct of, 181–186
    dream analysis by, 8–9
    drive/structure model of, 66–68
    on ego, 126
    evolution in analytic thought by, 41–42
    fear of splitting theories by, 103
    fixation and, 111–112
    on formulation, 41–42
    on integration anxiety, 113
    Kohut's view of, 58
    on mental functioning, 63
    Mitchell and, 83–85
    on narcissism, 29
    on object relations, 190
    on Oedipal complex, 7, 22, 31
    on pedagogy, 54
    on perceptual identity, 48
    on perversion, 108–109
    on psychosexual bisexuality, 13
    on reality principle, 126–127
    relational theory of, 85–87
Fromm, E., 111

G

Gaddini, E., 112–113
Gedo, J., 38, 45, 132, 135, 136, 137, 141,
        145 146, 171
Gender, 125–126
Gender identity, 125–126

General theory, vs. clinical theory,
        131–134
Genes, 76
Genitality, 123–128
Glover, E., 111–112, 153–154, 155
Goldberg, A., 31, 55, 63, 64, 137
Goldner, V., 125–126
Grandiosity, 140
Greece, 69–70
Green, A., 132, 185, 192
Greenberg, J., 50, 65–66, 69, 70–71, 72–73,
        75, 136, 141, 185–186
Grotstein, J. S., 137, 207
Group pathology, 108–109
Group scenes, 14
Groupthink, 57
Guilty Man, 177
Guntrip, H., 176–180, 186, 188–189

H

Hamilton, V., 9–10, 144, 149, 163, 165
Hartmann, H., 151
Hebb, D. O., 43
Hermeneutic methodology, 44–45
Historical position, 104–105
Hoffman, I., 74, 75, 184
Holt, R., 57, 147, 148
Homosexual anxiety, 27–28
Homosexual fantasies, 24
Homosexuality, 25
How Does Analysis Cure? (Kohut), 7, 58
Humanities, 48–51

I

Id, 103, 111
Identification, 124–125
Identity, 101–102
Ignorance, 140
Inattentional blindness, 49–51
Indoctrination, 163
Infantile sexuality, 12, 14–15, 29–30
Innovation
    culture of, 56–57
    emphasis on, as impediment to

progress, 4, 17–18
  introduction of, 58–59
  tradition and, 51–55, 58–59
Instability, 67
Instinct, 29, 85
  death, 181–186
  life, 103
Integration anxiety, 113
Integrative thinking, 60–61, *see also*
      Comparative-integrative
      analysis
Intersubjective agreement, 36–38, 43

J

Jacobson, L., 84
Judgment, 41
Jung, C., 41
Juvet, G., 211

K

Kant, 82
Kernberg, O. F., 113, 163–164, 166–168
Kihn, Thomas, 39, 99
Kipling, Rudyard, 65, 83
Klein, George, 131
Klein, Melanie, 108, 113–115
Kleinian Freudians, 117–118
Kleinian school, 113–115, 117–118, 132
Knowledge, 75, 139–140
Kohut, Heinz, 172, 177
  on classical framework, 46–47
  contributions of, to analytic thought,
    3–5
  dream analysis by, 8–33
  established knowledge and, 51–55
  focus of, on self psychological
    formulations, 43–45, 149
  inability of, to perceive classical
    theory, 35–36, 38–41
  integration attempts by, 66–67
  Oedipal complex and, 7–8, 36–38
  perspective of, on psychoanalytic
    tradition, 17–18
  serial analysis and, 144–145

  view of Freud, 58
Kriegman, J., 75–76, 77, 101
Kris, A., 162
Kuhn, T. S., 121, 128, 159

L

Laplanche, J., 61, 98
Latent dreams, 9, 12–13
Latin American psychoanalysts, 133–134
Layton, L., 125
Leacock, Stephen, 139–140
Lewontin, R., 46
Life instinct, 103
Loewald, H., 106, 112–113, 156, 157
Love, 57, 123, 124–125

M

MacLennan, H., 162–163
Mahler, M. S., 140
Manifest content, 8–10, 12–13, 21
Maternal transference, 15
Matte-Blanco, I., 186
McDougall, Joyce, 108
Meehl, Paul, 63, 168
Mental functioning, 63
Metaphors, 112
Michels, R., 120
Mistakes, usefulness of, 31–32, 37–38
Mitchell, Stephen, 12, 19, 50, 65–66,
      69–71, 73, 80–81, 100, 185–186
  contradictions in, 80–85
  Freud and, 83–85
Mixed model, 106–107
Mock trial memory, 25–27
Model curriculum, 151–157
Modell, A. H., 68, 71, 73, 139, 168
Modification, 121–122
Monadic perspectives, 13–14
Morrison, A. P., 13
Multiplicity, 101–102
Mutuality, 78–79
Mythification, 114–115

N

Narcissism, 29, 38, 57
Narcissistic injury, 29–30
Natural sciences, 45–47
Negation, 107
Negative oedipal, 29–31
Neil, Fred, 98
Nothingness, 192

O

Object relations, 114, 125, 179–180,
    189–192
Object relations theory, 176–178
Observations, 42, 46
Occidental modes of thought, 70
Ocnophilic attachment, 39
Oedipal resistance, 8
Oedipus complex, 4, 6
    attacks on, 56
    centrality of, 127
    Freud on, 7, 22, 31
    invisible, 27
    Kohut and, 7–8, 36–38
    negative, 29–31
    overlooked in Kohut's dream
        interpretations, 10–33
    scientific challenges to, 36–38
Ogden, T. H., 104, 113–114, 129, 150, 187,
    188–191
One-person perspective, 13
Operational thought, 79
Oral character, 39
O'Shaughnessy, E., 27

P

Paradigms, 121
Paradoxes, 68–71, 74–75, 81, 110
Paradoxical thought, 110–111
Paranoia, 25
Paranoid position, 188
Paranoid-schizoid position, 101–102, 188
Paraphilia, 107–108
Parental relationship, 15, 16, 19
Pars pro toto principle, 100

Part-whole relationships, 44–45, 48
Pedagogy, 54
Perception, 49–51, 74–75
Perceptual identity, 48–49
Personality Structure and Human
        Interaction (Guntrip), 176
Perverse sexuality, 107
Perversion, 108–109, 110
Phallic imagery, 21, 23, 24
Phallic-oedipal phase, 125
Phillips, A., 116–117
Philobatic attachment, 39
Physical sciences, 45–47
Physics, 45–46, 47
Pine, F., 137, 145
Pizer, S., 111
Planck, Max, 58
Pluralism, 131, 140–141, 170, 205, 212, see
        also Comparative-integrative
        analysis
Polanyi, Michael, 47
Polarities, 107
Primal scene concept, 14–15, 187–188
Primary identification, 87
Prisonhouse of Psychoanalysis, The
        (Goldberg), 31
Procrustes, 127
Professional training, 139–140
Projective tests, 201–202
Proscribed vocabulary, 94
Psychoanalysis
    analytic attitude toward, 96–98
    dialectical thinking in, 59
    intersubjective agreement in, 36–38, 43
    pluralism in, 91–93
    theoretical conflicts in, 3, 5–6
Psychoanalysts
    flexible attitude of, 135–137
    training of, 139–140
Psychoanalytic education
    class example, 175–203
    criticisms of, 163–167
    generativity vs. stagnation, 167–171
    model curriculum, 151–157
    provisional evaluation of, 157–159
    repressive climate of, 161–163

significance of comparative-integrative approach for, 147–173

Psychoanalytic history, 98–102

Psychoanalytic practice, relevance of comparative-integrative approach for, 131–146

Psychoanalytic research tradition, 17–18

Psychoanalytic theories
arrested development of, 107–113
extension of, 121–122
Kohut's contributions to, 3–5
splitting within, 102–107

Psychoanalytic Theory, Therapy, and the Self (Guntrip), 178

Psychology, disarray of, 205

Psychosexual bisexuality, 13

Psychosocial stages, 78–79

R

Rangell, L., 110, 118, 119–120, 129, 132, 154, 165, 170, 207

Rapaport, D., 35, 40, 114, 152

Rapprochement, 140–141

Reality principle, 127

Regressed ego, 179–186

Reisner, S., 85, 86–87

Relatedness, 78–80

Relational-conflict model, 82

Relational deprivation, 29–30

Relational drives, 77

Relationalists, 14–15

Relational/structure model, 76–77
Freud and, 85–87
incompatibility between drive/structure model and, 65–67
integration of, 68–69, 75–78
persistence of, 70–71

Repression, 76–77, 108–109

Resistance, 29

Richards, A. D., 62

Rickman, J., 14

Rothenberg, A., 31

Rothstein, A., 38

Rubin, J. B., 99, 112, 144

S

Sandler, J., 105

Sartre, Jean-Paul, 175

Schafer, Roy, 15, 35, 40, 50, 92, 93, 95, 98, 114, 115, 120, 132, 141, 153, 154, 155

Schizoid Phenomena, Object Relations, and Self (Guntrip), 176–177

Schizoid position, 188

Scholl, Brian, 49

Schwaber, E. A., 95

Scientific evolution, 55–56

Scientific progress, 4, 206
as barrier, 40
impediments to, 41
influence of, on the scientist, 47

Scientific reasoning, 15–17

Scientific spirit, 1

Scot, Clifford, 140

Self-deception, 37

Self-definition, 78–80

Self-objects, 177–178

Self-preservation, 122

Self psychologists
conflicts between other psychologists and, 5–6
oral character of, 39

Self psychology, 155
attempts to integrate, 66–67
emergence of, 55–56
Kohut's focus on, 4–5, 43–45
object relations theory and, 177–178
promotion of, 58–59
in psychoanalytic tradition, 17–18
two-person perspective of, 13–14

Self-state dreams, 8

Self-theory, 116

Sensation, 189

Serial analysis, 142–145

Sexual fantasies, 11–12, 20–21, 29–30

Sexual identity, 125–126

Sexuality
drive theory and, 86–87
infantile, 12, 14–15, 29–30
perverse, 107

Shame, 23, 25
Shane, E., 138
Shichman, S., 78–80
Sibling rivalry, 22
Simon, B., 127, 128
Slavin, M., 75–76, 77, 101
Spezzano, C., 121–122
Staats, Arthur, 205
Steele, R. S., 44
Stein, S., 143–144
Stepansky, P. E., 17–18
Stern, Donnel, 96, 209
Subjective contour completion, 48
Sublimated aggression, 115, 134
Supportive treatment approaches,
     194–196
Sutherland, J. D., 161
Suzuki, S., 160
Symbolism, of camera, 23–25

T

Thanatos, 186
Theoretical conflicts, 3
Theoretical disloyalty, 109
Therapeutic relationship, 142
Three-person psychology, 13–14
Tolerance, 96
Toronto Institute for Contemporary
     Psychoanalysis, 148
Total composite psychoanalytic theory,
     118–120
Totalitarianism, 109–111, 161–163

Tradition
     innovation and, 51–55, 58–59
     protection of, 120–121
Tragic Man, 177
Transference paradigms, 46
Transgression fantasies, 19
Transitional space, 69
Triangularity, 19, 25
True self, 77
Two-person perspective, 13–14

U

Uncertainty principle, 46
Unconscious, 100

V

Voyeurism, 11–12, 19, 22

W

Wallerstein, R. S., 92, 129, 131–132, 133,
     134–135, 147, 158, 160, 163,
     165–166, 205
Weinshel, E. M., 134–135, 158, 160,
     165–166
Western philosophical tradition, 69–70
Wilde, Oscar, 56
Winnicott, D. W., 53, 69, 105, 142–143,
     144, 160
Wolf, Ernest, 58
Womb, 188–190, 191, 202